ALIENS & UFOs

Messengers or Deceivers?

JAMES L. THOMPSON

Second Printing, May 1994

International Standard Book Number
0-88290-469-8

Horizon Publishers' Catalog and Order Number
1006

Printed and distributed
in the United States of America by

Horizon
Publishers
& Distributors, Incorporated
P.O. Box 490 Bountiful, Utah 84011-0490

Foreword

It may surprise you to learn from this book that sightings of unidentified flying objects (UFOs), not to mention contacts with and even abductions by purported "space people," are *much* more common than their discussion in the main-stream media might lead you to expect—unless you have had a sighting yourself or have been contacted or abducted! Or perhaps you have studied the phenomenon as James Thompson has. If not, you may also be surprised to learn the extent to which people who think a lot about UFOs have become enamored with the occult and the so-called New Age. What does it all mean to a Latter-day Saint? Brother Thompson has given that question much more thought than most of us, and he provides some highly perceptive insights in this volume.

From 1962 until about 1980, I gave the question of UFOs quite a bit of thought. Indeed, a book that I wrote, *The Utah UFO Display,* was published in 1974 (and is now long out of print). I interviewed about twenty UFO witnesses or groups of witnesses from a file of about 80 sightings that had been collected by Joseph Hicks, a junior-high teacher in Roosevelt in the Uintah Basin of Utah. My goal was to be scientific. I considered the several explanations that had been put forward and concluded that none was sufficient although all had some elements of truth or possible truth. Then as now, many UFO sightings were misinterpretations of natural or conventional phenomena such as the planet Venus. A few were simply lies or hoaxes. Because they have been seen throughout history, they could hardly be secret weapons of somebody's air force. One can apply much psychology in understanding the witnesses, but mass hallucinations or other psychological phenomena cannot explain the UFOs. In my thinking, one could not scientifically eliminate the "visitors-from-another-planet" hypothesis, which was the main idea at that time—and the main target of UFO debunkers.

Nevertheless, as I delved into the various aspects of the UFO phenomenon, it became increasingly apparent that the UFOs could hardly represent true explorers from another world. For one thing, as Thompson describes, they *wanted* to be seen; they were putting on a *display.* I was perplexed by it all and concluded in my book that "they are putting on a show for our benefit. Why? What are they trying to prepare us for? What's the point of all this conditioning? One thing is certain: in a few areas of the world, such as the Uintah Basin, their display is having a powerful effect upon the collective thinking of the inhabitants. It is becoming the stuff of legend and folklore. Perhaps if we keep our minds open and remain patient, we shall someday know why."

After writing the book, I became increasingly disturbed about what was going on. The "contactees," as we called them then, were becoming more numerous, and their stories were becoming more difficult to shrug off. With such experiences, it became virtually impossible to maintain an objective, detached, scientific approach to the study of UFOs. My religious interpretations were becoming more important than science. But I could not accept the idea that our visitors were from Enoch's Zion, for example, or that they were angels who were preparing for the Lord's Second Coming. There were too many signs of *evil,* too much resemblance to spiritualism and other occult matters. It was easier to imagine that "false Christs, and false prophets," were showing "great signs and wonders; insomuch that, if it were possible, they shall deceive the very elect." (Matt. 24:24, see also Joseph Smith Matt. 1:22)

I am amazed at the intensity with which the UFO phenomenon has become associated with contactee and abduction stories, which now seem paramount. There has been a profound influence on (at least) Western collective thought, which is increasingly involved with the New Age religion and the occult. The world is being taught an alternative to the return of the Savior!

James Thompson has examined these matters in much depth. He provides some answers, tentative at least, to the questions that I posed at the close of my book—and he poses many questions of his own. As a lawyer, he knows the limitations of his knowledge and investigative abilities, not to mention the strange nature of the evidence, so he is never dogmatic. As a devout Latter-day Saint, he has a body of revealed knowledge—Father Lehi's iron rod—to hold on to, and that he does. His love of his Redeemer and the gospel message shines through in every discussion, and his probing of the enigma is as extensive and deep as that of any UFO researcher known to me. You have much to learn as you read these pages, and you can learn much from this volume. And perhaps you can help to restrain the flood of evil that is rising in the world. Read in the proper spirit, this book can help you do so.

Frank B. Salisbury, Ph.D.
North Logan, Utah

Table of Contents

Part I
The
Gospel View
Of The
Universe

Most investigators and researchers of Unidentified Flying Objects (UFOs) and their "alien" pilots are unable to reach any tentative conclusions about the phenomenon because modern philosophy imposes no limitations on what is possible. Because they believe that there are no restrictions, limits, or universal laws (what we might term eternal principles of truth), theorists cannot confine the UFO phenomenon to anything that is knowable—it has become a dogma of modern intellectualism. In this Part I, revealed Gospel knowledge is used to establish parameters to the search for extraterrestrial life—to construct a *paradigm* within which to analyze the phenomenon. In other words, before answering the question "What is probable?," the question "What is possible?" must first be answered.

1

Are UFO Experiences
A Frequent Phenomenon?

The 1991 Roper Organization Survey

The Roper Organization was commissioned in 1991 to conduct a survey of American adults to determine the extent of American participation in the UFO phenomenon.[1] The survey was commissioned by the Bigelow Holding Company, a consortium of UFO groups and scientists, for the purpose of alerting the mental health profession that patients with claims of close encounters are not merely delusional. The results of the survey were published in late 1992, along with a plea to mental health professionals by John E. Mack, M.D., Professor of Psychiatry at the Harvard Medical School,[2] and as of this printing were still sending shock waves through the mental health profession, as well as the media. Three Roper "Omnibus" polls (July, August, September of 1991) involving a total of 5,947 adults, repeated a battery of eleven questions, five of which were key indicator questions. Some questions were pointed, others were subtle indicators of a suppressed abduction experience, while one was a mere control question inserted to determine how many "yea-sayers" were participating. Surprisingly, only one percent responded affirmatively to the control question, "Hearing or seeing the word TRONDANT and knowing that it has a secret meaning for you." The pollsters made up the word Trondant.

The survey was conducted so precisely that the results are given a margin of error of only plus or minus 1.4 percent. The most pointed question asked if the respondent had seen a UFO. The affirmative response was a surprising seven percent of all American adults.[3] That is seven percent of 185 million, or a total of 12.95 million adults.

---

[1] Unusual Personal Experiences: An Analysis of the Data from Three National Surveys, The Bigelow Holding Company, Nevada (1992).

[2] *Ibid.*, p. 7.

[3] *Ibid.*, p. 7.

In surveys there is a segment of the adult population known as the Political Social Actives (PSAs), which is made up of those who participate in the community. This can be with the PTA, at polling places, at church, etc. This PSA segment of society remains a constant 10 percent of the general population. What is interesting is that PSAs responded affirmatively to the survey questions almost 50 percent more often than the average American adult. To the above question regarding having seen a UFO, for instance, the PSA response was 10 percent.[4]

The survey asked if the participant had experienced the following, which are indicators (in the opinion of the commissioners) of a prior UFO abduction. Included are the questions and the responses, both average and PSA.

Seeing a ghost. [Av 11%   PSA 16%]

Feeling as if you left your body. [Av 14%   PSA 23%]

Seeing a UFO. [Av 7%   PSA 10%]

Waking up paralyzed with a sense of a strange person or presence or something else in the room. [Av 18%   PSA 28%]*

Feeling that you were actually flying through the air although you didn't know why or how. [Av 10%   PSA 18%]*

Experiencing a period of time of an hour or more, in which you were apparently lost, but you could not remember why, or where you had been. [Av 13%   PSA 17%]*

Seen unusual lights or balls of light in a room without knowing what was causing them, or where they came from. [Av 8%   PSA 11%]*

Finding puzzling scars on your body and neither you nor anyone else remembering how you received them or where you got them. [Av 8%   PSA 9%]*

Having seen, either as a child or an adult, a terrifying figure—which might have been a monster, a witch, a devil, or some other evil figure in your bedroom, closet, or somewhere else. [Av 15%   PSA 19%]

Having vivid dreams about UFOs. [Av 7%   PSA 10%]

To the uninitiated, many of these questions may appear to be unrelated to the UFO phenomenon. What do bedroom visitations, unnoticed scars, and unusual lights in the house have to do with UFOs? Are these not spiritual or psychological manifestations that should be dealt with in those terms? The commissioners of the survey concluded that, based upon their inside knowledge of the UFO phenomenon, anyone who answered affirmatively

---

[4] *Ibid.*, p. 31.

to four out of the five questions followed by "*" was likely to have been abducted by aliens without his or her knowledge. Is this a credible conclusion for scientists and doctors to reach? You be the judge as you examine the materials included herein.

Interestingly, the survey commissioners were quite surprised at the eight percent response to the question dealing with unusual lights inside. They are of the opinion that this phenomenon is so uniquely associated with the UFO phenomenon that it is a clear indicator of UFO activity. However, anyone who researches spiritual experiences knows that such a phenomenon is clearly present in many spiritual encounters, both good and evil.

Based on the survey results, two percent of American adults answered affirmatively to four of the five key indicator questions, resulting in a likelihood that 3.7 million have been abducted.[5] This is a staggering statistic. Is there really a large body of experts who believe that millions of American adults have been abducted and taken on board UFOs for examination and related procedures? Apparently so.

There is no demographic preference for who sees UFOs and who does not. An LDS Bishop is just as likely to have a sighting over Salt Lake City as an Australian aborigine in the bush or a Russian fisherman on a trawling ship. Thousands of Americans have reported encountering UFO occupants. Hundreds complain of being abducted, examined, and worse. The statistics are constant worldwide.

Through the years of pondering the UFO enigma and its implications, I, as all observers, had developed certain ephemeral viewpoints as I weighed new information gathered while reading gospel commentaries, while watching new and improved episodes of *Star Trek*, or while glancing discretely to the left in the supermarket checkout lines. In the same way most of us attempt to decipher events related to the Second Coming, I would take each new piece of UFO information, analyze it, and attempt to make it fit into an appropriate pigeon hole I had already created in a previous attempt. It would have been easy to dismiss the entire phenomenon as a large-scale chic hoax, a cultural craze, or a modern reflection of massive abnormal psychology. However, the possibility of human visitors from other planets was always very real also, especially in light of our understanding that we are not Heavenly Father's only children in the universe.

---

5 *Ibid.*, p. 48.

There is much to be considered when attempting to understand and discern the UFO phenomenon. We might even feel that the subject is unworthy of our attention because of its former prominence among the fringe element, the crackpots and misfits of society. The silence of the Lord on the subject might also persuade us to ignore whatever it is that "others" are saying they see in our skies. These feelings are no longer justified, in light of the astounding numbers of honest people that are claiming close encounters with UFOs, especially when we consider the tremendous impact the phenomenon is having on American and world cultures, religions, and politics. The effects of the UFO phenomenon are overwhelming and far reaching, even here in the safe haven of LDS culture and life.

The 1992 LDS Extraterrestrial Life Survey

As a substructure for this work, and out of sheer curiosity, I developed a questionnaire for the purpose of surveying members of The Church of Jesus Christ of Latter-day Saints for their viewpoints on the subjects addressed herein. The questionnaire, "EXTRATERRESTRIAL LIFE SURVEY," was circulated throughout the United States, based roughly on per capita LDS Church membership in the respective geographical areas. I requested that people I knew in Oregon, California, Idaho, New York, Connecticut, and Utah pass out questionnaires to members of their congregations. Just under 100 completed surveys were returned to me in January of 1992. The questions were presented in order from general to specific, and were formulated to be clear, and not leading.

Listed below are the questions asked in the survey. Following the questions are the results of the survey expressed in percentages of responses assigned to each possible answer.

1. Do you believe that any form of life exists on planets other than Earth? Yes _____ No _____ No opinion _____

2. Do you believe that human-like life ("aliens") exists on planets other than Earth? Yes _____ No _____ No opinion _____

3. Do you believe that aliens travel in space ships to planets other than their own? Yes ____ No ____ No opinion ____

4. Do you believe that aliens have indirectly contacted humans (e.g., electronic signals, telepathy)? Yes ____ No ____ No opinion ____

5. Do you believe that aliens have travelled into Earth's atmosphere? Yes ____ No ____ No opinion ____

6. Do you believe that aliens have landed on Earth? Yes ____ No ____ No opinion ____

7. Do you believe that aliens have landed on Earth and contacted humans directly? Yes ____ No ____ No opinion ____

8. Do you believe that humans have gone onto alien space ships? Yes ____ No ____ No opinion ____

9. Do you believe that angels use space vehicles to travel to Earth? Yes ____ No ____ No opinion ____

10. Do you believe that God uses space vehicles to travel to Earth? Yes ____ No ____ No opinion ____

11. Have you ever seen an alien space craft or UFO? Yes ____ No ____

12. Do you know anyone that claims to have seen an alien space craft or UFO? Yes ____ No ____

The responses to the twelve questions on the survey were as follows:

1.	Yes (95%)	No (04%)	No opinion (01%)
2.	Yes (85%)	No (10%)	No opinion (05%)
3.	Yes (44%)	No (37%)	No opinion (19%)
4.	Yes (25%)	No (52%)	No opinion (23%)
5.	Yes (44%)	No (40%)	No opinion (16%)
6.	Yes (39%)	No (43%)	No opinion (18%)
7.	Yes (25%)	No (46%)	No opinion (29%)
8.	Yes (12%)	No (61%)	No opinion (27%)
9.	Yes (02%)	No (06%)	No opinion (92%)
10.	Yes (02%)	No (06%)	No opinion (92%)
11.	Yes (08%)	No (92%)	
12.	Yes (27%)	No (73%)	

Although demographic information was gathered regarding the sex, age, educational level, and geographical region of the respondents, there were no significant statistical variations between any of these groups.[6]

Following the questions on the survey, the respondents were invited to share any personal encounter experiences or experiences of other LDS Church members. Approximately six percent of the respondents shared such an experience, mostly those of relatives.

A High Percentage Of LDS UFO Encounters

Are the survey results significant? One statistic that jumps out is the response to question number 11. The question does not ask for an opinion but queries, "Have you ever seen an alien space craft or UFO?" Eight percent of the respondents answered "yes." If this statistic holds true throughout the general LDS population, there are more than a half million LDS members who have personally witnessed a UFO!

Remember that the national adult average identified in the Roper Organization survey was seven percent, while the response rate of those actively participating in the community (PSAs) was ten percent. I believe that the statistic accurately represents the rate of UFO sightings among LDS Church members. Statistically, many of such sightings are explainable as misidentified flying objects or naturally occurring phenomena. However, as we see below, this still leaves us with a high number of genuine UFO encounters in our own ranks.

Also significant is the response to question number 12, "Do you know anyone that claims to have seen an alien space craft or UFO?" Twenty-seven percent of the respondents answered "yes" to this question. This translates into approximately two million LDS Church members who personally know someone who has experienced a UFO encounter.

It is interesting, yet predictable that the percentages of "yes" responses declined as more specific questions were asked. Most members believe that extraterrestrial life exists millions of miles out in space, but few believe that aliens have been in their back yards. What is significant is the response to questions number 5 and 6, asking about the respondent's belief that "aliens" have travelled into Earth's atmosphere or landed on this planet. The "yes"

---

6 *Extraterrestrial Life Survey*, Bountiful, Utah, 1992.

responses were a significant 44% and 39%, respectively, hovering at about 3.5 million LDS members. The "unsure" responses to these questions were 16% and 18% respectively (another 1.3 million). These figures show that the UFO phenomenon has made a significant impression on LDS Church membership. The great significance of this fact will become increasingly apparent as you read this work.

How would the respondents to the LDS survey have differed in their responses to the Roper Organization survey? We can only guess, of course, but some significant issues present themselves in the Roper survey that were not covered in the LDS survey. For instance, the commissioners of the Roper survey preceded their "UFO" question with two supernatural category questions: seeing a ghost and having an out-of-body experience. These questions were included to indicate to the respondent that unusual, "fringe" types of questions were about to be presented. A secondary reason for including these questions was that such experiences are actually related to the UFO phenomenon, but in what way, the commissioners were not sure. Affirmative responses to all of the paranormal category questions were higher than expected, however. The pollsters were shocked at the high number of affirmative responses to all of the questions.

An interesting demographic differentiation in affirmative responses exists in the Roper surveys. The older groups reported fewer UFO-related experiences, while those in their twenties and thirties have had significantly more encounters with UFOs, aliens, and night visitors. From my many conversations with LDS Church members, I suspect that even higher numbers would respond affirmatively to the paranormal-category questions. The paranormal encounters seem clearly spiritual in nature. Then, one asks, how are they related to the UFO phenomenon? That question is the very reason for the research and analysis in this book—to attempt to discern how all of the "Unsolved Mystery" phenomena that are becoming so prominent in our modern culture are related, and why they are becoming so prevalent in these latter days.

No other planets have yet been discovered by astronomers outside of our own solar system, with a possible exception of one in early 1992. Yet many scientists postulate that there exist numerous planets circling myriad stars in our universe. Of these planets, some estimate that a low percentage (still, thousands of planets) are capable of sustaining life. Although it would be statistically nearly impossible for life to exist on such planets from an evolutionary viewpoint,[7] scripturally, we know that many are populated with transplanted human and other life forms. Being armed with this knowledge, it would be easy for us to say "yes," we are most likely being visited by our brethren from one or more of these distant planets. There are, however, certain patterns to the forms of visitation, the forms of communication, and the content of such communication from the bulk of these UFO encounters that give us great pause.

The Approaches Taken In This Book

Are UFOs real objects? Does their presence represent a physical phenomenon? Most scientists initially found it too difficult to accept the existence of UFOs. Many, however, came to find the evidence too compelling to ignore, and began accepting the possibility of extraterrestrial life and its visitation to Earth. Many of these, with no religious training or background, for the reasons discussed herein, are beginning to rethink the "extraterrestrial visitors" assumption. Now, having accepted the possibility of extraterrestrial life, they, like laymen, are finding great difficulty in ascertaining whether or not UFOs are manifestations of extraterrestrial visitation, or something else.

Though the Church at present has no official position stated on the UFO phenomenon, we can survey the volumes of UFO literature, search the scriptures and the prophets, and attempt to understand the UFO phenomenon within a Gospel framework. Taking certain gospel principles as true and universal, we have the advantage over most who try to make sense of UFOs and their "extraterrestrial" occupants. With the Gospel as our guide we can further analyze the UFO "message" to mankind.

To unravel the tangle of "UFOlogy" (the study and body of UFO reports) and how it relates to the Gospel, we first survey the UFO literature and look closely at those who are "victims" of close encounters with UFOs and their occupants. In so doing, we examine what the scriptures, prophets, and others have revealed about the existence and nature of extraterrestrial life in our universe, and whether or not they enlighten us concerning the current UFO enigma. We next survey the history of UFO phenomena, in their various forms and manifestations, including LDS accounts at all levels. Finally,

---

[7] *Nature,* "UFO, APPENDIX," by Dr. Frank B. Salisbury, October 1969, p. 2.

we analyze the "message" and other information we are receiving from UFOs and related sources, and weigh in the balance the nature, origin, and character of these, our "space brothers."

The UFO phenomenon is real and widespread, and I predict it will have far-reaching effects in coming years. After years of close observation and several months of intense research, I present my conclusion about UFOs and their "extraterrestrial occupants":

It is possible that the Earth is periodically visited by interplanetary craft piloted either remotely or by extraterrestrial human occupants. However, many UFO sightings and alien encounters appear to correspond better to traditional supernatural phenomena. There is often little difference between aliens and the evil spirits, poltergeists, and related counterfeit angelic apparitions that are manifested with increasing frequency. Because we know these paranormal phenomena to be Satanic deceptive apparitions, it is quite possible that many UFO sightings and encounters have similar origins and purposes.

I attempt herein to fully document cases and testimonies that provide our database, and statements and conclusions of the world class experts that have investigated them, reaching conclusions similar to mine. I invite you to analyze the data in a thoughtful, prayerful manner. Whether or not your conclusions are the same as mine, by reading these materials you will at least have received an education regarding phenomena that will take on greater prominence and significance in our very near future.

2

Extraterrestrial Life In
The Standard Works

An Infinite Number Of Earths

Before we can intelligently discuss the existence and nature of life elsewhere in our universe, we are wise to first seek enlightenment from the Lord on the subject. When we gain a knowledge of what He has revealed on the treatise, we can *then* apply our acquired insights to attempt to fill any gaps left by the scanty information gained from this primary source of revelation—The Standard Works of the Church of Jesus Christ of Latter-day Saints. The Standard Works are surprisingly clear, yet concise, in answering the question, Does life exist on planets other than Earth? The universe is immense and filled with "kingdoms," as latter-day revelation informs us: "And there are many kingdoms; for there is no space in which there is no kingdom; and there is no kingdom in which there is no space, either a greater or a lesser kingdom." (*Doctrine and Covenants* 88:37.)

As God revealed the immensity and substance of His kingdom and dominion to Moses, he began to gain an appreciation of the magnitude of the creative works of God.

> And worlds without number have I created; and I also created them for mine own purpose; and by the Son created I them, which is mine Only Begotten. And the first man of all men have I called Adam, which is many. But only an account of this earth, and the inhabitants thereof, give I unto you. For behold, there are many worlds that have passed away by the word of my power.[1] And there are many that now stand, and *innumerable* are they unto man; but all things are numbered unto me, for they are mine and I know them. [Moses 1:33-35, emphasis supplied.]

---

[1] Concerning the "passing away" of planets President Joseph Fielding Smith explained that this does not indicate that planets die or disintegrate:

HOW EARTHS PASS AWAY. This passing away does not mean that earths grow old and die, becoming cold, lifeless bodies, wandering through space, perhaps to disintegrate, be broken up and in some unknown manner be recreated, by some natural force working on the energy in the universe. We have every reason to believe that *the passing away of an earth simply means that it will undergo,* or has undergone, *the same definite course which is destined for our earth*, and the Lord has made that perfectly clear. *This earth is a living body.* It is true to the law given it. It was created to become a celestial body and the abode for celestial beings. (D & C 88:17-26, Isa. 51:6-7; Ps. 102:25-26) [*Doctrines of Salvation,* Vol. 1. p. 72]

This scripture clarifies the truth of a number of important Gospel topics. Not only does the revelation proclaim the existence of other life-sustaining planets and the existence of life on those planets, it informs us that humans, children of our Heavenly Father, live on those planets.

Our conception of what "human" implies, however, must be tempered by a look at what it means on Earth. As we scan human life on this planet, we find some races of man that are three feet tall, and some that are seven feet tall; some with black skin, some with red, and others with white or yellow; some have flat, rounded facial features, while others have thin, narrow characteristics. We find many sizes, shapes, and colors of humans, with divergent features and attributes all on this single planet. All of these normal variations of human appearance are "in the image of God." (Genesis 1:26.) The image of God could easily have even greater divergence on some of the other planets referred to in the above scripture. How much divergence, we do not know, although we would expect our brothers and sisters to appear more or less like we do, within reasonable variations.

As the Prophet Joseph Smith was engaged in rendering a more accurate translation of the New Testament, he came upon John 5:29, which reads: "And [the dead] shall come forth; they that have done good, unto the resurrection of life; and they that have done evil, unto the resurrection of damnation." In relation to this statement Joseph had many questions regarding the multiplicity of human destinations in the eternities. While contemplating the question, a wonderful vision was opened to Joseph and Sidney Rigdon at Hiram, Ohio, February 16, 1832, as recorded in Section 76 of the *Doctrine and Covenants*. Among the many marvelous and important truths revealed to them in the vision, they heard a voice bearing record that Jesus Christ is the Only Begotten of the Father, adding, "That by him, and through him, and of him, the *worlds are and were created*,[2] and the inhabitants thereof are begotten sons and daughters unto God." This latter-day testimony makes clear that there is life on other planets, human life just like Earth's own children of Adam and Eve, and that all of these humans are children of God, and therefore, literally, our brothers and sisters.

---

[2] The Apostle Paul also understood and taught that Jesus Christ is the creator of numerous worlds. In his epistle to the Hebrews, Paul explained that God "Hath in these last days spoken unto us by *his* Son, whom he hath appointed heir of all things, by whom also he made the *worlds*; . . . Through faith we understand that the *worlds* were framed by the word of God, so that things which are seen were not made of things which do appear." (Hebrews 1:2; 11:3.)

Joseph Smith taught that "It has been the design of Jehovah, from the commencement of the world, and is His purpose now, to regulate the affairs of the world in His own time, to stand as a head of the universe, and take the reigns of government in His own hand. . . ." [*Teachings of the Prophet Joseph Smith*, p. 250]

The question immediately arises from a reading of Moses 1:33-35: How many worlds does "worlds without number" and "innumerable" constitute? We could suppose that such a representation merely indicated to the ancients that a large number is involved, and that in those times men dealt in hundreds, or perhaps thousands, and God did not wish to confuse Moses with truly larger numbers. However, the meaning of "worlds without number" and "innumerable" was made clear to Enoch as he comprehended the number in vision and exclaimed: "And were it possible that man could number the particles of the earth, yea, *millions of earths* like this, *it would not be a beginning to the number of thy creations*; . . ." (Moses 7:30.) The number of particles that make up millions of earths like this is indeed, a very great number. God informed Moses, and understandably so, that it is not possible for the limited human mind to fully comprehend all of God's works:

> And behold, thou art my son; wherefore look, and I will show thee the workmanship of mine hands; but not all, for *my works are without end*, and also my words, for *they never cease*. Wherefore, no man can behold all my works, except he behold all my glory; and no man can behold all my glory, and afterwards remain in the flesh on the earth. [Moses 1:4-5]

The extent of God's creations is staggering to the finite human mind. Worlds, truly without number has He created. If we ascribe to each world approximately 80 billion human inhabitants during its telestial tenure,[3] and trillions upon trillions of plants and animals, it is no wonder that a man could not remain in the flesh after having comprehended the fullness of God's stewardship.

The People Of Zion Live On A Terrestrial Planet

The Standard Works say little else about other worlds and their inhabitants generally, but much is said about one group of people that left this planet to live on another—the people of Zion. Because so many Church members

---

3 This number is based on Church Family History Department estimates of the cumulative population of this world during its six thousand year temporal existence.

assume that extraterrestrial visitors could be translated beings ministering to Earth from other planets—or, because in our search for extraterrestrial life it is important to establish scripturally the existence or nonexistence of human life on foreign worlds, we endeavor here to pinpoint what happened to Zion and its inhabitants.[4]

As the Lord revealed to Enoch his Earthly ministry and the eventual results thereof, Enoch was privileged to see his own future:

> And it came to pass that the Lord showed unto Enoch all the inhabitants of the earth; and he beheld, and lo, Zion, in process of time, was taken up into heaven. And the Lord said unto Enoch: Behold mine abode forever. . . . And after that Zion was taken up into heaven, Enoch beheld, and lo, all the nations of the earth were before him; And there came generation upon generation; and Enoch was high and lifted up, even in the bosom of the Father, and of the Son of Man; and behold, the power of Satan was upon all the face of the earth. . . . And Enoch beheld angels descending out of heaven, bearing testimony of the Father and Son; and the Holy Ghost fell on many, and they were caught up by the powers of heaven into Zion. [Moses 7:21-27]

This passage, when analyzed with other verses in Moses, Chapter 7, helps us gain an understanding of where Zion is. Enoch testified of events that were yet future to him. He said Zion would be "taken up into heaven," [5]although he failed here to identify the exact final location of Zion. In this passage Enoch himself was taken to "the bosom of the Father," and the Lord said to Enoch, "Behold mine abode forever." These statements, however, were made in connection with Enoch's visit to the throne of God, at which time he was shown all things pertaining to the kingdoms of God—past, present, and future. The scripture, standing alone, does not necessarily indicate that *Zion* was taken to God's bosom or abode—only that Enoch beheld God's bosom or abode.

The passage is further enlightening because it indicates an ongoing connection between Zion and the Earth, even after Zion is taken. This it does by suggesting that others were translated to Zion after its removal and that angels continued to travel between Zion and the Earth. President Spencer W. Kimball confirmed this by answering the question: "Is man earthbound?

---

4 Some latter-day prophets and apostles have alluded to the possibility that another group or groups of people have likewise been taken to another planet, such as the Ten Lost Tribes of Israel.

5 In *The Book of the Secrets of Enoch*, Enoch describes ten heavens, all with varying qualities of life.

Largely so, and temporarily so, yet Enoch and his people were translated
from earth, and the living Christ and angels commuted." (*The Teachings
of Spencer W. Kimball*, p. 445.)

An interesting example of ongoing communication between Zion and the
Earth is illustrated in the Dead Sea Scrolls.[6]

> An extremely unusual son was born to Lameck. The child's body was white as snow,
> with parts as red as a rose. His long hair was white as wool, and his eyes were piercing
> and brilliant. He was able to talk immediately and, according to Lameck, apparently
> conversed with the Lord. Lameck, concerned and disturbed, wondered if the boy were
> his own or possibly had been conceived by one of the "watchers" or "sons of heaven."[7]
> He discussed the matter with his wife, BatEnosh, who swore that the boy was Lameck's.
> Lameck took his problem to his father, Methuselah, who in turn sought counsel from
> his father, Enoch, who previously had been taken (translated) into heaven. Enoch told
> Methuselah to assure Lameck that his son had been sent from God to do a great work
> on the earth and that his name should be called Noah. [*Christ's Eternal Gospel*, p.
> 155, rendering parallel translations from The Book of Lameck, The Book of Noah,
> and The Book of Enoch from the scroll "A Genesis Apocryphon," the Dead Sea Scrolls]

Zion's process of reaching the above-indicated state of perfection was not
quick or easy, as we learn from Moses: "And all the days of Zion, in the
days of Enoch, were three hundred and sixty-five years. And Enoch and all
his people walked with God, and he dwelt in the midst of Zion; and it came
to pass that Zion was not, for God received it up into his own bosom; and
from thence went forth the saying, ZION IS FLED." (Moses 7:68-69.)[8] We
cannot tell from these scriptures precisely where God planted Zion and its
inhabitants. This latest passage suggests they were taken to the Lord's "bosom."
This is supported by Enoch's own statement, "And thou hast taken Zion to
thine own bosom, from all thy creations, from all eternity to all eternity;
and naught but peace, justice, and truth is the habitation of thy throne; and
mercy shall go before thy face and have no end; . . ." (Moses 7:31.) Still,
none of these scriptures absolutely points us to the *precise* location of Zion,
or of God's "bosom," if Zion is truly there.

This actual event of translation of the city of Zion along with its geographical
surroundings and underpinnings, being physically removed from Earth and

---

[6] This is not, of course, scripture that is necessarily accepted as containing true doctrine
by the Church. However, the passage is instructive, and the reader is free to determine
the value of the information.

[7] The concept of giants being born to normal human women impregnated by "watchers"
or "sons of heaven" is quite controversial among Christian scholars and UFOlogists alike.
For a fuller treatment of this subject see Chapter 3.

[8] See also, *Doctrine and Covenants* 38:4; Genesis 5:24; and Hebrews 11:5.

taken elsewhere, is affirmed in modern scripture also. God declares that Enoch and the people of Zion were "separated from the earth," and that God "received" them to Himself: "Wherefore, hearken ye together and let me show unto you even my wisdom—the wisdom of him whom ye say is the God of Enoch, and his brethren, Who were separated from the earth, and were received unto myself—a city reserved until a day of righteousness shall come—a day which was sought for by all holy men, and they found it not because of wickedness and abominations; . . ." (*Doctrine and Covenants* 45:11-12; See also, *Inspired Version*, Genesis 14:32-34)

In this latter-day revelation we also learn that the city of Zion will return to the Earth—to the city of New Jerusalem in Jackson County, Missouri—at the time when "a day of righteousness shall come." Of that glorious day, "the Lord said unto Enoch: Then shalt thou and all thy city meet them there, and we will receive them into our bosom, and they shall see us; and we will fall upon their necks, and they shall fall upon our necks, and we will kiss each other; . . ." (Moses 7:63.) Both of these scriptures further reinforce the fact that Zion is with God, but again, we receive no directive or qualification of what it means for noncelestial beings to be "with God."

In all of the above material, we learn that Zion and its surrounding countryside is somewhere with God, but we cannot be sure if it is physically "with" God, or physically "near" God, on a nearby planet. Of the planet on which God resides, modern scripture informs us:

> The angels do not reside on a planet like this earth; But they reside in the presence of God, on a globe like a sea of glass and fire, where all things for their glory are manifest, past, present, and future, and are continually before the Lord. The place where God resides is a great Urim and Thummim. This earth, in its sanctified and immortal state, will be made like unto crystal and will be a Urim and Thummim to the inhabitants who dwell thereon, whereby all things pertaining to an inferior kingdom, or all kingdoms of a lower order, will be manifest to those who dwell on it; and this earth will be Christ's. [D & C 130:79]

God's planet is a celestial world. Our limited understanding of the doctrine of translation informs us that translated beings are raised from a telestial existence to a terrestrial state. We can safely assume that the city of Zion and the portion of the Earth taken with it was likewise elevated to a terrestrial state. The obvious question is, Are terrestrial beings living on a terrestrial portion of Earth, compatible with a celestial world and beings, for an extended period of time? Other than our understanding that in the eternities, beings of a higher order may minister to beings of a lower order, but not vice versa,[9]

---

[9] *See e.g.*, D & C 88:81-91.

we cannot venture an informed guess about their compatibility. We know from Moses that "Enoch and all his people walked with God, and he dwelt in the midst of Zion," (Moses 7:69); but again, this is a case of a being of a higher order ministering to beings of a lower order.

It is possible that Enoch and his city dwell "near" God's celestial planet instead of on it. We learn from the writings of Father Abraham that there exist planets and stars *near* God's dwelling place, as Abraham instructs as he sets out the hierarchy of the planets and stars.

> And I, Abraham, had the Urim and Thummim, which the Lord my God had given unto me, in Ur of the Chaldees; And I saw the stars that they were very great, and that one of them was nearest unto the throne of God; and there were many great ones which were near unto it; And the Lord said unto me: These are the governing ones; and the name of the great one is Kolob, because it is near unto me, for I am the Lord thy God: . . . And thus there shall be the reckoning of the time of one planet above another, until thou come nigh unto Kolob, which Kolob is after the reckoning of the Lord's time; which Kolob is set nigh unto the throne of God. . . . [Abraham 3:1-17]

Although no definitive answer is found in these scriptures concerning the exact dwelling place of Zion, our reasoning that Zion is on one of the planets near God instead of with God on His own celestial planet appears to be supported by Joseph Smith's explanation of the process of perfection of translated beings. The Prophet explains, "Many have supposed that the doctrine of translation was a doctrine whereby men were taken immediately into the presence of God, and into an eternal fullness, but this is a mistaken idea. Their place of habitation is that of the terrestrial order, and a place prepared for such characters He held in reserve to be ministering angels unto many planets, and who as yet have not entered into so great a fullness as those who are resurrected from the dead." (*Teachings of the Prophet Joseph Smith*, p. 170)

This statement apparently eliminates any possibility that Zion is on God's celestial planet because translated beings are not "taken immediately into the presence of God," but to a "place of habitation" of a "terrestrial order." Therefore, God's "bosom" seems to be either figurative language for "a godly place," or a place or planet in space near God. This long discussion demonstrates that this Earth is visited by beings from Zion and beings from God's presence. Therefore, we know that beings from at least two other planets visit here on a regular basis. Are these the beings that pilot the thousands or even millions of UFOs that are reported in our skies? The question is premature at this point. However, the discussion of the nature of these beings is important in answering the question later in our discussion.

All of these "regulations" regarding the status of translated beings do not take into account the changed status of Zion and its inhabitants at the time of the Lord's resurrection. We learn through revelation that all of these beings, translated before the resurrection, were with Christ in the resurrection, and have received the "fullness" of which Joseph Smith spoke above. (*D & C* 133:54-55) This, of course, does not change the initial status of these translated persons as we have discussed them, but it could change their current status regarding the abode of Zion—they could *now* be celestial beings living on God's planet. However, we know that Zion and its inhabitants remain as a single body, and will return to the *terrestrialized* Earth as an intact city, and will unite with New Jerusalem, a city built on the American continent by the Saints. This indicates a "terrestrial" status for Zion.

> [A]nd righteousness and truth will I cause to sweep the earth as with a flood, to gather out mine el⌐ct from the four quarters of the earth, unto a place which I shall prepare, an Holy City, that my people may gird up their loins, and be looking forth for the time of my coming; for there shall be my tabernacle, and it shall be called Zion, a New Jerusalem. And the Lord said unto Enoch: Then shalt thou and all thy city meet them there, and we will receive them into our bosom, and they shall see us; and we will fall upon their necks, and they shall fall upon our necks, and we will kiss each other; and there shall be mine abode, and it shall be Zion, which shall come forth out of all the creations which I have made; and for the space of a thousand years the earth shall rest. [Moses 7:62-64]

The changing of the location of the Lord's "bosom" and "abode" to New Jerusalem on this Earth in the near future are further indications that such words are not used as literal pinpoints of God's celestial dwelling place, but are figurative terms indicating a quality of life and communion with God.

The Order Of The Universe

Father Abraham discerned the order and makeup of the universe by means of the Urim and Thummim.

> And I, Abraham, had the Urim and Thummim, which the Lord my God had given unto me, in Ur of the Chaldees;
> And I saw the stars that they were very great, and that one of them was nearest unto the throne of God; and there were many great ones which were near unto it;
> And the Lord said unto me: These are the governing ones; and the name of the great one is Kolob, because it is near unto me, for I am the Lord thy God: I have set this one to govern all those which belong to the same order as that upon which thou standest.
> And the Lord said unto me, by the Urim and Thummim, that Kolob was after the manner of the Lord, according to its times and seasons in the revolutions thereof; that one revolution was a day unto the Lord, after his manner of reckoning, it being one

thousand years according to the time appointed unto that whereon thou standest. This is the reckoning of the Lord's time, according to the reckoning of Kolob.

And the Lord said unto me: The planet which is the lesser light, lesser than that which is to rule the day, even the night, is above or greater than that upon which thou standest in point of reckoning, for it moveth in order more slow; this is in order because it standeth above the earth upon which thou standest, therefore the reckoning of its time is not so many as to its number of days, and of months, and of years.

And the Lord said unto me: Now, Abraham, these two facts exist, behold thine eyes see it; it is given unto thee to know the times of reckoning, and the set time, yea, the set time of the earth upon which thou standest, and the set time of the greater light which is set to rule the day, and the set time of the lesser light which is set to rule the night.

Now the set time of the lesser light is a longer time as to its reckoning than the reckoning of the time of the earth upon which thou standest.

And where these two facts exist, there shall be another fact above them, that is, there shall be another planet whose reckoning of time shall be longer still;

And thus there shall be the reckoning of the time of one planet above another, until thou come nigh unto Kolob, which Kolob is after the reckoning of the Lord's time; which Kolob is set nigh unto the throne of God, to govern all those planets which belong to the same order as that upon which thou standest.

And it is given unto thee to know the set time of all the stars that are set to give light, until thou come near unto the throne of God.

Thus I, Abraham, talked with the Lord, face to face, as one man talketh with another; and he told me of the works which his hands had made;

And he said unto me: My son, my son (and his hand was stretched out), behold I will show you all these. And he put his hand upon mine eyes, and I saw those things which his hands had made, which were many; and they multiplied before mine eyes, and I could not see the end thereof.

And he said unto me: This is Shinehah, which is the sun. And he said unto me: Kokob, which is star. And he said unto me: Olea, which is the moon. And he said unto me: Kokaubeam, which signifies stars, or all the great lights, which were in the firmament of heaven.

. . . If two things exist, and there be one above the other, there shall be greater things above them; therefore Kolob is the greatest of all the Kokaubeam that thou hast seen, because it is nearest unto me.

Now, if there be two things, one above the other, and the moon be above the earth, then it may be that a planet or a star may exist above it; and there is nothing that the Lord thy God shall take into his heart to do but what he will do it. [Abraham 3:1-17]

An important fact that we learn from this scripture passage is that Kolob is not the celestial planet on which God dwells, nor a terrestrial planet on which Enoch dwells. The Lord tells Abraham that Kolob is not only "nearest" unto God, clarifying that it is not God's abode, but Kolob is not even a planet—it is a "Kokob, which is a star . . . the greatest of all the Kokaubeam," signifying stars. We can infer, however, that there are planets near Kolob, which is the nearest global body to God's planet:

And thus there shall be the reckoning of the time of *one planet above another, until thou come nigh unto Kolob*, which Kolob is after the reckoning of the Lord's time;

which Kolob is set nigh unto the throne of God, to govern all those planets which belong to the same order as that upon which thou standest. [Abraham 3:9]

There are, therefore, planets "nigh" unto Kolob. It is probably on one of these near ones that Zion resides. This passage also exhibits another interesting point that we learn from Abraham—that it is often the revolutions[10] of these great stars, not always of inhabited planets, that establish the bench-marks for the measurement of time throughout the universe. "And the Lord said unto me: These are the governing ones; and the name of the great one is Kolob, because it is near unto me, for I am the Lord thy God: I have set this one to govern all those which belong to the same order as that upon which thou standest." (Abraham 3:3) We discuss the "reckoning," or possibly the "relativity" of time among the various "classes" of stars and planets below. This may become important in our discussion of the origins of UFOs and their occupants.

Classes Or Clusters?

In rendering translations of Facsimile No. 2 accompanying the Book of Abraham, Joseph Smith revealed that there exists not only classification and hierarchy among the planets and stars, but that groups of stars and planets are organized into "orders," as indicated by the above passage also. Earth, and all other planets of its order, are governed by Kolob. The word "order," of course, is not defined for us here and we cannot tell from the scriptures if "order" indicates a class or family of planets, or a general location of concentrically clustered groups of planets. Because many of the governing stars and planets seem to be located in the same general location—near God's celestial planet, we could infer that the former definition (classes) is more likely. However, because groups of the governed orders appear to be grouped in close concentric proximity to one another, the latter is possible.

The fact that Earth belongs to Kolob's order indicates two things: there must be something uncommon or unique about the Earth because it belongs to what appears to be a distinguished order; and, there exist other orders, of which Earth is not a member.[11] We have little information regarding

---

10 When the scriptures speak of revolutions of stars or planets, we lack information concerning whether "revolution" refers to the body revolving on its own axis (rotation,) or orbiting around another star or planet. This is made apparent from Joseph Smith's translation of Figure 5 of Facsimile No. 2, discussed below.

11 Although the existence of this fact may seem obvious, its significance will vary with a definitive answer to the question, How do the "orders" of planets vary?

these observations other than to note that this earth enjoys the distinction of having the Savior live His life here. This Earth is unique of all of God's Creations because of these truths.

Joseph Smith's translation of Figure 2 (Facsimile 2) supports the idea that the great governing stars and planets regulate groups of planet "classes" or "families" rather than concentric clusters:

> Fig. 2. Stands next to Kolob, called by the Egyptians Oliblish, which is the next grand governing creation near to the celestial or the place where God resides; holding the key of power also, pertaining to other planets; as revealed from God to Abraham, as he offered sacrifice upon an altar, which he had built unto the Lord.

The global body Oliblish, which is second closest to God, regulates a group of planets not associated with Earth. Many Book of Abraham commentaries appear to indicate that these governing systems are merely moons revolving around planets, planets revolving around suns, and solar systems revolving around larger systems, until we arrive at galaxies revolving around systems at the center of which are "the governing ones."[12] The fact that the governing ones are clustered near the celestial planet of God, and their governed systems are far away from God's abode indicates that this is not the case—not entirely, anyway. In other words, the concentric nature of the commentaries' theoretic systems does not allow for the grouping of the governing ones near God's planet, with their governed systems being far away in space. However, the concentric nature of our solar systems and galaxies provides for partial correctness of this theory. The breakdown of the theory comes in the nonconcentricity of the entire system.

The Measurement Of Time

To further aid in our understanding of the nature of the universe, Joseph Smith rendered translations of Abraham's hand-drawn Facsimiles that accompanied the Book of Abraham. These translations bear strong witness of the divine calling of Joseph as a prophet, seer, and revelator, as well as provide us with valuable information regarding the order of the universe. The translation of Figure 1 of Facsimile 2 of the Book of Abraham confirms much of what has already been discussed in the scriptures treated above.

---

[12] *See, e.g.*, George Reynolds and Janne M. Sjodahl, *Commentary on the Pearl of Great Price*, p. 309.

Fig. 1. Kolob, signifying the first creation, nearest to the celestial, or the residence of God. First in government, the last pertaining to the measurement of time. The measurement according to celestial time, which celestial time signifies one day to a cubit. One day in Kolob is equal to a thousand years according to the measurement of this earth, which is called by the Egyptians Jah-oh-eh.

The correlation between a "thousand-year celestial day" and a "cubit" is illustrated by Hugh Nibley in his explanation of Figure 4 (Facsimile 2): "The sky-vessel is called 'the ship of 1000 cubits long,' suggesting the designation of the above celestial Sokar-ship as 'also a numerical figure, in Egyptian signifying one thousand.' (Fac. 2, Fig. 4.)" The "space/time" relationship is elucidated in Nibley's statement, "Clement of Alexandria, an Egyptian, says that the ship symbol signifies 'that the Sun, taking its way through the sweet and moist air begets time, and hence is a symbol of time' (*Strom.*, V, XL7, 41, 3; Hopfner, *Fontes*, p. 371)." (*The Message of the Joseph Smith Papyri, an Egyptian Endowment*, pp. 137-38)

I have somtimes listened while Gospel Doctrine instructors, and others, have assumed that there exists a difference in the comprehension of the passing of time between beings of these various classes of planets and stars, at a "1 day/1,000 year" ratio. A possible explanatin of the principle is that the Kolob class (or classes) of planets and stars revolve at a much slower rate, and the passing of time is universally comprehended as one thousand years (as we comprehend them) per revolution. However, the former explanation could be true—that is, "Earth class" beings could live or comprehend a thousand years in the same real time a "Kolob class" being lives or perceives a day.

All of this presupposes that God even experiences time (and space) in a way like man does. The truth is, we do not know the answers to these time/space questions. Throughout the centuries theologians, philosophers, and scientists have attempted to discern the relativity of time throughout the universe, which fact alone indicates that the subject is repeatedly thrust into the conversation by some unknown source. Is the discussion legitimate, or is it a red herring surreptitiously raised to confuse the issues of the nature of God or the nature of "aliens"? We might assume that these are unrevealed mysteries, and our preoccupation with them will prove unfruitful. We discuss these issues here, however, because they are raised in the "UFO/alien visitation" literature to a large extent. Again, before we can intelligently judge the validity of such "alien" assertions, we must garner all of the intelligence that God has revealed on the subject, no matter how little, as in this case. Some small amount of enlightenment may be had by H. Donl Peterson, who quotes Elder James E. Talmage and others in his book, *The Pearl of Great Price, A History and*

Commentary (pp. 113-14). Therein, Elder Talmage and others briefly discuss measurements in units of time among the various orders and planets. The representations are not definitive, however.

Finally, the translation of Figure 4 (Facsimile 2), the one thousand cubit solar bark, signifying one thousand years of time to a day of time, informs us that Oliblish also measures time in like manner as Kolob. Unfortunately, we are no more enlightened concerning time relativity, but we are informed a little more regarding the structure of the universe.

> Fig. 4. Answers to the Hebrew word Raukeeyang, signifying expanse, or the firmament of the heavens; also a numerical figure, in Egyptian signifying one thousand; answering to the measuring of the time of Oliblish, which is equal with Kolob in its revolution and in its measuring of time.

How The "Governing Ones" Govern

The translation of Figure 5 is possibly the most interesting, and confusing of all of the explanations of Facsimile 2. It appears to teach us concerning the organization of governing stars and planets, and their governed groups.

> Fig. 5. Is called in Egyptian Ensih-go-on-dosh; this is one of the governing planets also, and is said by the Egyptians to be the Sun, and to borrow its light from Kolob through the medium of Kae-e-vanrash, which is the grand Key, or, in other words, the governing power, which governs fifteen other fixed planets or stars, as also Floeese or the Moon, the Earth and the Sun in their annual revolutions. This planet receives its power through the medium of Kli-flos-is-es, or Hah-ko-kau-beam, the stars represented by numbers 22 and 23, receiving light from the revolutions of Kolob.

Figure 5 is said to represent Ensih-go-on-dosh, a governing "planet," defined as a "star." This instructs us that the words "star" and "planet" are sometimes used interchangeably to signify "star." The Egyptians believe it to be the Sun, although we receive no specific endorsement of their belief. The translation further informs us that Ensih-go-on-dosh, or possibly the Sun, "borrows" its light from Kolob, through a governing power or medium called Kae-e-vanrash. The structure of the sentence implies that this Kae-e-vanrash "governs fifteen other fixed planets or stars," among which are our own Sun, Earth, and Moon. The last principle we learn from Figure 5 is that the Sun (Ensih-go-on-dosh) receives its light indirectly from Kolob, through Kli-flos-is-es or Hah-ko-kau-beam (note the plural suffix "beam"), either a star with two names, or two distinct stars, one of which is the intermediate transferor of light and power. However the medium operates, it is interesting to know, though modern science might not accept the principle, that these orders of stars from the governing to the governed are linked in a way that power and energy are circuited through them from the greater to the lesser, regardless of their relative position or proximity.

More Planets = Interplanetary Travel?

The Standard Works leave no room to doubt that life exists on other planets. They make clear that many millions of planets, possibly billions, or more, exist in our universe—planets peopled with children of our Heavenly Father— humans that appear essentially like us.[13] Regarding questions of interplanetary communication and travel, the Standard Works shed little light beyond that which is discussed above. However, latter-day prophets and apostles have commented on the topic and have assured us that such interplanetary communication and travel exists at some level or another. We know for sure that the possibilities of interplanetary communication and travel are greatly enhanced by the sheer number of planets peopled by humans. Seeing in our own history that 100 years can elevate humans from horse and buggy to the planets, there is little difficulty in assuming that other planets, more righteous perhaps, have enjoyed longer bursts of technological revelation enabling interplanetary intercourse.

---

13 "And God said, Let us make man in our image, after our likeness: . . ." (Genesis 1:26.)

3

Latter-day Prophets Speak About Extraterrestrial Life

Modern Prophets Speak With Authority

Before initiating a discussion of what latter-day prophets have said concerning the multiplicity of worlds and their respective natures and inhabitants, it may be necessary to provide a reasonable basis for some to believe that these men possessed abundant personal knowledge of such matters. It also may be prudent to establish a reliable reporting system, in order to properly authenticate any purported statements by latter-day prophets. Therefore, I shall endeavor to use only properly reported statements herein, or note unauthenticated reports.

It must be remembered that all scientific knowledge ultimately comes from God, as was taught by Joseph Smith: "If there was anything great or good in the world, it came from God. . . . The learning of the Egyptians, and their knowledge of astronomy was no doubt taught them by Abraham and Joseph, as their records testify, who received it from the Lord." (*Teachings of the Prophet Joseph Smith*, p. 251) President Spencer W. Kimball further taught that sometimes God's technological gifts to mankind remain inferior to revelation when man is seeking higher knowledge of God's creative works: "Astronomers have developed powerful telescopes through which they have seen much, but prophets and seers have had clearer vision at greater distances with precision instruments such as the Liahona and the Urim and Thummim, which have far exceeded the most advanced radar, radio, television, or telescope equipment." (*The Teachings of Spencer W. Kimball*, p. 445) In all cases, the reader is free to discern the authoritative value of each statement concerning the planets, their natures, their inhabitants, and travel and communication between them.

Joseph Smith Understood Extraterrestrial Life

Joseph Smith, the Prophet of the latter-day restoration, was, in my mind, as qualified as any prophet to speak on topics concerning the cosmos and its inhabitants. As with all prophets claiming any insight into the nature of the planets and the inhabitants thereof, Joseph Smith had to acquire his information through revelation. He was allowed to look into the eternities on various occasions, viewing and discerning the creations of God, as in the vision recorded in Section 76 of the *Doctrine and Covenants*. In performing the work of translating the Book of Abraham, and in similar pursuits, Joseph Smith gained the very same understanding of the universe held by Father Abraham, as recorded by Joseph in his journal:

> October 1.—This afternoon I labored on the Egyptian alphabet, in company with Brothers Oliver Cowdery and W. W. Phelps, and during the research, the principles of astronomy *as understood* by Father Abraham and the ancients unfolded to our understanding, the particulars of which will appear hereafter.[1] [*History of the Church*, vol. 2, p. 286, emphasis supplied]

Like Abraham, Joseph had complete access to and training in the use of the Urim and Thummim. It should be remembered that during Joseph's annual visits to the place where the golden plates were buried, he was taught by the angel Moroni. These instructional encounters included, along with explanations of the scriptures and gospel doctrines, training in the use of the Urim and Thummim. Joseph's Urim and Thummim was the very same possessed by the brother of Jared. (D & C 17:1) Joseph also possessed the "seer stone" which he used as a Urim and Thummim.[2] Besides its use as

---

1   Despite this promise, little else was offered on the subject by Joseph in the *History of the Church*. William W. Phelps did refer to these "records found in the catacombs of Egypt," however, in passing on some information he claimed to have originated with Joseph concerning the age of what he termed "this system." He said that "eternity . . . has been going on in this system, almost two thousand five hundred and fifty five millions [2,555,000,000] of years." *Times and Seasons*, V, (January 1, 1845), page 758. Whether "this system" refers to our solar system, one of the higher orders of systems comprising our universe, the universe itself, or Heavenly Father's eternal kingdom, we have no answer. I infer that it refers to God's Kingdom/universe, based on the use of the term "eternity." What is unique about the statement is that in Joseph Smith's day, no one spoke of the age of the universe in terms of billions of years. Now, scientists guess, based on their perceived status of an oscillating universe theory, that its age could be in the 2.5 billion year range. Recent guesses augment this figure to 10 to 15 billion years.

2 Joseph retained the seer stone throughout his life. As of the time of President Joseph Fielding Smith, the seer stone was still in the possession of the Church. (*Doctrines of Salvation*, Vol. 3, p. 225)

a translating device, the Urim and Thummim was used to see things from God's vantage point. Joseph later explained what it is that one sees in a Urim and Thummim as he described the future state of this earth and its celestial inhabitants.

> The angels do not reside on a planet like this earth;
> But they reside in the presence of God, on a globe like a sea of glass and fire, where all things for their glory are manifest, past, present, and future, and are continually before the Lord.
> The place where God resides is a great Urim and Thummim.
> This earth, in its sanctified and immortal state, will be made like unto crystal and will be a Urim and Thummim to the inhabitants who dwell thereon, whereby all things pertaining to an inferior kingdom, or all kingdoms of a lower order, will be manifest to those who dwell on it; and this earth will be Christ's.
> Then the white stone mentioned in Revelation 2:17, will become a Urim and Thummim to each individual who receives one, whereby things pertaining to a higher order of kingdoms will be made known; . . . [D & C 130:6-10]

Therefore, a Urim and Thummim is a device used by its operator to see all things past, present, and future of a lower or higher order, if the operator is so authorized.[3] Abraham explained that it was through the use of the Urim and Thummim that he was able to discern the nature of the cosmos. (Abraham 3:1)

Joseph Smith not only translated the Book of Abraham, but also rendered interpretations of Facsimiles 1 through 3, No. 2 of which contained explanations of Abraham, Chapter 3, as cited above. Based on the foregoing, it cannot be doubted that Joseph Smith possessed superior knowledge concerning the cosmos. It is possible, in fact, that he knew as much as, or more than, any other prophet on Earth.

We cannot assume that Joseph considered the topic of the cosmos inappropriate for discussion and instruction among the Brethren of the early restoration, inasmuch as he taught it to them himself: "I also gave some instructions in the mysteries of the kingdom of God; such as the history of the planets, Abraham's writings upon the planetary systems, etc." (*Teachings of the Prophet Joseph Smith*, p. 118) Joseph said, speaking of William M'Lellin, Brigham Young, and Jared Carter, "I exhibited and explained the Egyptian records to them, and explained many of the things concerning the dealing of God with the ancients, and the formation of the planetary systems. (*History*

---

[3] "And the things are called interpreters, and no man can look in them except he be commanded, lest he should look for that he ought not and he should perish. And whosoever is commanded to look in them, the same is called seer." (Mosiah 8:13)

of the Church, vol. 2, p. 334) Commenting on this quote by Joseph Smith, President Joseph Fielding Smith added:

> There is a prevalent notion in the world today that before the time of Columbus, Galileo, and Copernicus, all ancient people believed that the earth was flat and the center of the universe. From the writings of the Scriptures, and more especially those which have come to us in this dispensation, we know that the ancient peoples, when they were guided by the Spirit of the Lord, had the true conception of the universe. The Lord revealed to Abraham great truths about the heavenly bodies, their revolutions, times and seasons, and these were published by the Prophet Joseph Smith before modern astronomers were familiar with these facts. From the writings of Abraham we learn that the Egyptians understood the nature of the planets.[4] Moses also recorded much about this and other worlds, but because of the unbelief and apostasy from truth, these writings were eliminated from his writings. In the Book of Abraham we find the following:
>
>> But the records of the fathers, even the patriarchs, concerning the right of Priesthood the Lord my God preserved in mine own hands; therefore a knowledge of the beginning of the creation, and also of the planets, and of the stars, as they were made known unto the fathers, have I kept unto this day, and I shall endeavor to write some of these things upon this record, for the benefit of my posterity that shall come after me.
>
> We learn from the Book of Mormon (Helaman 12:13-15) that the Nephites understood the nature of the planets. It was not until apostasy and rebellion against the things of God that the true knowledge of the universe, as well as the knowledge of other truths, became lost among men. [*Teachings of the Prophet Joseph Smith*, p. 118, footnote 2]

Not only did Joseph teach that there exist millions of worlds that are inhabited by beings, just like those that dwell on Earth, but he also specifically taught that animals inhabit those planets. Some, he instructed, are quite unlike those found on Earth: "I suppose John saw beings [in heaven] of a thousand forms, that had been saved from ten thousand times ten thousand [100,000,000] earths like this,—strange beasts of which we have no conception: all might be seen in heaven." (*Teachings of the Prophet Joseph Smith*, p. 291)

Brigham Young Also Knew Of Life On Other Planets

President Brigham Young too, was quite clear in speaking of the existence of millions of life-sustaining earths like our own.

> There is a Power that has organized all things from the crude matter that floats in the immensity of space. He has given form, motion and life to this material world. . . . He is the Father of all, is above all, through all, and in you all, he knoweth

---

[4] Abraham himself taught the Egyptians about the cosmos.

all things pertaining to this earth, and he knows all things pertaining to millions of earths like this. [*Discourses of Brigham Young*, 11:120; 11:41]

According to Brigham Young, it was from one of these earths that our father Adam brought the lifeforms that are now here.

[Adam] was the person who brought the animals and the seeds from other planets to this world, and brought a wife with him and stayed here. You may read and believe what you please as to what is found written in the Bible. Adam was made from the dust of an earth, but not from the dust of this earth. [*Journal of Discourses*, 3:319]

President Young further explained that God has been creating worlds like ours for a very long time.

The Organized Universe—The creations of God—the worlds that are and the worlds that have been,—who can grasp in the vision of his mind the truth that there never has been a time when there have not been worlds like this. There is an eternity of matter, and it is all acted upon and filled with a portion of divinity. Matter is to exist; it cannot be annihilated. Eternity is without bounds, and is filled with matter; and there is no such place as empty space. And matter is capacitated to receive intelligence. [*Ibid*. 7:2]

Brigham Young also teaches us in this statement that matter is not only plentiful, but it is eternal, cannot be destroyed, and can be impregnated with spirit intelligence. The following statement by President Young expounds on these principles.

[Matter] is brought together, organized, and capacitated to receive knowledge and intelligence, to be enthroned in glory, to be made angels, Gods—beings who will hold control over the elements, and have power by their word to command the creation and redemption of worlds, or to extinguish suns by their breath, and disorganize worlds, hurling them back into their chaotic state.[5] This is what you and I are created for. [Ibid, 3:356]

Joseph Fielding Smith Taught Of Extraterrestrial Life

President Joseph Fielding Smith has also taught that Heavenly Father has countless planets inhabited by His offspring.

EARTHS CREATED FOR MAN. The Lord declared to Moses that his great work and glory is "to bring to pass the immortality and eternal life of man." For this purpose

---

5 This statement does not necessarily indicate that the divine extinguishing of planets actually occurs (although we have no direct revelation concerning the lives or cycles of stars), but only that Gods have such power. The quote should be considered in light of the statement by President Joseph Fielding Smith quoted in Chapter 2. This teaching is supported by Orson Pratt in the *Journal of Discourses*, vol. 19, p. 290.

earths have been made and are now being built; and *the Lord's purpose is to provide for his children immortality and eternal life, not only on this earth, but on the countless earths throughout the universe.* They are numberless to man, yet our Father knows them all and they are numbered unto him. The Lord has said: "And as one *earth shall pass away,* and the heavens thereof even so shall another come; and there is no end to my works, neither to my words." [Footnote cites Moses 1:27-40]

. . .

Other earths, no doubt, are being *prepared as habitations for terrestrial and telestial beings,* for there must be places prepared for those who fail to obtain celestial glory,[6] who receive immortality but not eternal life . . . ." [*Doctrines of Salvation*, vol. I, pp. 72-74]

This last statement demonstrates a heretofore undiscussed principle—that there exist millions[7] of planets in our universe peopled by those who have been born on other worlds, who have died and been resurrected, and having failed to obtain a celestial glory, were assigned to a specially prepared planet of a terrestrial or telestial nature to act as their eternal inheritance. The existence of such planets and their inhabitants raises many questions regarding the spirits of such planets, their death and resurrection, and interplanetary contact of the inhabitants of those worlds with other worlds.

Spencer W. Kimball Taught
Of Extraterrestrial Life

Speaking of the time when the righteous will have obtained the creative powers of Godhood, President Spencer W. Kimball offered some enlightening comments about life on other worlds that may help answer some of the questions raised above.

We take one element, and we transform it and organize it into another . . . . You look out there in the starry night and you see the sky is filled with stars. There are in the

---

6 President Smith, as well as other prophets, made clear that the planets created for probationary life, like Earth, will be eventually inherited only by those who obtain celestial glory: "MANY CELESTIAL EARTHS. This earth on which we dwell, like many that have gone before, is destined to become a celestial sphere and the righteous shall inherit it forever." [*Doctrines of Salvation,* vol. II, p. 26]

7 The number of such terrestrial and telestial planets would necessarily be twice the number of "probationary state" planets, because each probationary planet becomes the celestial abode of its righteous inhabitants, leaving the necessity of two new planets for those who inherit the other two levels of glory.

universe numerous bits or quantities of materials—gases and other elements—which brought together in the proper way can create an earth and can eventually produce fruit trees, and grain fields, and forests.

All of that is possible, and you are the men the Lord has chosen to do this work. Now it will take a long while, of course, for us to learn enough to be able to do that, but we're on our way. Every week we learn more about the priesthood. Every week we learn better how to handle it. The time will come when we will not only create with our wives the mortal tabernacles which our earthly children occupy, but we will be able to expand our efforts and extend them and go out into the great eternities. And we will be able to produce great families of spirit children who in turn may return to that planet which you will have organized and will have made habitable. And those children will be permitted to go to those planets or earths, and there they will receive mortal bodies to have their schooling process so that eventually they also can return to their Heavenly Father. [*The Teachings of Spencer W. Kimball*, p. 53]

In responding to some of the questions raised above, President Kimball asked and answered the following:

Is man earthbound? Largely so, and temporarily so, yet Enoch and his people were translated from earth, and the living Christ and angels commuted.

Is there interplanetary conversation? Certainly. Man may speak to God and receive answers from him.

Is there association of interplanetary beings? There is no question.

Are planets out in space inhabited by intelligent creatures? Without doubt.

Will radioed messages ever come between planets across limitless space? Certainly, for there have already been coming for six thousand years, properly decoded, interpreted, and publicized messages of utmost importance to the inhabitants of this earth. Dreams and open vision, like perfected television programs, have come repeatedly. Personal representatives have brought warning messages too numerous times to mention, and it is our testimony to the world that God lives and abides in his heavenly home, and the earth is his footstool, and only one of his numerous creations; that Jesus Christ the Son of that living God is the Creator, Savior, and Redeemer of the people on this earth who will listen and obey; and that these interstellar messages—call them what you will, visions, revelations, television, radio—from the abode of God to man on this earth continue now to come to the living prophet of God among us this day. [*The Teachings of Spencer W. Kimball*, p. 445]

Not only does President Kimball confirm the existence of life on other planets, but he also affirms the existence of interplanetary travel and communication. However, a narrow reading of this statement limits President Kimball's remarks to "official" ecclesiastical communications and travels— prayer, revelation, and angelic visitation. We have already established that God, angels, and translated beings travel here from at least two different planets. Whether or not President Kimball intended to restrict his accounts of interplanetary travel and communication to a "God to Earth" context, we cannot be sure, but a slightly broader reading of his remarks leaves the door wide open for liberal interplanetary intercourse.

Who Ministers To This Earth?

If we consider interplanetary exchange in a strictly angelic sense, the question, from how many planets could Earth be visited?, becomes a narrow one because of the following scripture:

> In answer to the question—Is not the reckoning of God's time, angel's time, prophet's time, and man's time, according to the planet on which they reside? I answer, Yes. *But there are no angels who minister to this earth but those who do belong or have belonged to it.* The angels do not reside on a planet like this earth; But they reside in the presence of God, on a globe like a sea of glass and fire, where all things for *their* [8] glory are manifest, past, present, and future, and are continually before the Lord. [D & C 130:4-7]

Only those angels who have been, or will be born on this earth can perform angelic ministrations here. Because this angelic class of beings resides on God's celestial planet,[9] we know that most angelic ministrations are limited to visitors from that planet. Certain translated beings, however, as already discussed, minister to this Earth "angelically," who probably do not reside on God's celestial planet. These citizens of Zion most likely live on a terrestrial planet near God's celestial planet. Other translated beings such as Moses, Elijah, John, Alma the younger, the Three Nephite apostles, possibly Melchizedek and his city of Salem,[10] and other individually translated persons who at times minister to this Earth, *may* dwell on planets other than Zion's terrestrial abode—we do not know where they are.[11] All of this merely tells us that the Earth has exchange with at least two other planets—possibly more. This is limited to "ecclesiastical" exchanges, however. The scriptures cast little light on our greater question of whether "exploratory" exchange between probationary planets is allowed, and if so, whether Earth is a participant therein.

If we are seeking to establish a pattern or to extrapolate a rule from what we have learned so far, there are certain principles that come to mind. We have little indication from the scriptures whether or not the rule that "Earth's

---

[8] Note that the Urim and Thummim is also for the benefit of the angels, not just for God.

[9] None of this indicates, however, that angels that belong to other worlds do not simultaneously reside on God's celestial planet. In fact, we must assume that such is the case in light of Joseph Smith's teaching that God's throne is surrounded by "sanctified beings from worlds that have been." (*Mormon Doctrine*, pp. 65-66)

[10] Inspired Version, Genesis 14:32-34.

[11] Although the scriptures are not specific concerning the whereabouts of these translated persons and groups, there are indications that all translated beings are with Zion.

only ministers are from Earth" applies to angels who minister to other planets. It is possible that angels from other planets are assigned to minister to planets other than their own. We have the teaching of Joseph Smith that translated beings who are pursuing a course of advancement have as their terrestrial habitation "a place prepared for such characters [that] He held in reserve to be *ministering angels unto many planets.*" (*Teachings of the Prophet Joseph Smith*, p. 170) This could indicate that individual translated beings minister to many planets, or that the *group* of beings ministers to many planets, but each individual is sent only to his home planet. If the former is true, which is quite possible from the text of the statement, this is a strong indication that there exists a distinct rule among other planets regarding interplanetary ministration. The egocentric thought that this earth may be different than other worlds, and that a separate set of rules may apply, is further supported by Earth's uniqueness due to the personal (temporal) and sacrificial presence of the universal Savior. This uniqueness, however, leads us only to an indication of "quarantine" of this earth that does not exist among other worlds. If there exists such a limitation at the angelic ministration level, there could well exist the same limitation at the social/exploration level as well.

Eternal Principles Are Universal

Presiding Bishop Orson F. Whitney once delivered an address to the Saints in which he illustrated that our own Earth is just like the multitude of other probationary planets in our universe.

> "Man proposes but God disposes," and the history of this world, or any other world which has passed through a similar probation and been redeemed and glorified by the power of God and obedience to the principles of righteousness, is one vast exemplification of that great truth . . . .
> The earth upon which we dwell is only one among the many creations of God. The stars that glitter in the heavens at night and give light unto the earth are His creations, redeemed worlds, perhaps, or worlds that are passing through the course of their redemption, being saved, purified, glorified and exalted by obedience to the principles of truth which we are now struggling to obey. Thus is the work of our Father made perpetual, and as fast as one world and its inhabitants are disposed of, He will roll another into existence, He will create another earth, He will people it with His offspring, the offspring of the Gods in eternity, and they will pass through probations such as we are now passing through, that they may prove their integrity by their works; that they may give an assurance to the Almighty that they are worthy to be exalted through obedience to those principles, that unchangeable plan of salvation which has been revealed to us . . . . A man must obey the same principles now that were obeyed two

thousand years ago, or six thousand years ago, or millions of ages ago, in order to attain the presence of His Father and God. [*Journal of Discourses*, vol. 26: pp. 195-96]

This statement emphasizes that all of the planets and their inhabitants are governed by the same set of laws and eternal principles. We shall see in later chapters that this is an important principle to keep in mind while attempting to determine the nature and origin of phenomena related to UFOs and their occupants.

Orson Pratt likewise spoke of the "sameness" of the "worlds without number" referred to in the scriptures:

Notwithstanding the unnumbered worlds which have been created, out of each one of these creations the Lord had taken Zion (in other words a people called Zion) to his own bosom. What does this signify? Are we not to understand that all these creations were fallen worlds? . . . I mention these things to show that we have, in the revelations that God has given, many indications, that there are worlds beside our own that are fallen; also that we may see that the Lord has one grand method, for the salvation of the righteous of all worlds—that Zion is selected and taken from all of them . . . . I think it was necessary, so far as mortality is concerned, and indicates that the inhabitants of these different planets are fallen, as we are. It does not say so, in so many words, but I can see that they must be fallen, and for that reason the Lord withdraws his presence from them, and visits them in their hour, and time, and season, and then withdraws from them, leaving them to ponder in their hearts the commandments given them. [*Journal of Discourses*, vol. 19: p. 293]

Elder Pratt's ongoing fascination with "Zion" is demonstrated in this segment of a discourse on the subject. He appears to be speaking of the "earthly" Zion that is created on each planet during its temporal existence rather than the translated Zion, wherein cities of Zion are translated to terrestrial planets.

In a discourse given on March 14, 1875, Orson Pratt continues his thoughts on the subject:

Then what? He [Christ] withdraws. What for? To fulfill other purposes; for he has other worlds or creations and other sons and daughters, perhaps just as good as those dwelling on this planet, and they, as well as we, will be visited, and they will be made glad with the countenance of their Lord. Thus he will go, in the time and in the season thereof, from kingdom to kingdom or from world to world, causing the pure in heart, the Zion that is taken from these creations, to rejoice in his presence.

But there is another thing I want you to understand. This will not be kept up to all eternity, it is merely a preparation for something still greater. And what is that? By and by, when each of these creations has fulfilled the measure and bounds set and the times given for its continuance in a temporal state, it and its inhabitants who are worthy will be made celestial and glorified together. Then, from that time henceforth and for ever, there will be no intervening vail between God and his people who are sanctified and glorified, and he will not be under the necessity of withdrawing from one to go and visit another, because they will all be in his presence. It matters not how far in space these creations may be located from any special celestial kingdom where the Lord our God shall dwell, they will be able to see him at all times. Why? Because it is only the fall, and the vail that has been shut down over this creation, that keep us from the presence of God. Let the vail be removed, which now hinders us from beholding the glory of God and the celestial kingdom; let this creation be once perfected, after having passed through its various ordeals, after having enjoyed the light of the countenance of our Lord, in our hour and in our season, and let all things be perfected and glorified, and there will be no necessity for this vail being shut down. [*Journal of Discourses*, vol. 17, p. 332]

Elder Pratt continues,

The people who are thus glorified are said to be taken into the bosom of the Almighty; as Enoch says—"Thou hast taken Zion from all these creations which thou hast made, and thy bosom is there," &c. He does not mean that the Lord God is right within a few rods of every individual; this would be an impossibility, so far as the person is concerned; but he means that there is a channel of communication, the privilege of beholding Zion, however great the distance; and the privilege of enjoying faculties and powers like this is confined to those high and exalted beings who occupy the celestial world. All who are made like him will, in due time, be able to see, to understand and to converse with each other though millions and millions of miles apart. [*Ibid.*, pp. 332-33]

Seeing The Light

Concerning the question of whether or not many of the twinkling celestial bodies in our night skies are celestialized planets, as suggested above by Bishop Whitney, and enhancing his teachings concerning the physical relationships between the creations of God scattered throughout the universe, the ever-prolific Orson Pratt described the future state of our planet and then conjectured concerning the ability to see, or communicate with a celestial planet:

And the earth will at that time have no more need of the light of a luminary like our sun, or any artificial light, for it will be a globe of light; for when God makes this earth immortal, he will make it glorious like the inhabitants that will be permitted to live upon it. . . . . It is doubtful whether the children of mortality on other worlds, will ever behold the light of this earth, after it is made eternal, unless they happen to catch a glimpse of it by vision . . . .

Let me say a few words on these different worlds of which I have spoken. They are stretched out in the immensity of space, are infinite in every direction, and they are inhabited. I doubt very much, whether any of these worlds are celestial. I do not think we could behold them, unless by vision, if they were celestial. They are worlds in various stages of progression, some more glorious than others, inhabited by beings prepared to dwell upon them, beings who are the sons and daughters of God, or the sons and daughters of his children . . . . [*Journal of Discourses*, vol. 19, pp. 290-92]

In this same vein, Orson Pratt gave a great deal of thought to the problems of interstellar communication as they relate to the inhabitants of celestialized planets, as reflected in the following statement:

> Now, supposing we were immortal beings, and we stood upon one celestial world, away in a distant part of space, and others dwelling upon another celestial world innumerable miles distant from us, there may be a process by which we could communicate one to another, and ideas be exchanged, from world to world, without adopting the slow process of communication by light or electricity. Well, says one, "I thought that light was transmitted more rapidly than anything that we could conceive of." Light proceeds from one luminary to another, at the rate of 185,000 miles per second. Can anything be swifter than this? . . . There may be a process of communication by means of celestial, heavenly light, that will far outstrip the natural light which proceeds from yonder luminaries in our heavens. It may be that this natural light travels very slowly, compared with the light that proceeds forth from celestial worlds, wherever they may be situated . . . . His method of conveying intelligence is far more rapid than that [sic] that of light. Light, how slow! Only 185,000 miles in a second. It would take three and a half years at that rate for light to come from one of the nearest fixed stars. A long time to wait, especially if yon [sic] were in a hurry to get an answer to any message you may send; you would have to wait three and a half years for the message to go, and probably for the same time, for the returning answer. [*Ibid.*]

Although these mental exercises may appear to be little more than old-fashioned attempts to reconcile religion and nineteenth-century science, the point is well taken that we have little knowledge concerning Heavenly Father's methods of universal travel and communication. The subject becomes prominent as we discuss below, in that UFO occupants' claims regarding similar subjects are recently deemed worthy of scientific consideration and research.

Interplanetary Communication

Before leaving the discourses of Orson Pratt, it is interesting to note that he spoke to the subject of communication between probationary planets as well:

> And do these [probationary] worlds communicate one with another? Why not; is the Lord limited in the process of communica[tion?] . . . . What a happy state and condition, not only to study these things pertaining to this little world we inhabit, but to extend our researches to our neighboring worlds, learning the laws, institutions, and governments of the peoples that inhabit them, also their history, and everything pertaining to them, and then extending our researches still further. [*Ibid.*, p. 292]

Unfortunately, Elder Pratt never left us with any indication of how this communication with, and study of other telestial worlds is accomplished. He may have been referring to the type of research limited to prophets who have the privilege of viewing beyond our own sphere of existence. He may have alluded to another principle not well known among the Church membership generally.

Extraterrestrials Among Men Anciently?

As indicated in Chapter 1, the concept of giants being born to normal human women impregnated by "watchers" or "sons of Heaven" is quite controversial among Christian scholars and UFOlogists alike. Our first indication of the enigma is found in Genesis 6:4, which reads:

> There were giants in the earth in those days; and also after that, when the sons of God came in unto the daughters of men, and they bare *children* to them, the same became mighty men which *were* of old, men of renown.

As cited in Chapter 1 above, Noah's father, Lameck, was worried that Noah may have been the offspring of one of these "sons of God."

> An extremely unusual son was born to Lameck. The child's body was white as snow, with parts as red as a rose. His long hair was white as wool, and his eyes were piercing and brilliant. He was able to talk immediately and, according to Lameck, apparently conversed with the Lord. Lameck, concerned and disturbed, wondered if the boy were his own or possibly had been conceived by one of the "watchers" or "sons of heaven." He discussed the matter with his wife, BatEnosh, who swore that the boy was Lameck's. [*Christ's Eternal Gospel*, p. 155, rendering parallel translations from *The Book of Lameck, The Book of Noah, and The Book of Enoch* from the scroll "*A Genesis Apocryphon*," the Dead Sea Scrolls]

Some Christian scholars believe that these "sons of God" were a certain class of angels set on earth as watchers, even protectors, who became renegades and began indulging in inappropriate earthly activities.[12] Some UFOlogists believe that these sons of heaven were large humans from another planet, who, during a mission to Earth, impregnated many earth women resulting in the birth of giant human children.[13]

---

[12] This position is somewhat strengthened by the verses of Genesis immediately following the statement, which reflect God's determination to destroy the Earth's inhabitants because of their great wickedness.

[13] The premier champion of this "angels=aliens" theory is the ever prolific Erich von Daniken, best known for his book, and the motion picture based thereon, *Chariots of the Gods*. In his book, *Signs of the Gods*, von Daniken, as in his other dozen or so books on the subject, pursues his extraterrestrial deity through any scripture or other written record that makes any mention of flight, fire, light, cloud, transportation, vision, visitation, markings on the ground, art, religion, legend, or miraculous occurrence. His critics

sometimes assert that his quantum leaps in logic and unfounded philosophical skyscrapers demonstrate that he is one of the least intellectual writers of our time. However, in his untiring efforts to justify his position on extraterrestrial sources of our religious history, he occasionally flushes out some interesting tidbits of research.

Von Daniken "cites" *The Book of Enoch*, wherein God chastises the angels: "Why have you done like the children of earth and begot giant sons?" In Chapter 18 of *The Book of the Secrets of Enoch*, (*The Apocrypha and Pseudopigrapha of the Old Testament in English*, R. H. Charles, D.Litt., D.D., Ed., (Oxford at the Clarendon Press: 1913, Vol. II), Enoch speaks of the "Grigori," a race of "soldiers" with human appearance held at bay in the fifth heaven, being of gigantic size, whose faces were withered and melancholy and whose mouths were silenced. Enoch is told that three of these followers of Satanail, the one who rebelled, broke through to the Earth and "saw the daughters of men how good they are, and took to themselves wives, and befouled the earth with their deeds, who in all times of their age made lawlessness and mixing, and giants are born and marvellous big men and great enmity." (Verses 1-6)

Von Daniken further cites in support of his "angels=aliens impregnated Earth women" theory, Chapter 100 of *Kebra Nagast*, which he claims to be an ancient Ethiopian writing, which purportedly says:

> But every daughter of Cain with whom the angels had consorted became pregnant, but could not give birth and died. And of the fruits of their wombs some died, and others came forth; they split their mother's womb and came out of the navel. When they were older and grew up, they became giants . . . . [*Signs of the Gods*, p. 117]

Of course, von Daniken's giants are the very same that appear throughout mythology as cyclops, etc., and must, therefore, be the very beings responsible for the famous "ruts" and megalithic temples of Malta. This is how von Daniken reasons, anyway.

The LDS Church has a somewhat more conservative understanding of the meaning of "sons of God" and "giants," derived no doubt from Moses 8:18, wherein the hearers of Noah's calls to repentance said:

> Behold, we are the sons of God; have we not taken unto our selves the daughters of men? And are we not eating and drinking, and marrying and giving in marriage? And our wives bear unto us children, and the same are mighty men, which are like unto men of old, men of great renown. And they harkened not unto the words of Noah.

From this scripture we can easily infer that the entire "giants" theory is probably due to a minor mistranslation or earlier misunderstanding of Genesis. There were giants, men of large stature in the Old Testament, but they were only men so far as the scriptures or prophets inform us.

In support of the "angels=aliens" theory, proponents point us to the Old Testament Hebrew word for giants used in Genesis, "nephil" or "naphal," which they say literally means "the fallen ones," or, "those who are fallen down." They infer from this strained definition that these are beings who came from the sky. As intriguing as this sounds, a look at a Hebrew and Chaldee Dictionary (*See e.g., Strong's Exhaustive Concordance of the Bible, Dictionary of the Hebrew Bible*, p. 79, words nos. 5303-5307), reveals that nephil merely means a feller, or lumberjack, and naphal means one who has failed or has been overcome. Although there were and are giants on the Earth, they most likely have not resulted from unions of aliens or angels with human women.

Having arrived at this conclusion, however, it is quite interesting, if true, that Lameck, a prophet of God, felt that his superhuman child might possibly be the illegitimate offspring of one of the enigmatic "watchers" or "sons of heaven." He was not alone in these assumptions. The subject pops up in scholarly literature and dissertations throughout recorded history, ancient and modern.

A Universal Hierarchy Of Nobility

After confirming many of the teachings already discussed concerning the plentiful existence of human life on millions of Earthlike planets, Elder B. H. Roberts spoke of the "noble ones" that stand at the head of each of these world families, and their mutual association in the eternities:

> It is seen that our Prophet taught the eternity of intelligence; also the existence of intelligences in other worlds than ours. The Presiding Intelligence to that order of things and beings to which we belong, is represented as standing among the intelligences appointed to life on our earth, "and among these were many of *the noble and great ones*." And the Presiding Intelligence said: "*These I will make my rulers;* for he stood among those that were spirits, and He saw that they were *good*." *The noble and great ones* are made rulers then; and doubtless the principle here operating in respect of those intelligences appointed to our earth, operates in all worlds and world systems. Some of the "good and the noble and the great ones" stand at the head of worlds and world groups, forming grand presidencies, in order and gradation, based upon their power and their appointment, which in turn depend upon their character, their nobility, greatness, and their worthiness, measured by their capacity to serve. Each one of such "rulers," and each "intelligence," independent in the sphere in which he is appointed to act, yet, nevertheless, acts in harmony—through the attainment of knowledge, of truth—with all other exalted and sanctified intelligences. These are the "rulers" in the universe, the Divine Beings who make up David's "congregation of the mighty," in which God, "more intelligent than them all," standeth and judgeth "among the Gods."
> [*History of the Church*, vol. 2, pp. 394-97]

There exist many theological theories and statements regarding the existence of life on other planets—in the Church and out. Such theories, however, do little to address the issue of interplanetary visitation and communication, a subject of great importance in light of the UFO phenomenon. At the time of this writing there are no official declarations or policy statements from the LDS Church leadership concerning these questions.

4

Scriptural
Spacecraft?

Who Believes That Angels Pilot UFOs?

I can think of no better way to begin this chapter than to say, some people will believe anything. You will remember that in our EXTRATERRESTRIAL LIFE SURVEY we asked LDS Church members "(9) Do you believe that angels use space vehicles to travel to earth?" Question number ten made the same query about God. Not surprisingly, only two percent of those questioned responded that they believe that angels use spacecraft when travelling between the planets to minister to their various inhabitants. The same respondents believed that God uses such a craft. An obvious reason for this statistically significant response is that LDS people appreciate that our Heavenly Father is omniscient and omnipotent, and in the words of the immortal Captain James T. Kirk in *Star Trek V,* "Excuse me—excuse me, I'd just like to ask a question—what does God need with a star ship?"

With this low percentage of LDS believers in mind, the contrast with other sectors of society that believe that Unidentified Flying Objects ("UFOs") in our Earthly skies are piloted by divine messengers is astounding. Anyone involved with the occult, from astrology to phone-in psychic readings, is a statistically good candidate to believe that UFOs are piloted by ministering spiritual beings. This subject is discussed in depth in Part III. Many liberal Christian churches have high percentages of membership that likewise accept this belief. These two categories already put us into the tens of millions of believers. Most disturbingly, however, many average people with transitory Christian beliefs who are moderately exposed to UFO literature and other media accounts are beginning to take on composite spiritual beliefs about UFOs. Erich von Daniken's "aliens=Gods/angels" books have sold in the tens of millions, and the motion picture based on his book *Chariots of the Gods* has been viewed by a like number. These average people who are being swayed by "every wind of doctrine" are precisely those who need to be taught

51

the Gospel—searching, open-minded neighbors. Although it is possible that UFOs have spiritual origins, we have every indication that they are not piloted by ministering angels.

UFOs In The Bible

There exist many books touting man's "alien" origins and claiming that the Bible is laden with tales of UFO visitations to Earth. These writers cite scriptures, generally from the Old Testament, that refer to flying chariots and other objects as evidence of divine dependence on mechanical vehicles for mobility not only between planets, but also on the Earth's surface. Herein is a summary of the arguments which are typically presented with reference to the Bible.

Chariots Of Fire

The assumption of the prophet Elijah is frequently cited and held to be especially descriptive of an ancient flying chariot:

> And it came to pass, as they still went on, and talked, that, behold, *there appeared* a chariot of fire, and horses of fire, and parted them both asunder; and Elijah went up by a whirlwind into heaven. And Elisha saw *it*, and he cried, My father, my father, the chariot of Israel, and the horsemen thereof . . . . [2 Kings 2:11-12]

Interestingly, the LDS version of the Bible cross-references this passage to Abraham 2:7 and Ezekiel 1:4. Abraham 2:7 reads:

> For I am the Lord thy God; I dwell in heaven; the earth is my footstool; I stretch my hand over the sea, and it obeys my voice; I cause the wind and the fire to be my chariot; I say to the mountains—Depart hence—and behold, they are taken away in an instant, suddenly.

The LDS annotators cross-reference Abraham 2:7 with 2 Kings 2:11, the assumption of Elijah, and to Isaiah 66:15, which says:

> For, behold, the Lord will come with fire, and with his chariots like a whirlwind, to render his anger with fury, and his rebuke with flames of fire.

Although we can somewhat easily interpret God's elemental chariots as being merely descriptive of His comings and goings as being with power and celebration, the chariot of fire that took Elijah into heaven may have a more functional character. A look at the sight beheld and described by Elisha includes "horses of fire" complete with "horsemen." UFO theorists say that these are mere descriptions of mechanical apparatus that propelled the craft, but it could well be that Elisha was shown a vision that accompanied Elijah's assumption, for the purpose of imbuing the occasion with power and authority—which has been the result. There are those who are always quick to explain away ancient reports by "interpreting" them away, saying that the report is phrased in the terms and understanding of the time. Even if true, however, this is not a license to interpret every flying object or miracle as having a UFO origin—which has become the practice of these "angels=aliens" protagonists. "Horses" just may mean "horses."

The Camp Of Israel Led By A UFO

Another proffered evidence of the Biblical UFO phenomenon is the pillar that accompanied Israel on its exodus from Egypt, across Sinai, to the Promised Land.

> And the Lord went before them by day in a pillar of a cloud, to lead them the way; and by night in a pillar of fire, to give them light; to go by day and night:
> He took not away the pillar of the cloud by day, nor the pillar of fire by night, *from* before the people. [Exodus 13:21-22]

> And the angel of God, which went before the camp of Israel, removed and went behind them; and the pillar of the cloud went from before their face, and stood behind them:
> And it came between the camp of the Egyptians and the camp of Israel; and it was a cloud and darkness *to them*, but it gave light by night *to these:* so that the one came not near the other all the night.
> And Moses stretched out his hand over the sea; and the Lord caused the sea to *go back* by a strong east wind all that night, and made the sea dry *land*, and the waters were divided.
> And the children of Israel went into the midst of the sea upon the dry ground: and the waters were a wall unto them on their right hand, and on their left.
> And the Egyptians pursued, and went in after them to the midst of the sea, even all Pharaoh's horses, his chariots, and his horsemen.
> And it came to pass, that in the morning watch the Lord looked unto the host of the Egyptians through the pillar of fire and of the cloud, and troubled the host of the Egyptians,
> And took off their chariot wheels, that they drave them heavily: so that the Egyptians said, Let us flee from the face of Israel; for the Lord fighteth for them against the Egyptians. [Exodus 14:19-25]

These verses inform us of some interesting characteristics of this pillar. First, we are told that the *Lord* went before Israel in the pillar. We can understand this to mean that He led them by the means of the pillar. However, we are next told that "the angel of God, which went before the camp of Israel, removed and went behind them." This gives us a more focused view of the nature of the pillar, that it was an angelic presence. UFO theorists conjecture that the pillar was possibly UFO exhaust, as evidenced by its dark cloudiness at times, and light at others. Therefore, they conclude that the "angel of God" was in a craft or device that exhausted a misty substance that could be lit up or left dark. Protagonists further claim that the "east wind" that blew and parted the sea and dried its floor in a single night was an antigravity field generated by the craft. This antigravity theory, they say, is supported by the fact that the Lord was able to remotely take "off their chariot wheels." And finally, because the Lord "looked unto the host of the Egyptians through the pillar of fire and of the cloud" as he troubled them with these difficulties, the pillar was more of a device than a presence.

God's Use Of Devices

Does God use "devices" to carry out His divine purposes? Hugh Nibley answers, "yes." In referring to Joseph's Smith's use of the Urim and Thummim and the Seer Stone to translate the Book of Mormon, Brother Nibley describes how Joseph would translate for hours, never opening the plates.

> "I frequently wrote day after day," E. W. Tullidge recalls, "often sitting at the table close by him, he sitting with his face buried in his hat, with a stone in it, and dictating hour after hour with nothing between us . . . . He used neither manuscript nor book to read from . . . the plates often lay on the table without any attempt at concealment, wrapped in a small linen table cloth." David Whitmer confirms this: "He did not use the plates in the translation, but would hold the interpreters to his eyes . . . and before his eyes would appear what seemed to be a parchment, on which would appear the characters of the plates . . . and immediately below would appear the translation in English." [*The Message of the Joseph Smith Papyri, an Egyptian Endowment*, p. 51.]

Why God uses "gadgets," as Brother Nibley terms them, is not apparent. He evidently reserves invisible miracles for occasions when He warts it understood that a miracle is occurring. Otherwise, God provides an Ark of the Covenant, a serpentine staff, a Urim and Thummim, or a luminous set of stones to act as a medium through which the benefit is conferred on man.

We are left with the question then, Does this mean that God might employ the use of flying machines to transport Himself and His servants? The obvious response is, he might—but He does not have to use such devices. One thing we can be sure of, this open possibility does not account for the millions of UFO sightings that are reported in these latter times.

The Wheels Of Ezekiel

The most vivid of all Biblical descriptions of flying "vehicles" is that of the prophet Ezekiel. With a little imagination, we can appreciate why Biblical UFO adherents believe that Ezekiel saw a genuine UFO.

And I looked, and, behold, a whirlwind came out of the north, a great cloud, and a fire infolding itself, and a brightness *was* about it, and out of the midst thereof as the colour of amber, out of the midst of the fire.

Also out of the midst thereof *came* the likeness of four living creatures. And this *was* their appearance; they had the likeness of a man.

And every one had four faces, and every one had four wings.

And their feet *were* straight feet; and the sole of their feet *was* like the sole of a calf's foot: and they sparkled like the colour of burnished brass.

And *they had* the hands of a man under their wings on their four sides; and they four had their faces and their wings.

Their wings *were* joined one to another; they turned not when they went; they went every one straight forward. As for the likeness of their faces, they four had the face of a man, and the face of a lion, on the right side: and they four had the face of an ox on the left side; they four also had the face of an eagle.

Thus *were* their faces: and their wings *were* stretched upward; two *wings* of every one *were* joined one to another, and two covered their bodies.

And they went every one straight forward: whither the spirit was to go, they went; *and* they turned not when they went.

As for the likeness of the living creatures, their appearance *was* like burning coals of fire, *and* like the appearance of lamps: it went up and down among the living creatures; and the fire was bright, and out of the fire went forth lightning.

And the living creatures ran and returned as the appearance of a flash of lightning.

Now as I beheld the living creatures, behold one wheel upon the earth by the living creatures, with his four faces.

The appearance of the wheels and their work *was* like unto the colour of beryl: and they four had one likeness: and their appearance and their work *was* as it were a wheel in the middle of a wheel.

When they went, they went upon their four sides: *and* they turned not when they went.

As for their rings, they were so high that they were dreadful; and their rings *were* full of eyes round about them four.

And when the living creatures went, the wheels went by them: and when the living creatures were lifted up from the earth, the wheels were lifted up.

Whithersoever the spirit was to go, they went, thither *was their* spirit to go; and the wheels were lifted up over against them: for the spirit of the living creature *was* in the wheels.

When those went, *these* went; and when those stood, these stood; and when those were lifted up from the earth, the wheels were lifted up over against them: for the spirit of the living creature *was* in the wheels.

And the likeness of the firmament upon the heads of the living creature *was* as the colour of the terrible crystal, stretched forth over their heads above.

And under the firmament *were* their wings straight, the one toward the other: every one had two, which covered on this side, and every one had two, which covered on that side, their bodies.

And when they went, I heard the noise of their wings, like the noise of great waters, as the voice of the *Almighty*, the voice of speech, as the noise of an host: when they stood, they let down their wings.

And there was a voice from the firmament that *was* over their heads, when they stood, *and* had let down their wings.

And above the firmament that *was* over their heads *was* the likeness of a throne, as the appearance of a sapphire stone: and upon the likeness of "the throne *was* the likeness as the appearance of a man above upon it.

And I saw as the colour of amber, as the appearance of fire round about within it, from the appearance of his loins even upward, and from the appearance of his loins even downward, I saw as it were the appearance of fire, and it had brightness round about.

As the appearance of the bow that is in the cloud in the day of rain, so *was* the appearance of the brightness round about. This *was* the appearance of the likeness of the glory of the Lord. And when I saw *it*, I fell upon my face, and I heard a voice of one that spake. [Ezekiel 1:4-28]

Ezekiel continues his narrative in Chapter 10, describing the "object's" takeoff.

THEN I looked, and, behold, in the firmament that was above the head of the cherubims there appeared over them as it were a sapphire stone, as the appearance of the likeness of a throne.

And he spake unto the man clothed with linen, and said, Go in between the wheels, *even* under the cherub, and fill thine hand with coals of fire from between the cherubims, and scatter *them* over the city. And he went in in my sight.

Now the cherubims stood on the right side of the house, when the man went in; and the cloud filled the inner court.

Then the glory of the Lord went up from the cherub, *and stood* over the threshold of the house; and the house was filled with the cloud, and the court was full of the brightness of the Lord's glory.

And the sound of the cherubims' wings was heard *even* to the outer court, as the voice of the Almighty God when he speaketh.

And it came to pass, *that* when he had commanded the man clothed with linen, saying, Take fire from between the wheels, from between the cherubims; then he went in, and stood beside the wheels.

And *one* cherub stretched forth his hand from between the cherubims unto the fire that *was* between the cherubims, and took *thereof*, and put it into the hands of *him that was* clothed in white linen: who took it, and went out.

And there appeared in the cherubims the form of a man's hand under the wings.

And when I looked, behold the four wheels by the cherubims, one wheel by one cherub, and another wheel by another cherub: and the appearance of the wheels *was* as the colour of a beryl stone.

And *as for* their appearances, the four had one likeness, as if a wheel had been in the midst of a wheel.

When they went, they went upon their four sides; they turned not as they went, but to the place whither the head looked they followed it; they turned not as they went.

And their whole body, and their backs, and their hands, and their wings, and the wheels, *were* full of eyes round about, *even* the wheels that they four had.

As for the wheels, it was cried unto them in my hearing, O wheel.

And every one had four faces: the first face *was* the face of a cherub, and the second face *was* the face of a man, and the third face of a lion, and the fourth face of an eagle.

> And the cherubims were lifted up. This is the living creature that I saw by the river of Chebar.
>
> And when the cherubims went, the wheels went by them: and when the cherubims lifted up their wings to mount up from the earth, the same wheels also turned not from beside them.
>
> When they stood, *these* stood; and when they were lifted up, *these* lifted up themselves *also:* for the spirit of the living creature *was* in them.
>
> Then the glory of the Lord departed from off the threshold of the house, and stood over the cherubims.
>
> And the cherubims lifted up their wings, and mounted up from the earth in my sight: when they went out, the wheels also *were* beside them, and *every one* stood at the door of the east gate of the Lord's house; and the glory of the God of Israel *was* over them above.
>
> This is the living creature that I saw under the God of Israel by the river of Chebar; and I knew that they *were* the cherubims.
>
> Every one had four faces apiece, and every one four wings; and the likeness of the hands of a man *was* under their wings.
>
> And the likeness of their faces *was* the same faces which I saw by the river chebar, their appearances and themselves: they went every one straight forward. [Ezekiel 10:1-22]

Many UFO books attempt to show a "UFO/history/religion" connection from Ezekiel's vision. They further generally offer an artist's conception of the "craft" described in great detail in the scripture. NASA *Saturn V* engineer, Josef F. Blumrich, attempted in 1968 to debunk the theory that "Ezekiel's Wheel" was a flying craft. He published a book in 1973 entitled *The Spaceships of Ezekiel*, in which he described how his debunking effort became a successful design venture. He writes, "Seldom has a total defeat been so rewarding, so fascinating, and so delightful!" His design is simple, resembling a domed upside-down loudspeaker with four vertical landing gear adorned with propellers. Although this type of undertaking might be enjoyable to an engineer, it is incongruous that beings that are capable of intergalactic flight could fly around in Earth's atmosphere in propeller-driven craft.

As a footnote to Ezekiel's experience, Ezekiel reports that he encountered an oddly colored "man" in connection with this "craft."

> And he brought me thither, and, behold, *there was* a man, whose appearance *was* like the appearance of brass, with a line of flax in his hand, and a measuring reed; and he stood in the gate. [Ezekiel 40:3; cross-referenced from Ezekiel 1:7 (color of craft's feet.)]

The "flax" or "measuring reed" in the fellow's hand is a point of interest to UFO investigators. UFO occupants are sometimes said to carry rods in their hands.

Biblical UFO proponents cite many more examples from the Bible—generally, anything that flies, floats (clouds), or shines is proffered as evidence for their theory.

Enoch's Escort

In the beginning of *The Book of the Secrets of Enoch*, the 365-year-old prophet recounts an unusual event that gave rise to an intriguing encounter:

> And when I was asleep, great distress came up into my heart, and I was weeping with my eyes in sleep, and I could not understand what this distress was, or what would happen to me. And there appeared to me two men, exceeding big, so that I never saw such on earth; their faces were shining like the sun, their eyes too were like a burning light, and from their lips was fire coming forth with clothing and singing of various kinds in appearance purple, their wings were brighter than gold, their hands whiter than snow. They were standing at the head of my couch and began to call me by my name. And I arose from my sleep and saw clearly those two men standing in front of me. And I saluted them and was seized with fear and the appearance of my face was changed from terror, and those men said to me: "Have courage, Enoch, do not fear; the eternal God sent us to thee, and lo! thou shalt to-day ascend with us into heaven, and thou shalt tell thy sons and all thy household all that they shall do without thee on earth in thy house, and let no one seek thee till the Lord return thee to them . . . ."
>
> It came to pass, when Enoch had told his sons, that the angels took him on to their wings and bore him up on to the first heaven and placed him on the clouds. And there I looked, and again I looked higher, and saw the ether, and they placed me on the first heaven and showed me a very great Sea, greater than the earthly sea.
>
> They brought before my face the elders and rulers of the stellar orders, and showed me two hundred angels, who rule the stars and their services to the heavens, and fly with their wings and come round all those who sail. [Chapters 1, 3 and 4]

Later chapters relate how Enoch was shown the workings of the planets and stars and the myriad angels assigned to oversee those functions. The most interesting aspect of these accounts is the description concerning the appearance of the angels and their mode of transportation. The assertion that the angels possessed "wings" which enabled them to fly from one heaven to another is most fascinating in light of our knowledge that angels do not have wings—not as part of their anatomy anyway. Could this indicate that they used something with wings for transportation as some would have us believe? Functionally, wings are not necessary for flight—not interstellar flight anyway—not for God, not for angels, or for UFOs. Therefore, Joseph Smith's explanation of such symbolic representations to the ancients seems more likely an explanation.

> Q. What are we to understand by the eyes and wings, which the beasts had?
>
> A. Their eyes are a representation of light and knowledge; and their wings are a representation of power, to move, to act, etc. [D & C 77:4]

UFOs In Egyptian Religious Texts

In drawing parallels between the ancient Gospel and other religions of antiquity, Hugh Nibley makes reference to interplanetary visitations by beings from other worlds who commute for purposes related to man's spiritual welfare.

> The ,unding and building of the Egyptian temple and the establishing of its rites is always done, according to Mrs. Reymond's study, by beings who sail from other worlds, and, when their work is done, 'the Shebtiw seem to have sailed away again' (E. Reymond, *Mythical Origin*, p. 27). Some such space travel (often indicated in the Coptic Gnostic writings) is indicated in C. T. 162 (II, 403f): 'He takes the ship of 1000 cubits from end to end, and he sails in it to the stairway of fire.' All of which most cogently brings to mind Joseph Smith's interpretation of the ship-figure (fig. 4) in Facsimile II of the Book of Abraham: ' . . . a numerical figure in Egyptian signifying one thousand; answering to the measuring of time . . . .' Very common are references to the dead King's being hauled by cables to heaven or rowed thither by crews of the Unwearied or the Imperishable Ones (i.e., unsetting stars). The sky ship can make the trip both ways: 'I go down among the weak ones (hasw, uninitiated) . . . . I have seized on to the cable of the Hnt-mn-it.f; I row in my seat in the divine ship. I have gone down upon my throne in the divine ship. I control, none being near my throne in the divine ship; I am in control, not being without a boat, my throne being in the divine ship at Heliopolis' (C. T. 151, II, 257). [*The Message of the Joseph Smith Papyri, an Egyptian Endowment*, p. 138]

Brother Nibley adds to this colorful description of ancient space travel:

> It is in the solar ship that the initiate joins his father on the horizon. One steps into the Sun-ship just as it reaches that place where the sky touches the earth at the horizon as the water meets the land at the sacred wharf of the pyramid or temple. It is a ship that carries one in a state of effortless suspension through the void between the worlds. [*Ibid.*, p. 135]

Remembering that all of this describes the transporting of the dead king's soul to his eternal resting place, much like our own celestial kingdom, the resemblance to reports by abductees of the "state of effortless suspension through the void between the worlds" is remarkable. Perhaps they have a common origin, as we discuss below.

One last interesting aspect discussed by Brother Nibley is the purported means of propulsion of these great Solar Barks:

> As the ship moves on, we remember that after all it is the Solar-bark, a Skyship, "Moving in Light" (Thausing, *Gr. Tb.*, p. 9). [*Ibid.*, p. 236]

In UFO literature there are many accounts of UFO occupants describing the propulsion system of their ship to their guest. One such description is that of an LDS Priesthood bearer, Udo Wartena, who's account is cited later in this work. According to his account, his hosts explained the mechanics of their craft to him, and then revealed to him that they focused on a distant

star and used its energy to draw them through space at speeds greater than
the speed of light. He then adds, "My host specifically mentioned 'skipping
upon the light waves.'" The similarity between "skipping upon the light waves"
and "moving in light" from the above citation is significant.

As a postscript to Egyptian religious accounts of space travel, it is noteworthy
that in Facsimile 2, Figure 3, of the *Book of Abraham*, there is a figure sitting
on a throne, riding in a thousand-cubit Solar Bark, which Joseph Smith
describes in his interpretation:

> Fig. 3. Is made to represent God, sitting upon his throne, clothed with power and
> authority; with a crown of eternal light upon his head; representing also the grand
> Key-words of the Holy Priesthood, as revealed to Adam in the Garden of Eden, as
> also to Seth, Noah, Melchizedek, Abraham, and all to whom the Priesthood was
> revealed.

Joseph Smith Visited By UFOs?

It is surprising how many UFOlogists point to the events of the Restoration
as evidence of early extraterrestrial contact with humans on Earth. They are
fascinated with scriptures like the following:

> I saw a pillar of light exactly over my head, above the brightness of the sun, which
> descended gradually until it fell upon me. It no sooner appeared than I found myself
> delivered from the enemy which held me bound. When the light rested upon me I saw
> two Personages, whose brightness and glory defy all description, standing above me
> in the air. [*Joseph Smith—History* 1:16-17]

> While I was thus in the act of calling upon God, I discovered a light appearing in
> my room, which continued to increase until the room was lighter than at noonday,
> when immediately a personage appeared at my bedside, standing in the air, for his
> feet did not touch the floor . . . . Not only was his robe exceedingly white, but his
> whole person was glorious beyond description, and his countenance truly like lightning.
> The room was exceedingly light, but not so very bright as immediately around his
> person . . . . After this communication, I saw the light in the room begin to gather
> immediately around the person of him who had been speaking to me, and it continued
> to do so until the room was again left dark, except just around him; when, instantly
> I saw, as it were, a conduit open right up into heaven, and he ascended till he entirely
> disappeared, and the room was left as it had been before this heavenly light had made
> its appearance. [*Ibid.* 1:30-43]

While Latter-day Saints do not link the angelic visits which herald the
gospel's restoration with UFOs, the similarities between Moroni's visit and
Star Trek special effects are regarded as noteworthy by UFOlogists. There
are other aspects of Joseph's experiences that intrigue UFO researchers as well.

Keep in mind the many religious parallels to UFO sightings and other close encounters as the UFO literature is surveyed in Part II. The similarities between UFO encounters and spiritual apparitions (good and evil) are marked.

Part II
Flying Saucers
And
Extraterrestrials—
What Is Going On?

Part II is intended to present an overview of the secular literature reporting unidentified flying objects and alien life observations. Public library bookshelves and other popular literature, as well as weekly television programs, are packed with stories telling and retelling of the hundreds of thousands of UFO sightings and close encounters that have been reported to date. The close encounter reports shared herein are "representative" of a survey of such literature. These accounts are related as they appear in the literature, often in the verbatim narratives of the witnesses, and are presented at full face value for the purpose of conveying what is occurring in the UFO phenomenon.

Whether the narratives reflect observations of "nuts and bolts" flying machines piloted by unusual beings, or a form of mass hypnosis or hysteria, or some kind of psychic or paranormal phenomenon, there has emerged a high degree of congruity among thousands of reported observations and encounters that merit attention. The sightings and experiences reported herein are submitted as data for the purpose of analyzing the possible sources of such phenomena, which analysis is based on the unique LDS perspective gained through latter-day revelation. They are also provided to afford the reader a point of reference with which to evaluate the LDS accounts of UFO encounters related herein.

5

UFOs In The Sky

A History Of UFO Sightings

Reports of Unidentified Flying Objects of one kind or another in terrestrial skies have persisted for thousands of years. Not unexpectedly, observers of these phenomena have generally recounted what they observed in terms descriptive of technology and scientific understanding of the era, culture, or region. Although this in itself is not surprising, the details of such narratives create something of a yardstick by which the veracity or origin of the accounts can be measured. With few exceptions, the same yardsticks can be employed to examine modern UFO accounts as well.

Ancient UFO Reports

From the time man learned to write down on parchment or clay tablets the important details of his day, brief accounts of mysterious flying vessels have been inserted between other affairs of state. As discussed above, many believe that various accounts in the Bible have such origins. In ancient China, a legend of humanoid visitors in "flying carts" with gilded wings found its genesis, and the tale has been passed on for centuries. In Rome, "flying shields," sometimes accompanied by spurting fire, were widely reported. Written in the Sanskrit *Drona Parva* text are accounts of a superhuman race conducting aerial dogfights in flying vessels called "vimana." One translation renders specifics of an air battle thus: a "blazing missile possessed of the radiance of smokeless fire was discharged."

Two of the most famous remote reports of flying vessels are those that occurred in the skies over Nuremburg, Germany and Basel, Switzerland, in 1561 and 1566, respectively. During these spectaculars, thousands of local citizens were treated to a display of several large disks, spheres and tubes which appeared in the skies, and "danced" or weaved themselves about in something described as an aerial ballet. When finished, these objects suddenly resolved themselves into "fiery red" spheres, and disappeared. Numerous historical reports like these have come to light in recent years.

Famed UFO investigator and author Jacques Vallee has documented many similarities and parallels between the medieval "fairy faith" and modern accounts of UFO sightings, encounters, and abductions. The peasantry were so overwhelmed by their encounters with small humanoids who whisked them away, generally into underground complexes, and performed physical examinations, as well as reproductive experimentations, that they revered these "fairies" as a supernatural force to be reckoned with. One village documented how one of its prominent midwives was kindly abducted and taken to an underground area where a humanoid giving birth needed assistance. When the ordeal was over, the midwife was thanked, and returned to her village to tell the tale. Accounts like these are disturbingly similar to modern abduction accounts, as outlined in the following chapters.

UFO Reports In Recent History

The current era of UFO sightings actually began in the late nineteenth century—around the period of the great airships. With popularized reports of high-tech flying machines hitting the public press, stories of flying machine sightings proliferated into an American avocation. Although many such accounts were accurate reports of prototype gas-filled balloon craft flying overhead, making mysterious noises and sporting eerie, colored lights, others were preposterous, and obvious fabrications intended to attract attention to the reporters. First, newspaper reporters were known to fabricate such tales to boost circulation, then telegraph operators did it for the pure pleasure of telling the tales.

With the advent of giant airships developed by industrialists bent on assisting with skirmishes in Cuba and elsewhere around the world, tales of peculiar night encounters with futuristic voyagers abounded. Although it is true that a handful of experimental airships nocturnally[1] crisscrossed the United States at speeds of twenty to thirty miles per hour, tales of ultramodern craft moving at 200 miles per hour (or much faster) surfaced sporadically. These tales gave rise to accounts of people witnessing hieroglyph-speckled crafts piloted

---

[1] Experimental flights of these craft were conducted at night because hot air balloons fly better in cold weather, and supposedly, to protect pending patents.

by superhuman beings clad in space-type uniforms. Many reports, made by credible citizens of the period, were very similar to UFO accounts of today—rapid movements and departures and emanating light beams that probed and lifted.

UFO Expectations

As of 1900, physical descriptions of these mysterious, advanced craft were limited to airships of the period—the dirigible kind; no flying saucers and no "aliens," yet. This "airship" portion of UFO history illustrates a disturbingly consistent phenomenon that has perplexed researchers for decades. From the late nineteenth century through the present, the UFO phenomenon, although consistent in other respects, has manifested itself in the technological and cultural (including sciencefictional) trappings and expectations of the era. Although mentioned briefly above, this phenomenon warrants a separate discussion here.

As noted and discussed by Dr. Salisbury in *The Utah UFO Display*, UFOs appear to people of different cultures, beliefs, and experiences, in manners seemingly diverse than to those of dissimilar backgrounds. For example, the encounters at Fatima, Portugal, discussed later in this work, were "packaged" specifically for rural Portugese Catholics of the early twentieth century. Other encounters, in South America appear to be tailored to Catholics of that region. There is a slight difference in belief, and therefore, cultural expectation. The astute reader may say, "But the Fatima and other 'Madonna' sightings appear more like spiritual manifestations of some kind rather than a UFO experience." This observation is one that should be kept in mind as all UFO sightings are analyzed. UFO author Brad Steiger has observed, "A historical survey reveals that reports of strange objects in the skies are laced through documents of the ancient and recent past. Interestingly, the records seem to indicate that UFOs have adapted themselves to the cultural milieu and the technological capacities of the observers."[2] As stated frequently herein, many UFO researchers are turning from their "nuts and bolts extraterrestrial flying machine" explanations of UFO origins to more metaphysical interpretations. The line between "nuts and bolts" and "spiritual" becomes quite hazy as the overall UFO occurrence is examined.

---

[2] *The UFO Abductors*, p. 212.

The "tailoring" of these divergent manifestations becomes somewhat apparent in the following chapters. The differences are not limited to those of perception, either. The craft, the humanoids, and the "UFO message" and its means of deliverance are manifested in a diverse, yet somewhat predictable fashion. This is why Dr. Salisbury employs the word "display" in his title—to illustrate the "theatrical" aspects of the encounters. As we begin our survey of modern UFO accounts, I invite you to note this pattern, as well as others that you detect, and to discern for yourself the paradigm of the UFO encounter.

UFOs In The Twentieth Century

The first half of the twentieth century saw the rapid escalation of reports of UFOs, but again, the accounts were initially limited to airships, and later, airplane-like craft and rockets. However, by now, popular literature had become overrun with Jules Verne and H. G. Wells "wannabees," and science fiction paperbacks became an American staple. Popular writers and radio programs weaved tales of air and space travel that captured the imagination of most of America, and then the world. Stories of close encounters with aliens from Mars, Venus, Jupiter, and even the Moon became common. Dime novel and "mystery" magazine publishers did all they could to promote their science fiction bonanza by creating eye-witness accounts of exotic interplanetary rockets manned by inhuman aliens; bug-eyed, gill-breathing monsters, whose designs were generally imperialistic.

As the skies began to fill up with shiny airplanes, test rockets, and other experimental craft, and as the minds of the public became habituated to the idea of interplanetary space travel, reports of weird flying machines abounded around the world. These reports were often the creations of unscrupulous reporters and publishers wishing to boost careers and increase circulation. By the time H. G. Wells's 1898 book *War of the Worlds* hit the radio airwaves, the public was willing to believe. Other sighting narratives made by average citizens of the time were somewhat less sensational and often mistaken, yet reported by believable townsmen who lent credibility to the UFO "industry."

Public UFO Reports By Credible Witnesses

During World War II allied as well as enemy pilots and crewmen reported seeing small globes following them as they flew in formation. These "foofighters" (also known as "Kraut Balls") as the allied airmen came to call them, were thought by both sides to be the secret weapon of the other. Fliers complained of being followed by one to ten of these red, orange, or clear spheres, believing them to be the result of superior German technology. Allied pilots soon learned, however, that the spheres were harmless. Former B-17 bomber pilot Charles Odom told the Houston *Post* that the foofighters "looked like crystal balls, clear, about the size of basketballs" and that they would advance to within about 100 yards of the flight formation and "would seem to become magnetized to our formation and fly alongside . . . . After awhile, they would peel off like a plane and leave."[3] These observations were so widespread that most World War II fliers reportedly experienced them. Subsequent to World War II, many pilots continue to report the presence of these luminous, enigmatic spheres. This is especially true in aerial combat situations, such as in Korea and Vietnam.

The Modern Era Of UFOs

The modern era of UFOs was ushered in on June 24, 1947, when Kenneth Arnold, a respectable Boise, Idaho pilot observed what he described as "nine peculiar aircraft" flying in formation and maneuvering at approximately 1,700 m.p.h., a speed unattainable in 1947. Arnold was a sober professional and experienced aircraft observer. His mission that day was to locate a downed C-46 Marine transport plane. He was watching very carefully when the nine metallic discs came into view. Arnold rejected the publicity that came his way as a result of what he saw on that clear summer day. He had assumed that the unidentifiable aircraft belonged to the U.S. Military, and fully expected a reasonable explanation of why disc-shaped craft without tails were flying at phenomenal speeds near Mt. Rainier, Washington, just as soon as he contacted the General Manager of Central Aircraft at the Yakima Airport. The General Manager was slightly dubious of Arnold's report, however, which set Arnold on a path leading to Military Intelligence to learn if unmanned guided missiles were being fired in the region. There was none.

---

[3] Raymond Fowler, *The Watchers*, p. 70.

In the next hours and days, hundreds of reports flooded the air traffic airwaves and the media that others had seen clusters of Arnold's flying "saucers." This proliferation of flying saucer reports caused Arnold to later write:

> From then on, if I was to go by the number of reports that came in of other sightings, of which I kept a close track, I thought it wouldn't be long before there would be one of these things in every garage. In order to stop what I thought was a lot of foolishness, and since I couldn't get any work done, I went out to the airport, cranked up my plane, and flew home to Boise.

Arnold attempted a few times to investigate what he considered to be credible UFO sightings. However, when he learned that sensationalist publishers were using his name to promote their books and magazines he gave it up.

Arnold's sighting and report of June 24, 1947, remains one of the most credible UFO sighting reports to date.[4] Even Military Intelligence accepted Arnold's story as completely true, without concluding the origin of the discs. Even then, however, UFO debunkers were on the scene attempting to prove that Arnold had witnessed nothing more than natural phenomena that only appeared like flying "saucers skipping over the water" at 1,700 m.p.h.

The decade of the 1950s saw the shift of science fiction from paperbacks and magazines to the silver screen. Flying saucers and their alien pilots were now being imprinted onto the psyches of industrialized nations in panoramic technicolor. As hundreds of thousands, and even millions of theater goers were deluged with the extraterrestrial phenomenon, the numbers of reported sightings escalated proportionately. UFO protagonists claim that the proliferation of sightings was not the result of public "overeagerness" to see UFOs, but of more eyes watching the sky.

By the 1960s counterfeit UFOs were being mass-produced by any teenager with a dry-cleaning bag, balsa wood, and a candle.[5] High-altitude weather balloons and meteorological phenomena produced reflected atmospheric flashes that caused even the best-trained pilots to believe that they were witnessing a true-to-life UFO. Many unmistakable UFO sightings were retrospectively learned to be mere test flights of conventional aircraft outfitted

---

[4] Arnold reportedly did some writing on the subject later that tended to diminish his "disinterested" status.

[5] It is interesting how many of these inexpensive lighted hot-air balloons have appeared on the front pages of newspapers with headlines announcing the arrival of UFOs to the local community. The balloons provide impressive night sky effects, including high-speed formation maneuvering, and have fooled thousands of observers.

with special lights or other test gear. UFO debunkers, such as Philip Klass, began to investigate UFO sightings with the same vigor as UFO protagonists, apparently explaining most with normal terrestrial phenomena. These facts were also learned by the public, and the UFO craze gained some perspective in conventional circles.

The Controversy Over UFO Evidence

With the affluence and technological advancements of the 1950s came the availability of inexpensive, good quality photographic equipment. UFO reports began to be accompanied by photographs of flying saucers. Expert analysis revealed no evidence of counterfeiting in many of these photographs, though some were obvious fakes. It did not take long for people to learn that a snapshot of a Buick hubcap flying through the air, or a double exposure of eerie lights in the night sky could bring instant national fame, and sometimes fortune. While most of the genuine, at least unmanufactured photographs reveal mere obscure shapes and smudges in speckled skies, a few, still frequently reprinted in UFO books, present clear images of saucer or disc-shaped objects in clear skies.

UFO Photographs

One such photograph was taken in McMinnville, Oregon, on May 11, 1950, by Paul Trent. This photograph shows a clear image of an up-side-down-plate-looking craft, with a small, pointed dome in the middle of the top. The photograph is one of the few ever to pass the scrutiny of the famed Condon Committee, an investigative committee well-known for its unkind treatment of UFO witnesses. The Condon Committee concluded, "The simplest, most direct interpretation of the photographs confirms precisely what the witnesses say they saw." Modern photographic analysis confirms that the Trent photograph is authentic. The two photographs were recently subjected to thorough computer enhancement scrutiny. The results prove that (1) the photographs contain no wires to hang a UFO model—a favorite debunker claim; (2) the UFO is an actual three-dimensional image, not flat or superimposed; (3) the UFO was at least one kilometer away; and, (4) the UFO is twenty to thirty meters in diameter. Interestingly, however, debunkers fail to accept the photograph as authentic, not because of any signs of counterfeiting, but because of the Trent family's "laid-back" attitude about the photos. This scholarly conclusion is based on the fact that a debunker had found the negatives on the floor near the sofa, where the children had knocked them off the coffee table.

Another difficulty with the testimony of the Trents is they are "repeaters." A repeater in UFOlogy is someone who has received more than his or her fair allotment of UFO sightings—generally, just one. Although the status of repeater is often the death knell of one's credibility, it is, as we shall see below, very much a part of the UFO phenomenon. Photographic analysis aside, there remains a question concerning the time of day the Trent photographs were taken. This, however, appears to be a post-analysis debunker fall-back argument.

One of the most fascinating UFO photographic windfalls occurred in Northern Utah in 1952. Delbert Newhouse and his wife were driving near Tremonton when she spotted flashes in the clear day sky. Delbert, a military aerial observation photographer, happened to have his photographic equipment in the car with him; a 16mm hightech movie camera. When he realized that he was observing something very rare in 1952 aviation he reached for his camera and photographed a cluster of shiny discs flying in formation through the summer sky. Government Intelligence analyzed the film for thousands of hours, and finally pronounced it to be authentic. The only other possible explanation proffered by government analysts was that the shiny objects may have been a flock of seagulls, but their own data demonstrated that the reflective nature of the objects was too radiant for seagulls, or any other type of bird, and they opted not to further analyze the theory.

The 1960s and 1970s produced a flood of UFO sightings and other close encounters, together with prolific "evidence" of UFO existence. Hundreds of photographs were published depicting clear shapes of advanced flying machines. Educators, policemen, ministers, engineers, and civic leaders reported seeing discs, saucers, cylinders, and other strange flying objects. People above reproach, former skeptics, were now confirming what they had seriously doubted only a moment before becoming witnesses themselves. Airline pilots dodged flying discs buzzing around the 350 m.p.h. passenger planes as if they were standing still. Radar centers tracked bogeys on their screens travelling at thousands of miles per hour. Reconnaissance jets were scrambled around the globe only to be chased back to base or to see metallic discs disappear into high altitudes in a flash.

Again, UFO debunkers attempt to eliminate many of such encounters as mistaken observations of bright planets, meteors, and terrestrial aircraft. It is with fervent zeal that debunkers attempt to convince the public that *all* such reports are explainable by natural phenomena. This is just not so, however, as we see below.

The Gulf Breeze UFOs

In some cases, UFOs have "haunted" certain locations for weeks, or even months, allowing the local citizens to see them many times. In one such case, citizens were able to move in with sophisticated photographic equipment to record their presence. This is the case of the Gulf Breeze, Florida, sightings. There, in late 1987, Ed and Frances Walters, local prominent business people, as well as many others, reported numerous sightings of flying vehicles. Ed and Frances armed themselves with a polaroid camera (it is difficult to fake polaroid photographs), a video camera, and even a sealed four lens 3-D camera supplied by UFO investigators. In the book *The Gulf Breeze Sightings*, the entire UFO experience between November 1987 and May 1988 is set out in detail, accompanied by more than twenty of the most impressive UFO photographs in existence. During the six-month sighting period, 135 of the local citizens of Gulf Breeze confirmed having seen the same flying vehicles photographed by the Walterses, and published in the local newspapers.[6] Experts from Jet Propulsion Laboratories and NASA examined the photographs and a video tape for nearly a year, concluding that they were unable to find any indication of counterfeiting in either the photographs, the video tape, or in the person of Ed Walters, the primary photographer. Psychologists, UFO-sighting investigators, and polygraph experts have fully examined Ed and Frances Walters,[7] and concluded that there exists a low probability of a hoax on their part.[8]

---

[6] Since the publication of the Walterses' book, many more sightings have been reported in Gulf Breeze, Florida, but none so close and clear as during November 1987 through May 1988.

[7] With the exception of Frances undergoing a polygraph examination—she was never asked. Ed Walters reports that his examination was as grueling a two days as he has ever undergone.

[8] All of this is not to say that the Walterses were not inundated with debunking efforts to assassinate their characters. Approximately two years after their UFO sightings stopped, debunkers planted a model of one of the UFOs in the Walters's house, and found a young man who would testify that he was in on the entire hoax. The young man could not withstand the scrutiny, and confessed that he had been put up to the debunking effort.

Experts with the Mutual UFO Network (MUFON), an organization holding itself out to investigate and document reported UFO sightings, agree that the Walters case is the best-documented American case to date. I have interviewed many of the investigators in the Gulf Breeze study, and all of those interviewed assert that they absolutely believe that the sightings occurred, and that the Walterses were not perpetrating a hoax. In my interview of Duane Cook, the editor of the *Gulf Breeze Sentinel*, he revealed that he was quite skeptical of running the story at first, although he had the photographs and initial analyses of them in hand. The turning point for him was when he decided to ask his parents' advice, who were visiting from out of town. He expected their usual conservative high eyebrow at the thought of publishing such nonsense, when instead he was met with, "That's the thing we saw on our way into town the other night!" They had observed the same UFO as they were driving to Cook's house, but did not know what it was, and decided not to say anything about it. Of course, Cook ran the story.

The Gulf Breeze sightings produced over 60 photographs of the UFOs,[9] 41 of which were taken by the Walterses, none of which was ever claimed to show evidence of counterfeiting by photographic analysis experts. Because of the recent and well documented nature of the Gulf Breeze sightings, I refer to that case in this chapter and those below as a benchmark of what appears to be occurring in contemporary UFO sightings and encounters. However, I do not attempt in this Part II to analyze the true nature or origin of the UFOs referred to—I simply present the documented facts as they have been reported. Other cases are used as benchmarks of the "abduction" phenomenon, discussed below.

UFO Design

General UFO design appears to be more functional than aesthetic—new car models have better aesthetics than do most UFOs. Besides the basic rounded and contoured shape of the main body, the Gulf Breeze UFOs have what appears to be diamond and square-shaped "portals" which encircle the entire craft. The diamond-shaped portals are reported to radiate with bright light at times, while the square shapes appear completely dark. The portals

---

9 Not all of the UFOs were exactly alike. There does seem to be similarity between them, however, as between a particular manufacturer's line of automobiles.

are reported by some to be unequally spaced around the craft. The main body varies in reported color, "grey/blue to a rich orange-brown," sometimes changing color while being observed. Nearly all of the Gulf Breeze UFOs had a large bright light in the center on top,[10] and a "power ring" looking light on the bottom. Ed Walters recounts that the power ring was generally "bright white with a darker orange core."

The power ring seems to be of importance to the mobility of the UFOs, although this is merely an observation. For instance, often times the power ring would become very bright just before the UFO flashed away, or "winked out."[11] During normal operation[12] the inside of the power ring is described as a "twisting, throbbing mass of . . . silent energy storm." The photographs and video taken of the power ring support this description. In the Walters photograph #19, wherein the UFO is approximately 10 feet above the road, the bright light of the power ring is reflected off the road. Photographic analysis reveals that the light source was very bright, but experts were puzzled by the phenomenon that the light appeared to be confined to a specific area, and did not light up more of the road and surroundings. A final interesting feature of the power ring is that it appears to be the source of a blue beam reported by the Walterses and other observers.

The Blue Beam

Ed Walters's very first reported encounter with one of the UFOs was accompanied by his being trapped in such a blue beam. After describing how the UFO, appearing like it was "right out of a Spielberg movie that had somehow escaped from the film studio," just floated into his neighborhood,

---

[10] This feature is nearly universal in UFO reports.

[11] Observers, including Ed and Frances Walters, reported that when the UFOs left in a hurry, they did so in such a manner that left the observer wondering if the craft had dashed away at incomprehensible speeds, or if it had just "disappeared." Some of the photographs show streaking as if the UFOs had moved quickly. However, the 1 min. 38 sec. video tape shows only that the UFO was there in one frame, and gone in the next, indicating that it had instantly disappeared. Again, this characteristic is very common.

[12] Normal operation of the UFOs was to hover or move slowly from place to place, bobbing and weaving as they went. Less frequently, the UFOs could move great or short distances in a flash.

over his neighbors' houses,[13] Ed Walters says he dashed for his polaroid camera that he uses in his construction business. He recounts:

> It glided along without a whisper of sound.[14] There was no hum, no wind, not a single disturbance to the air, trees, or houses as it passed over them.[15] While rocking back and forth, it did not seem to spin, so I never saw all sides, only what was in the photographs.[16]

After Walters had taken several photographs, the UFO had moved directly over him, and as he looked up into the power ring he explains:

> Bang! Something hit me. All over my body. I tried to lift my arms to point the camera. I couldn't move them. They were blue. I was blue. Everything was blue. I was in a blue light beam. The blue beam had hit me like compression. It was pressing me firmly, just enough to stop me from moving.
>
> I screamed, with my mouth frozen half open, but the sound was hollow. Dead, like a vacuum. I couldn't even move my eyes or eyelids. I thought I was dying. I was trying to breathe, there was air, each breath shallow . . . .
>
> The best I can tell, this all took less than twenty seconds. Then my feet lifted off the ground. I screamed. A voice groaned in my head. "We will not harm you."
>
> I screamed again.
>
> The deep, computerlike voice said, "Calm down."
>
> But it was in my head, not my ears.
>
> I screamed, as well as I could, "Put me down!"
>
> A few seconds passed as I slowly rose away from the pavement. A dream? Hell no! This was real. The feeling of helplessness was the worst. No control—just a piercing smell, a little scent of ammonia mixed with heavy cinnamon that scorched, then stuck to, the back of my throat.
>
> My heart was pumping so hard I could feel its throb as it thumped against my unmoving chest. I could feel the thumping vibration pass down my legs.
>
> The voice groaned, "S-t-o-p i-t."
>
> I screamed, "S[____] you!"
>
> All this happened fast. Now I was about two feet above the street. I panted for air, but the smell stung my lungs. My brain started to black out, so I screamed, "Aagghh!"
>
> The scream was black and dull, just outside my mouth. Almost the way you feel if you dive to the bottom of a swimming pool with the pressure holding everything, even your own voice, close to you.
>
> The voice came back, but now it seemed to be female. An easy hum filled my head. Suddenly, from within my head, came the sharp vision of a dog. Then another and

---

13 After the *Gulf Breeze Sentinel* had published Walters' photographs of this UFO, witnesses came forward with testimony that they had also seen the UFO that evening near the Walters's home.

14 In all of the reports of these Gulf Breeze UFOs, the observers are unanimous that none of the UFOs made an audible sound.

15 This lack of disturbance of the air is likewise significant, because many reports indicate that a UFO would flash a quarter mile in a second, just over the observer, then back to the original position in a like amount of time, with no wind, sound, or sonic boom. Again, this is a very common feature in UFO sightings.

16 *The Gulf Breeze Sightings*, p. 28.

another. I was confused. What are these dogs? Rapid visions, one after another, on and on. It seemed that I could almost see words beneath the dog visions. Something was flashing dog pictures in my head just as if they were turning the pages of a book.[17] The hum continued. I had the sensation I was four feet above the ground.

Wham! I hit the pavement hard and fell forward on my knees. The blue light was gone. The hum was still in my head, but it quickly decreased and was gone, like the hum of a speeding car as it races by. I collapsed onto my chest into the middle of the road, filling my lungs with real air. My stomach turned and I choked, trying not to throw up.[18]

Ed Walters says that as he rolled to his back he saw a small airplane entering the area's airspace, and assumes that the plane scared the UFO away in the nick of time.[19]

If not for the photographs that Ed Walters was able to take during this sighting, it would be an encounter that he would never have reported—understandably. If not for the photographs being determined to be authentic by leading photographic experts, Ed Walters's story would be nearly impossible to accept as anything but contrived. Although thousands claim to see UFOs, Ed Walters's account is pivotal because of the photographs. There exists so little credible, tangible evidence of UFO encounters that Ed Walters's bonanza of photographic confirmation renders it the best case for analysis.

The UFOs returned many times, and made many attempts to abduct Walters. Investigators feel, after subsequent events, that Ed Walters had closer ties with these UFOs than he realized, or remembered, and there was a specific purpose for their repeated attempts to pick him up.

The blue beam described by Ed Walters was repeatedly seen by six Gulf Breeze residents in all,[20] and was photographed from a distance and up close by Walters. We learn of other properties and functions of the blue beam in similar encounters had by Ed and Frances Walters. On one occasion, Ed recounts he was scurrying out the back door to get a photograph of a UFO he spied behind his house when a blue beam flashed down at him and hit

---

17 In a later encounter, Ed Walters reports that the UFO attempted to distract him with flashed pictures of naked women. Although this, in itself, could tend to detract from the credibility of a UFO sighting, in this case, it lends some credence. Ed reports that the UFO flashed indiscriminate pictures at him; naked women that are not generally thought of as "attractive." Apparently, the UFO was not aware of certain aspects of Earth culture and male preferences. Ed was not distracted.

18 *The Gulf Breeze Sightings,* pp. 29-30.

19 As observed below, UFO pilots may be surprised by unnoticed traffic entering their field of control. If this occurred here, it could be the reason the UFO abandoned its design to abduct Ed Walters.

20 Interestingly, some reported the blue beam being "shot" into the water in the Gulf of Mexico.

him on the leg. Rather than just having the effect of rendering Ed's leg useless or paralyzed, the beam effectively froze the leg in its three-dimensional position. Ed's momentum carried him forward, with his leg "pinned" where it was, slightly injuring him as he hyperextended the knee. Ed, with the assistance of Frances, was barely able to pull himself free of the blue beam. However, on another occasion when Frances dodged a blue beam that was near her, she reports that "[l]eaves and bits of gravel swirled around and within the beam."[21] Besides attempting to elevate Ed Walters with the blue beam, the pilots of the UFOs evidently use the blue beam as a transportation device to exit and enter the UFOs.

Telepathic Communication

An important aspect of the above-detailed Ed Walters first encounter is the apparent communication between the UFO and Walters. During many subsequent attempts to pick up Walters, he heard voices coaxing him into the open, and telling him not to resist. The voice would assure him that he was in no danger, not from the UFO anyway, and that he should go with them. Other times, the voice insisted that he was indeed in danger, and that going with the UFO would help him. The voice soon began calling him by a new name, "Zehaas." Ed had no idea why it called him by this name, but the voice, nearly always female after the initial communication, beckoned him, "Zehaas, Zehaas."[22] Not only did Ed Walters hear the computerlike voice, and the later female voice, but he also heard, or apparently overheard, human voices speaking in Spanish, and sometimes in other languages that he did

---

21 *The Gulf Breeze Sightings*, p. 179.

22 Walters was contacted by a woman who explained that "Zehaas" was very close to the pronunciation of the spanish word "cejas," meaning eyebrows. He noted that he has very dark, bushy eyebrows, and sensed that the hairless UFO occupants liked them. As ridiculous as this explanation sounds, other men report a feeling that they have been selected, at least in part, because of the bushiness of their eyebrows and other body hair. They observe that they "feel" physically admired by their abductors, and that there exist certain physical characteristics of humans that these abductors intend to breed into their own species, as discussed below. "Ed," in *Intruders: The Incredible Visitations at Copley Woods* (Budd Hopkins, 1987) reports, "At that time in my life my hair was thick and coal black, and I don't know if they told me or I just had the impression that they liked my coal-black hair, and they liked my . . . they like our features. They like our skin, and they like our eyebrows and they like our hair." (At p. 139)

not recognize. The Spanish voices, evidently of an abducted Earth couple, were accompanied by the sound of a crying baby.[23] In Ed Walters's limited understanding of the Spanish language, he heard the man complain that they were provided with nothing but bananas to eat. The man observed that "they," their captors, never seemed to eat anything but bananas themselves. In addition to the voices, Ed heard ambient sounds like doors, clanks, bumps, compressed air releases, and other background noises. All of this latter communication resembled eavesdropping, or inadvertently overhearing conversations, as if something had gone awry with the UFOs' communications systems, into which Ed Walters had evidently been plugged in some way.

In addition to the voices, Ed Walters often heard the hum in his head, like that of his first encounter, just before a sighting would occur. This is the purported reason he was able to have his cameras ready to photograph the UFOs when they appeared. The many opportunities to photograph the UFOs is a point of great interest in the Gulf Breeze sightings. The UFOs allowed Ed Walters, and others, to photograph them. However, early on Ed heard the voice say in Spanish, "Los fotos son prohibido [photographs are prohibited]," just as he took another. Just then, the female voice, sounding suddenly earthly, said, "You can't expose them. They won't hurt you. Just a few tests. That's all." The implication was clear that the voice belonged to an Earth woman, acting in concert with the UFO pilots.[24] However, the plea not to expose the UFOs is contrary to the overwhelming evidence that they wanted Ed Walters and others to photograph them.[25] This inconsistency is one that has not escaped any of the investigators, or Ed Walters. Ed Walters muses, "if they want people to know about them, why don't they just land in the middle of the Orange Bowl?"

Ed Walters is not the only person in the Gulf Breeze area to claim that he heard voices from the UFOs. The "hearing" of voices during UFO sightings

---

[23] The presence of the baby is significant in light of the UFO reproductive experimentation discussed below.

[24] Many who have reported seeing UFO occupants report that those who look different than us are sometimes accompanied by Earth humans, or hybrids—half alien, half human.

[25] Although they wanted some to see them, the UFOs appeared to go to great lengths to ensure that certain others did not see them. Investigators soon discovered that the UFOs disappeared instantly when Ed Walters gained knowledge of the investigators' presence. Sensing that the UFOs were "plugged into" Ed's sensory perceptors, the investigators withheld information from him, enabling them to witness the UFOs themselves on a couple of occasions.

7

Extraterrestrial Visitors

The Nature Of UFO Occupants

As we enter the world of sightings of, and encounters with, alien beings, we quickly perceive that this is the *"Twilight Zone"* of UFOlogy. With the advent of direct contact with extraterrestrials, or whatever UFO occupants are, no clear answers present themselves concerning alien visitations to Earth—rather, the confusion intensifies. The answers we do begin to formulate leave us quite uncomfortable. Descriptions of the physical makeup of these extraterrestrial visitors vary widely. Accounts of such beings range from human looking, blonde-haired, blue-eyed men, to tiny, fur-clad gnomes with little in the way of facial features.

Some UFO proponents have attempted to categorize aliens into four or five basic groups. While some believe that the wide variety of alien forms is the result of our being visited by beings from different planets, others believe that we are visited by extraterrestrial humans, who in turn bring an entourage of "assistants"—robots to collect specimens, monsters to scare the earthling natives away, and lesser life forms to perform dangerous or mundane tasks. Other aspects of the natures and origins of the occupants of UFOs, *e.g.* spiritual, metaphysical, electromagnetic, and psychic are discussed below in Part III. Interestingly, proponents of human/alien theories often believe that much of the visitation is by humans or humanoids from this planet.[1] Two major Earth/UFO theories are dominant.

---

[1] Other paranormal theories exist, postulating that UFOs and their occupants are from parallel worlds that exist on other planes, much like we view the existence of the spirit world.

The Subterranean Civilizations Theory

The first theory is that human civilizations live in little-known subterranean regions of the Earth. These earthlings enjoy the benefits of monitoring us without being observed by us. They have all of our technology, plus that of ancient advanced civilizations, and some of their own. There are people who profess to be former members of these civilizations. Recently, on a local radio talk show[2] the host conducted a telephone interview with a young (sounding) woman who calls herself Sharula Dux, who claims to be approximately 250 years old, and a former resident of an underground city, Telos, in the Mt. Shasta area of northern California. She said that this city possesses, among other things, a High Priest, for whom Sharula acts as a spiritual channeler to the surface world.

Sharula maintains that there exist more than 150 such subterranean cities around the world, which possess superior technology, and whose citizens live to extreme ages. The longevity is attributed to their toxin and radiation free environment, and certain "word of wisdom" lifestyles that they lead. Interestingly, accounts from UFO contactees also tell us that UFO occupants live to ages in the 1,000-year range. It is fascinating that both Betty Luca (an abductee discussed below) and Ed Walters, as well as others including some LDS abductees, indicate that they were taken under the water to subterranean complexes when abducted by UFOs. Significantly, these subterranean civilization theories have persisted for centuries.

The Returning Earthling Theory

The second theory explains that somewhere in Earth's history a human civilization possessing extraordinary technology left this planet and visits it from time to time. Accounts relate that these former earthlings have either moved to another planet,[3] or developed the ability of intergalactic travel at hyper-light speeds, causing their relatively short travels in space to translate into thousands of years to us. A subclass of this theory is that UFOs are piloted

---

[2] KSL Radio, Salt Lake City, Utah, March 9, 1992.

[3] Theories that we have descended from a race of humans from a fabled tenth planet in our solar system are proffered by some. The theory purports that our earthling forefathers returned to the home planet, but continue to visit us on Earth.

by our own descendants, who have mastered the science of time travel and have returned to help us.

The Extraterrestrial Human Theory

Having touched upon the human/alien theories which hold that unknown earthlings are actually responsible for flying saucers, and reserving the "gnome and fairy" theories for Part III, the bulk of extraterrestrial personage encounters recount that human-like[4] persons are visiting our planet. Many accounts report that UFO pilots are nothing more than Earth-like humans, sometimes sporting larger ears or some other minor deviation, but essentially like us. The bulk of contemporary narratives, however, claim that "small greys" are manning the UFOs.

Small Greys

Most persons touting alien encounters describe alien beings that stand three-and-one-half to five feet tall, having grey colored, hairless skin, proportional arms and legs, diminutive mouths and noses, no ears, and very large dark or black "almond" shaped eyes set in a bulbous head with a pointy chin. These are the type of aliens described by Ed Walters, as well as most abductees, discussed below. These abductees generally only retrospectively "remember" the aliens, after "hypnotic retrieval" sessions with psychologists. Sometimes the small greys are accompanied, if not led, by taller, human looking beings.

During my LDS mission to Italy in 1978-1979, a wave of sightings occurred in that country. The effect was so alarming that even the Italian Parliament debated the subject. On July 4, 1978, Italian Navy personnel ascended Mt. Etna and sighted "three red pulsating UFOs, one of which landed." They described it as being a "domed disc about 12 meters [40 feet] in diameter with red and yellow body lights." They then observed "two tall golden-haired, white-robed beings accompanied by three or four shorter beings wearing

---

4 The term "human-like" is used broadly here. As pointed out in Part I, humans on this Earth vary widely in size, color, characteristics, and appearance. If humans from other parts of the universe are actually visiting us, we could expect a reasonable amount of similarity or diversity without stretching the bounds of our understanding of the nature of humanity.

helmets and spacesuits." During an inquiry, the military personnel said they "felt a compulsion" to climb the slopes. The phenomenon of tall humans accompanied by small humanoids is common in reported observations of UFO occupants. Telepathic suggestion to rendezvous at a predetermined place is also a routine technique employed by UFO occupants.

Ed Walters experienced at least two occasions when he saw the small greys up close, in full consciousness. On the first occasion, he was in bed when he heard the family dog bark in an unusual manner. He recounts:

> The pistol in one hand, the camera in the other, I walked over to the French doors that lead from the master bedroom out to a screened-in porch overlooking the pool.
>
> Cloth miniblinds covered the glass. I could tell it was still dark out. Only the faint glow from the school's security lights, across the field behind us, showed around the edges of the blinds.
>
> I felt for the draw cord and pulled it down quickly, leaning forward as the blinds came up. On the other side of the glass was a small creature. Big black eyes stared into mine. Just inches separated us. I screamed and fell backward onto the floor as my feet got crossed. My head and shoulders hit the closet door.
>
> The creature just stood there, staring in at me. It was maybe four feet tall. A dark, grayish-black, box-like thing hid most of its body. The "helmet" over its head had a clear insert that revealed its eyes, really big eyes that covered the top half of its head. It grasped a glowing silver rod in its right hand . . . .
>
> I still had the pistol in my hand, so I quickly raised it and pointed it at the creature. I wasn't going to shoot unless it tried to get through the door.
>
> The creature stared at me with eyes that showed no fear. Eyes that were calm. Eyes that were almost sad. Eyes that somehow seemed curious.

Ed Walters decided to attempt a capture of this small grey and ran out the back door only to be attacked by the blue beam. It is interesting that Walters recounts that this being wore shielding only in the front. As the creature walked away, its back was unshielded. The entire encounter was an apparent attempt to get Walters out into the open to abduct him with the blue beam. From this we surmise that the creature felt no need to protect itself in the back because it knew that Walters would be "beamed up" if he pursued the creature. Ed Walters saw the blue beam shoot down from the UFO just a few minutes after its failed attempt to capture him, and took a photograph of it. He speculates that the creature was beamed up in the blue beam.

The use of the blue beam as a transportation device gives rise to Walters's second conscious encounter with the UFO occupants. Ed Walters narrates that one evening while driving his pickup through a remote area to a construction site,

> I pressed the gas pedal and rounded a curve. Everything turned bright white. The hood reflected a brilliant flash. Some of the "light" came through the windshield and hit my arms.

I yelled, "What the h__l?"

I really screamed, and at that moment, flash! Again I was being hit with a white beam. Almost like a flashcube going off inches from my eyes. It was extremely bright and left my eyes trying to refocus on the road. Within seconds, I realized I couldn't feel my arms. The sensation was the same as when your foot goes to sleep and you feel all those pin pricks . . . .

Still accelerating down the road, I knew I was in trouble. The truck swerved from side to side and was almost out of control because I couldn't watch the road curves and watch my hands control the steering wheel at the same time.

Only seconds had passed from the first flash of light. From overhead, and coming from behind, the UFO passed straight down the road in front of me . . . . I hit the brakes hard and came to a stop about 200 feet from the UFO . . . . By bracing my left arm on the steering wheel, I managed to shoot photo 19. I pulled out the film, preparing for another shot, when I noticed that the UFO was definitely moving closer.

I panicked, afraid the white flash could hit me in the truck cab. Out of the truck and onto the ground I pushed myself in a gasping rush. I was scared, and my chest heaved as I hyperventilated. I was trying to crawl under the truck. The camera was slung on my left wrist, and I dragged the shotgun with my right hand.

When I looked forward, down the road, the UFO wasn't there. I was halfway under the truck when it hit again. Flash? My legs stung and went numb from the knees down. I dug into the grass with my elbows and finally managed to make it to where my head was below the oil pan . . . .

A blue beam flashed from the UFO to the road. Five times it shot down. Each blue beam deposited a creature on the road close to the UFO . . . .

Finally all five began to move in lock-step toward me. Each one had a silver rod. They moved the rods up and down in their right hands as they marched down the middle of the road.

With this, Ed Walters decided to get into his pickup and flee, which he did, with great difficulty. These silver rods are apparently the same as that carried by the single small grey on the night it attempted to lure Walters out of the house. Apparently such a glowing silver rod is a technical device used by these beings as a stun gun, communicator, or some other environmental control device.

The Varied And Ephemeral Nature Of UFO Occupants

Descriptions of aliens, or whatever the beings are that occupy UFOs, range more widely than those offered above. "Moth-men" who fly without fluttering their wings have been reported around the world, as well as in the United States. Tiny two-foot-tall men with long white beards, or even giants, are commonly described. Many UFOlogists suggest that UFO occupants are ephemeral in nature, able to change their size, shape, and appearance at will.

Some contactees report that the beings are self described as being able to change their appearance. These facts raise many important questions for Latter-Day Saints, and for anyone else who is interested in the spiritual aspects of these phenomena.

Kathie Davis describes a childhood experience in which, after seeing a flash of bright, white light and hearing a loud noise, she wandered to a "house" with the door open, although there was snow on the ground. Inside, she met a "little boy" who took her into his "playroom," where a small mechanical device surreptitiously cut her leg while the boy distracted her. Upon taking the blood sample she recounts that the boy metamorphosed into a small, large-headed, grey-skinned person.[5]

Shootout At Kelley

On a hot August evening, Billy Ray Taylor, a guest at the Sutton family farm in the Kelley area of southwestern Kentucky, went out to the well for a drink of water. He came running into the house in a panic, reporting that he had just seen a flying saucer fly over and descend into a gully near the house. The family teased him about his attempt to frighten them until the dog began barking nervously, and hid under the house. Billy Ray and Mr. Sutton looked outside and saw a very short being approaching the house. They describe the creature as having a large, round head with big, luminous eyes, and long arms with "talons" on the end. The two men went directly for some firepower—a 20-gauge shotgun and a .22 rifle. As the creature neared the house, they both began blasting. It appeared to take a hit, tumbling head over heels through the air, and disappearing. The men went outside to check for more creatures, finding one on the roof and one in the tree. They shot the one on the roof, which likewise somersaulted through the air, and then the one in the tree. This creature "floated" to the ground, escaping with a limping dash.

Mr. Sutton began around the corner of the house in search of more creatures, when he came upon one at the corner. He shot it at point-blank range with the shotgun. He relates that he heard a loud hollow clink, like shooting a metal pail. The creature retreated, although it appeared to be uninjured.

---

5 *Intruders*, pp. 203-04.

The creatures surrounded the house, and the men shot at them through the windows, trying to calm the children between outbursts of fire. After three hours of this, the creatures finally disappeared. When it appeared that the creatures might be gone, the family dashed for the cars and drove to the nearest town for help.

The city and state police returned to the farm with the Suttons, and thoroughly investigated the incident. They brought along a photographer to make a detailed record of the investigation. The creatures were gone, but a luminous patch of liquid remained where one of the creatures had fallen after taking a blast. The police concluded their investigation early in the morning and returned to town to file their reports.

A short while later the creatures returned, again peering through the windows of the Sutton farm house. The men began anew their relentless firing of rifle blasts into the creatures through the doors and windows. After a couple of hours, the creatures departed for the last time. The only physical evidence of the second shootout was a house full of bullet holes. However, the police agencies involved were thoroughly convinced of the sincerity of Billy Ray Taylor and his hosts, the Suttons, and commented in their official reports that by the demeanor and attitude of the victims, the police believed their unusual story.[6]

Although we can begin making a composite perceptual sketch of the nature of UFO occupants from the tidbits of information we gain from alleged observers, it is not until we commence an analysis of abduction reports that we gain any understanding of their purposes for visiting the Earth as claimed. The "space brother" preachings of the 1960s begin to pale in comparison as we compile the data that are streaming into investigation centers in connection with abductions, and the story they tell is quite unsettling.

---

6 *The UFO Phenomenon*, Time-Life Books, Virginia, 1987 (*Mysteries of the Unknown* Series).

8
Extraterrestrial Abductors

Missing Time

In the past few decades many people have come forward telling of perplexing experiences wherein they have seen a UFO, then have gone about their business without apparent interruption, only to find that an hour or two of time has escaped them, and no memory of the "missing time" can be recalled. The continuum of the passing of time seems completely uninterrupted to these witnesses, at first at least—yet there exist inescapable signs that something unremembered has occurred to them. This phenomenon is reported throughout the world, as well as by LDS Church members. The Roper Organization poll cited in the Introduction reflects that up to 13 % of American Adults have experienced such a missing time episode.

Judi Moudy

Judi Moudy is the legal assistant of my former missionary companion, Stan Harter. As I discussed the details of Stan's encounter with him on the telephone, he related that his assistant came to speak with him of her own encounter, as she was preparing his dictated account. He told me that he was quite impressed with her account, as well as with her personally. He related that he has known Judi for a long while, trusts her completely, and *knows* that she is "incapable of lying." Judi tells of her encounter quite openly. Because it is so representative of abduction cases, we consider it first.

My encounter occurred when I was in high school. It was August of 1977 and I was living in Del City, Oklahoma, a suburb of Oklahoma City. I was fifteen years old at the time and had two friends spending the night. Rhonda, Julie, and I decided to sleep in my parents' travel trailer which was parked in the back yard. Our home was located on the last street in a subdivision and was adjacent to a large alfalfa field. It was about 11:00 p.m. and MUCH too hot and muggy to sleep. If you have ever been to Oklahoma City in August, you'll know what I mean. We fixed ourselves a coke and some popcorn and sat out in the front yard to talk. The adjacent town is Midwest City, where Tinker Air Force Base (home of the AWACS) is located, and my house is in the flight path of the east-west runway. Thus, I grew up with sonic booms, loud planes flying overhead and strange lights in the sky at night.

When Rhonda saw lights in the northern sky moving erratically, I told her it was probably just a plane coming in for a landing. All of a sudden the lights began moving toward us at a very high rate of speed. I had never seen a plane do this before. The lights kept coming toward us, getting bigger and brighter, until it was right over the field across the street. It was just breathtaking. Prior to this time, the crickets were chirping and dogs were barking. When the craft hovered over the field, all noises ceased.

The craft was cigar-shaped with lights around the top, bottom and center. The lights in the center actually looked like portholes as the light in this area was coming out of the holes inside the craft as if they were windows. The craft paused for about one minute, then slowly moved to the right to the far end of the field, then went straight down. Julie, the most adventurous of us three, took off running across the street to see where it landed. Rhonda and I followed, but when we got to the yard across the street we saw bright blue beams of light shooting through the alfalfa and coming straight at us. It was a very strange light—we could see the beginning of it, then it was as if someone turned off the source, and the beam separated itself and kept coming at us as if sections of pipe were being shot out. The beams were short at first, then kept getting longer and longer. Another strange thing was that there was a chain link fence at the corner of the yard across from us. When the beams became long enough to reach the fence, the light would *go over* the fence! Just past this fence was the concrete street. When the beam of light hit the concrete, it disintegrated into steam!

We kept watching the beams of light for some time. Suddenly we all became VERY sleepy. I looked at my watch and told Rhonda and Julie it was 12:30 and that we should get to bed because we had to get up at 6:00 a.m. for early morning marching band practice. The next thing I remember, we were back in my front yard walking toward the trailer. We were completely exhausted and went inside to go to bed. When we turned on the lights, we noticed that we each had dirt on our arms and legs. Earlier in the evening, Rhonda had given herself a manicure complete with bright red nail polish. She now had mud under her nails! I turned and looked at the clock; it was *3:00 a.m.* We couldn't understand what had happened. It seemed like I had just mentioned that it was 12:30 and that we should get to bed; we walked to the trailer and it was 3:00 a.m.

I debated on waking up my dad, but he had been ill with ulcers and moody for some time. So we all went to sleep. When we awoke the next morning, Rhonda and Julie had terrible rashes on their arms and stomachs. I didn't have a rash, but I developed a SEVERE headache which lasted for several days. I had never been bothered by headaches before, but I have suffered from migraines ever since that incident. We discovered that each of us had an identical inch-long cut on the outside of our index finger on our left hands.

We went outside to see if the craft was still there, but it was gone. We walked over to the field where it had been to see if there was any evidence of its presence. As we walked out through the field, the alfalfa was about neck high. Then we came upon an area where the alfalfa had been "burned" in the form of a triangle with three large circles at the ends [corners]. The alfalfa in the center looked similar to singed hair. We ran back to the house and told my parents, who were *very skeptical*. I finally convinced my dad to come to the field with us to look at the evidence. Julie's dad had already arrived and was now with us. After seeing the evidence our parents finally believed us.

Julie's dad had an interest in UFOs and knew of a researcher based in Norman, Oklahoma, named Hayden Hewes. Julie's dad called Mr. Hewes, and he came to my house that same afternoon to interview us. Mr. Hewes interviewed each of us separately with a tape recorder to be certain we each saw the same thing. Our stories concurred. Mr. Hewes took samples of the soil from the field, the alfalfa, and the dirt from under Rhonda's nails which he sent to a lab for analysis. Each sample was determined to have a high level of radioactivity.

My father was a civilian employee at Tinker Air Force Base at that time and called a friend of his who was working in the control tower that night to ask if anything strange had shown up on radar. The friend asked the reason for his inquiry and questioned him concerning what he had seen. My dad responded that his daughter had seen something strange in the sky and that he was just curious. The friend said he wasn't at liberty to give out any information, but the next day two gentlemen from the Air Force came to our house and interviewed us. They wouldn't give us any information either.

Reporters got wind of our story, did an interview, and printed it on the front page of the Daily Oklahoman newspaper. At the end of the article, Mr. Hewes requested anyone else who may have seen something that night to call his office. Twelve people called in, two of them police officers who wanted to remain anonymous.

Since my encounter, I have read almost everything I can get my hands on relating to UFO experiences. Unfortunately, most of the material seems fictionalized or sensationalized. Frankly, it scares me. It's hard for me to rationalize what may have happened to us—it just doesn't make intellectual sense. But I also don't know how to explain the loss of time and the identical scars.[1]

Judi's experience is much like those of thousands of others. The questions, What happened during the missing two and one half hours?; How did the girls become so dirty?; and, What are the identical cuts from? leap out at us and demand explanation. No explanation can be had absent the restoration of the girls' memories. However, others with similar experiences have remembered, or subsequently recalled what happened to them.

Between the time that Judi sent me a copy of her account, and the time we discussed it on the telephone (about a week), the television movie *Intruders* aired. To take advantage of the market hype generated by the network advertising for *Intruders* much of the week's television programming included UFO-oriented programs. As I rewatched my tapes of that week's UFO programs, I was especially impressed by the accounts coming out of Belgium and other areas concerning triangular UFOs. Thousands of official reports have been made to the Belgian government since 1987, including many from government employees—police, etc. These craft appear to be "cigar-shaped"

---

[1] Letter to Author, dated May 12, 1992.

when seen from the side, with a row of lights or lighted windows around the perimeter, as reported by Judi. When seen from below, however, witnesses report that the craft are actually triangular, having rounded, convex edges all around. The design is much the same as if one bent a pipe into a triangle and covered the inside hollow section with a covering, top and bottom.

The UFOs reportedly had white glowing lights on the underside of the three corners. It is interesting how precisely similar these reports are with Judi's 1977 report—cigar-shaped from the side, yet leaving a singed triangular impression in the alfalfa field with distinctly round markings at the three corners. This similarity did not escape Judi either.

The Betty And Barney Hill Abduction

One of the most famous UFO abduction cases, and the earliest to be widely reported, is that of Betty and Barney Hill. Their experience, as told in John Fuller's *The Interrupted Journey* (1966) and a series of *Look* magazine articles, typifies many contemporary abduction stories. The Hills were reportedly driving late at night in the fall of 1961. As they made their tedious journey through the White Mountains from Montreal to their home in Exeter, New Hampshire, they spotted a bright light in the night sky that began to follow them. Barney stopped the car to get a better look at the object, when they noticed that it was a craft with windows, through which the Hills could see occupants. When the Hills saw this, they jumped back into their car and drove home, arriving two hours later than they thought it should be.

Within a week or so the Hills started suffering from recurring nightmares wherein they were forcibly abducted and taken aboard a UFO. Their captors were small greys, with the exception of a taller leader and "doctor." This doctor is so described because his function was to perform certain physical examinations on the Hills. Betty was examined almost exclusively as to her reproductive organs. She describes under hypnosis an examination technique that was completely unfamiliar to her, or anyone else at the time:

> The examiner has a long needle . . . . He said he wants to put it in my navel, it's just a simple test . . . . And I'm telling him, "It's hurting, it's hurting, take it out." And the leader comes over and he puts his hand, rubs his hand in front of my eyes,

and he says it will be all right. I won't feel it . . . . He said it was a pregnancy test. I said, "That was no pregnancy test here."[2]

It was many years later that our own technology developed the correlating procedure of laparoscopy to perform *in vitro* examinations. In fact, laparoscopy was later applied to treat infertility by placing sperm and oocytes directly into an infertile woman's fallopian tubes for *in vivo* fertilization.

Barney Hill was similarly subjected to examination of his genitals, reporting that a circular instrument had been placed over the groin area, later resulting in the appearance of a circle of warts at the site of the instrument.

Other than their recurring dreams, the Hills had no conscious memory of the abduction. A few years later they sought psychiatric assistance, not understanding the reasons underlying stress they were experiencing in their lives and marriage. It was while under psychiatric hypnosis that the Hills independently recalled their harrowing experience of abduction and physical examination. While under hypnosis Betty was able to recall and draw a star chart she had observed on the UFO. Some feel that the chart she drew is extraordinary because it matches perfectly with far away star systems. Debunkers feel that the chart is insignificant because of the high probability of matching any given star pattern with a true charting, given the large number of stars in our universe.

Onboard Medical Examinations

The disturbing pattern of UFO abductions that appear to be inundating investigators are those in which abductees report being taken aboard UFOs and given medical examinations. Often, as with Betty and Barney Hill, these reported examinations are centered in human reproductivity. Stories abound that human semen and egg samples are collected during these abductions. Others, men curiously, claim that they are forced or enticed to breed with a female alien or human/alien hybrid. Generally, however, sperm samples are taken mechanically. Women further claim to be artificially impregnated with alien semen.

---

2 Raymond E. Fowler, *The Watchers: The Secret Design Behind UFO Abduction*, Bantam Books, New York (1990). Raymond Fowler cites the Betty Hill examination to compare with that of the subject of his book, Betty Andreasson Luca: "Oh! And he's going to put that in my navel! Ohhhh! Feel's like he's going around my stuff inside—feeling it—with that needle." Like Betty Hill, Betty Luca also received the benefit of the abductor putting his hand on her head to relieve her pain.

Many reports are surfacing that offspring of these human/alien reproductive experiments exist. Accounts are becoming more common that women who were in their first trimester of pregnancy are suddenly finding themselves no longer pregnant. Medical experts reportedly confirm that a *bona fide* pregnancy existed, and was then non-existent, leaving no trace that a pregnancy ever existed or that an abortion occurred. As much as this all sounds like fodder for selling supermarket tabloids, many UFOlogists are buying into the phenomenon. They report that upon the application of hypnotic retrieval to such a person, memories of multiple UFO abductions surface. In the first instance, generally in childhood, abducted youth are subjected to the taking of tissue samples. Later, as young adults, those who pass genetic muster are abducted for the taking of sperm[3] and ova. Sometimes, the abducted women are impregnated, generally artificially, and later the developing fetus is removed from the womb and a special therapy is applied to remove signs of pregnancy. Budd Hopkins documents in *Intruders* how multigenerational abductions have created experimentational bloodlines, evidently of high value to the abductors.

Antonio Villas-Boas

Before the medical examination/reproductive experimentation aspects of the UFO abduction phenomenon were widely reported, a young Brazilian student, Antonio Villas-Boas sheepishly reported a "rape" in 1957. Antonio was helping out on his father's farm, plowing a field by night, when an egg-shaped UFO landed within fifty feet of his tractor. The tractor turned off by itself as three or four short uniform-and-helmet-clad creatures exited the craft and came toward him. Antonio attempted to escape, but the creatures dragged him into the UFO. They took blood samples and removed Antonio's clothing. After rubbing his body with a clear liquid, the creatures put Antonio into a room by himself aboard the UFO. The room soon began to fill with a smoke, which made Antonio nauseous. A small, blonde, naked female

---

[3] Two of the men that Budd Hopkins worked with expressed that they had received vasectomies, due to an overwhelming, innate drive to do so. The one reports that he was later abducted for the purpose of mating with a hybrid woman. (*Intruders*, pp. 138-40.) He recounts (through tears of humiliation) that after the perfunctory sexual encounter (unemotional for her, traumatic for him), he was nearly thrown out of the UFO for his misdeed. He received an unequivocal telepathic message that his captors were not amused.

"woman" then entered the room, and after some prodding, was able to lower Antonio's defenses, and sexual intercourse ensued—twice. Antonio claimed that the liquid rubbed on him must have lowered his resistance to her promptings. Following intercourse, Antonio recounts that the woman pointed to her abdomen, and then to the stars. Investigators felt that her mute message indicated that a child would be born from their encounter.

After dressing and receiving a quick tour of the UFO, Antonio was ejected from the craft and left to himself. His story seemed more fantasy than fact at the time, except for a few items of latent evidence. Antonio became quite nauseous over the next few days, during which time strange sores developed over his body. He was later examined by a local physician who was unable to diagnose or cure his symptoms. Some experts have conjectured that his symptoms were very much like radiation poisoning. This possibility is echoed by the reports of others who are told by their abductors that their short stays on the UFOs are due to the fact that they will become ill if they stay too long. In any case, no matter how fantastic Antonio's tale appeared in 1957, the fact that many similar reports have surfaced since then, coupled with Antonio's reputation for honesty, have made his account one of the most accepted UFO "rape" cases in the abduction literature.[4]

Human Accomplices

Kathie Davis reported an eerie encounter at a mountain cabin that she and others had with three young men who were plainly unconventional. This encounter was accompanied by a UFO sighting,[5] and missing time for all involved, including the adult cabin owners. They all relate that the "leader" of the three did all of the talking, and was very interested in Kathie (not a good looking young woman). The behavior of the three was quite suspect. For instance, they mentioned that they were together because they played in a band. When asked what kind of music the band played, they first asked

---

[4] Jerome Clark, *UFOs in the 1980s,* Apogee Books (1990), p. 10; *The UFO Phenomenon,* Time-Life Books, p. 10.

[5] This UFO sighting is noteworthy in that Kathie Davis describes the UFO in terms of seeing "four lights descending, spinning like pinwheels." Other than reports of the main body of a UFO slowly turning on its axis, few accounts mention "spinning." This "spinning like pinwheels" description is the closest account I have located to the "Wheels of Ezekiel" UFO theory proffered by those of the "Biblical UFOs" bent.

what kind of music those present preferred, and then responded that it was the kind of music they played. This sort of seeking out appropriate responses to questions was prevalent during the encounter.

As Budd Hopkins questioned those present about the incident, they all reported that they had absolutely no recollection regarding the appearance of the two taller, quiet young men. They all, however, remembered every detail about the leader. After individual descriptions of the leader, Hopkins remarked to each that his or her characterization sounded like a description of Kathie, to which they each agreed there did exist a strong family resemblance. In light of the leader's unusual interest in Kathie's life and background, and the multigenerational genetic and reproductive research apparently occurring in the "Davis" family, Hopkins's implication was that this young man was an unknown brother of Kathie's, retained by the aliens after conception, performing reconnaissance missions for the UFO occupants. The concept of human agents of UFO occupants is not at all new.[6]

The Nursery

As an epilogue to the fetal removal phenomenon, some hypnotic retrieval attempts have unearthed memories of yet another abduction during which the donor of the ova or fetus, or in some cases, the contributing father, is given the hybrid child to hold and cuddle. After the "bonding" session is completed, the child is removed from the mother or father who is then returned to the bedroom or other place of abduction, without any memory of the abduction or the child. Theories attempting to explain all of such reproductive experimentation by aliens speculate that genetic manipulation is occurring, either to enrich alien gene pools or to regulate human evolution. A third possibility is that a hybrid race is being created for an unknown purpose. Of course, those of the Erich von Daniken bent claim that man was created by this very process,[7] and that the course of his evolution has always been determined by the genetic interference of our alien "fathers."

---

6 See generally, Jim and Coral Lorenzea, *Abducted,* Berkley Publishing Corporation; *e.g.,* "The Walton Affair," pp. 80-86.

' 7 Von Daniken theorizes that humans were created by altering the genes of Earth apes with genetic information of extraterrestrials. This explains the missing link in our evolutionary process according to von Daniken.

These hybrid babies are generally described as tiny and thin, often lying in small metal containers in the UFOs, having thin, greyish skin. The human women are very attracted to the babies, finding them almost irresistible—with hypnotic eyes. It is while "falling into" the babies' dark eyes that the women develop a sense that the babies are "wise," or "omniscient." A type of communication occurs between the women and the babies, during which the women become captivated by the great wisdom and intelligence of the babies, feeling a close kinship to them. Kathie Davis described her feelings about her little hybrid, Andrew, as she looked into his eyes as, "It's like the whole world was in this little baby's eyes. It was like, God, he knew, he *knew* what I felt. He just knew. I can't describe it. It was so intense, so euphoric or something. I was so excited, so up."[8]

During such an abduction experience of a psychotherapist called "Lucille," she gained information that offers an explanation of why these reproductive experiments are occurring. She "sensed" from her telepathic communication with the aliens that their society was "millions of years old, of outstanding technology and intellect but not much individuality or warmth." She wrote "the society was dying, that children were being born and living to a certain age, perhaps preadolescence, and then dying." She felt that there was "a desperate need to survive, to continue their race." Lucille explained, "It is a culture without touching, feeling, nurturing . . . basically intellectual. Something has gone wrong genetically. Whatever their bodies are now, they have evolved from something else. My impression is that they wanted to somehow share their history and achievements and their present difficulties in survival. But I really don't know what they are looking for." Lucille was shown a series of "holographic" images, remarking, "I saw a child about four feet tall, gray, totally their race, waving its arms . . . it was in pain and dying. I was told that this is what is happening now."[9]

The "Aliens" Have Something To Learn From Us

An underlying theme of many of these "nursery" abductions is a sense that the aliens are sorely lacking in "warmth" skills. Kathie Davis claimed that she was abducted and shown a small hybrid female child, and was told

---

[8] *Intruders*, p. 184.

[9] See *Intruders*, pp. 187-91, for a full narrative of Lucille's abduction experience.

it was hers. She described her strong feelings of love for this "beautiful" little half-human girl. She explained that the female aliens, distinguishable only by their emotional "feel," were interested in learning how she held, cuddled, and loved the child. On a subsequent abduction, Kathie's little girl, about four years old, joined in watching and learning as Kathie was told that an additional eight children had been produced from her removed ova. She was then allowed to hold the youngest of her many hybrid children. She recalled under hypnosis:

> They want to watch me . . . hold this . . . baby. They want . . . to feel how I love it. I shouldn't worry, 'cause she'll [the first female child] take care of it. I have something they can't give.
> [When asked "what?" she replied;]
> Something . . . to do with touch, and the human part . . . and they don't understand, but they'll learn. And they said I could name them. I would choose . . . .

Kathie noted that this undersized hybrid baby "was all pale . . . he looked dead, but he wasn't." When she began cuddling and kissing him, he suddenly gained strength and vitality. [10]

Lucille reports that in her encounter, she noted the difficulties of the alien race:

> We spoke about the lack of touching. I told them that some animals here can die within a day of birth if they are not licked and touched by their mothers or other loving caretakers, since that affects their perceptions of their bodily functions as well as of themselves. Strange as it may seem, I suggested their interpreting Ashley Montague's book *Touching*. [11]

Erased Memories

Most of these occurrences of abduction, and their often attendant reproductive system experimentation, are not "remembered" initially by the abductees. As in the case of the Hills, unexplained periods of "missing time" or recurring dreams or other subconscious manifestations of abduction and experimentation plague the person until psychological assistance is sought. Hypnotic retrieval of these repressed memories often recovers the memory of the missing time or forgotten period and the details of the abduction.

The conscious memories of the abduction appear to be purposely "erased" by the abductors. Some abductees claim to have been told by the aliens that because no one would believe them anyway, it would be better just to have

---

[10] *Ibid.*, p. 184, see also, *UFOs in the 1980s,* p. 10.

[11] *Ibid.*, p. 191

their memories erased. Other abductees have seemingly received forced amnesia through less beneficent means. Laura, Kathie Davis's sister, reports that hypnosis to help her lose weight had the opposite effect, making her eat everything in sight. When she called her hypnotist, upon hearing his voice she became homicidally violent. When taken to another hypnotist, it took several sessions to get her past an implanted posthypnotic suggestion that she would die if she were hypnotized or if she tried to remember her abduction experience.[12]

Hypnotic Retrieval

The practice of hypnotic retrieval is controversial because debunkers claim that those who perform the hypnosis "suggest" or "plant" ideas of abduction in the hypnotised person, even if it is done unintentionally. Debunkers fear that hypnotists inadvertently "lead" the hypnotized person, or "indicate" appropriate responses to questioning without intending to do so, thereby creating abduction memories. Budd Hopkins, presumably the foremost (or most experienced) UFO hypnotic retrieval expert, claims that he has certain "control points" by which he discerns abduction reports hypnotically retrieved. Hopkins claims that there exist certain consistent "details" in most genuine "retrieved" abduction cases that he withholds from the public. Because only he and his colleagues know what these details are, abductee wannabees have no way of knowing how to fake a hypnotic session with him. Some of these control points are specific examination and surgical techniques used by the abductors and specific hieroglyphs and other symbols seen while aboard the UFOs. Although this control point technique may satisfy Budd Hopkins, it does little to alleviate debunkers' fears of inadvertent memory implanting by the hypnotists.[13]

The Ed Walters Abductions

It may be no surprise that Ed Walters was also abducted by the UFOs that plagued his life for five months. He too had no conscious memory of being

---

12 *Intruders*, p. 12.

13 See generally, *UFOs in the 1980s,* pp. 1-13.

abducted, but was able to recall some details of abduction through hypnotic retrieval. He begins with a narration of what he consciously remembered about the abduction:

> In a fraction of a second my eyes caught the glow of the UFO about thirty-five feet above me. I flinched, and my right hand squeezed the shutter button, resulting in photo 39. Then, with the UFO just above a small oak tree, my eyes went completely white, just as if a flashcube had gone off in my brain. I could not tell if the whiteness was all around me, like a floodlight, or just within my head. Instantly I felt nothing, no sensations from my body, only a vague sense of falling.
>
> The next instant I was lifting my face and chest up off the sand at the edge of the water. My head pounded, and as I tried to stand, I stumbled in dizziness. Disoriented, I crawled up the beach twenty feet to the bench and sat there with my head in my hands.
>
> A smell from my hands was making me nauseated. Then it dawned on me. How could I fall to the ground while standing at the [camera] and get up a second later twenty feet away? I checked my watch and couldn't believe the time. It was 2:25 A.M. What had happened to the hour and fifteen minutes[14] between taking the photographs and finding myself on the beach?[15]

With the aid of regressive hypnosis Ed Walters claims that he is discovering that he was abducted and taken aboard the UFO on that occasion, as well as on other occasions during his life. He recounts three weird (terrifying, ocult-like) experiences that occurred at eight-year intervals in his life, wherein missing time was present. Walters again asserts that through hypnotic retrieval he has learned that he was abducted on these occasions also.

Although Ed Walters fails to offer details of why he was abducted, he believes that the abduction on the Gulf Breeze beach will be his last. He offers in support of this belief the following facts which occurred upon his waking the following morning.

> In the bathroom I ran a comb through my hair and felt a bump at the back of my head very close to the center of my neck. It felt bruised, and I went to the mirror to try to see what I could feel. When I looked into the mirror I couldn't see the lump, but as I turned around, I immediately saw more than I expected to.
>
> A large bruise, with a red dot in the center, was prominent between my eyes right at the bridge of my nose. Two more similar red marks were centered on my temples, each surrounded by a bruise. I was shocked.[16]

---

[14] Most reported UFO abductions are of short duration, lasting generally one to eight hours—usually closer to two. Although most of the time the UFO occupants are said to have no more interest in the abductees than to hurriedly complete their predetermined examinations and medical procedures, Kathie Davis reported that on more than one occasion she was told she had to leave because a delay would result in her illness.

[15] *The Gulf Breeze Sightings,* p. 263.

[16] *Ibid.,* p. 264.

Implanted Monitors

Researchers of the Ed Walters case believe it probable from their observations and Walters's reports that he was abducted as a child, at which time he received certain tiny implants around his head. The abductors could monitor Walters as well as communicate with him through the implants. Walters was monitored for an unspecified purpose by the communications implants and picked up at regular intervals for examination. This implantation and periodic pickup scenario is becoming quite common in UFOlogy.

All of this sounds uncomfortably like our own methods of tagging and tracking animals in the wild. In fact, some investigators are surprised at the high number of reported implants that appear to be occurring. Budd Hopkins claims in *Intruders* that the implanting of small "BB-like" objects in the abductee's inner ear or nose is becoming a disturbingly common complaint. The most common method appears to be the nose implant. Hopkins recounts that some of his abductees "have recalled a thin probe of some sort with a tiny ball on the end having been inserted in the nostril, and they feel pain when the probe apparently breaks through at the top of the nasal cavity."[17] Abductees similarly report such probes being placed into their noses or ears, and seeing no tiny ball until the probe is withdrawn. This, of course, would be at the time of removing the previously implanted device. Regardless of the point of penetration or final lodging, these tiny balls are evidently placed in close proximity to the subject's brain. A handful of children of abduction families in the Copley Woods area (Indianapolis) were discovered by Budd Hopkins to have suffered terrible nosebleeds during the night. One mother remarked to Hopkins that a doctor at the local hospital said her child had probably put a pencil or a similar object up his nose, and punctured the membrane, as evidenced by a small wound there. He then observed how it was peculiar that so many children had been brought into the hospital recently for identical wounds.[18]

Dreams Or Memories?

Ed Walters was only beginning his regressive hypnosis therapy when he published his book, so few details of his boarding the UFOs are reported

---

[17] *Intruders*, p. 44.
[18] *Ibid.*

therein. However, one initial indicator of suppressed memories mentioned in the book is a vivid, frequent dream, which later appeared to be a subconscious memory surfacing. In reciting the details of the dream, Walters reported:

> The dream would begin with me rising high in the sky and looking over a coastline. I could see the sandy beach with waves breaking on the shore. Sometimes I would recognize the beach but most often not. Then I would quickly descend and pass beneath the water into the ocean. I would gasp for air, in fear of drowning, but as I went deeper and deeper, I realized I was inside a container with a large diamond-shaped window.[19] Through the window I could see the water and fish. Shortly thereafter I saw a lot of bubbles passing in front of the window, followed by rising sand, which soon completely covered the glass. That's all I remember of it.[20]

Ed Walters writes that during some of his encounters with the UFOs, as he would attempt to avoid abduction, the voices he heard commanding him to step out into the clear and not resist would taunt him with clues about what was occurring in his life. Upon one failed abduction attempt the UFO voice said, "Zehaas . . . in sleep you know . . . we are here for you." After cursing at the UFO, Walters again heard, "Zehaas . . . sleep and know."[21] Interestingly, the before-cited Roper Organization poll found that a full 10% of the adult American poplation has experienced similar, vivid dreams.

Many abductees remember portions of their ordeals as bad dreams. Kathie Davis still refers to her experiences as her dreams. Mary M., an LDS abductee, thought for many years that she was only experiencing nightmares. It was when she began reading of the accounts of other abductees that she discovered that her nightmares were exactly like those of hundreds of others. She, like many so afflicted, has come to believe that more than "dreaming" is occurring in her life. Of course, for many, the answer could be nightmares—or phenomena not based in reality, or at least not the realms of the normal physical world.[22]

The Bedroom Encounter

In Walters's case, as well as the majority, a number of abductions or other encounters occur while the subject is cozy in his or her own bed. These

---

[19] The photographs of the Gulf Breeze UFOs reveal diamond-shaped portals surrounding the UFOs.

[20] *Ibid.*, p. 161.

[21] *Ibid*, p. 166; see also, p. 241.

[22] See generally, *UFOs in the 1980s,* pp. 1-13.

"bedroom encounters" are classic, and if the subject remembers anything at all, it is generally the very end of the encounter, having a foggy recollection of a small grey exiting the bedroom. Again, the Roper Organization poll reports that 18% of American adults have had this kind of terrifying bedroom experience.

Kathie Davis reports a few bedroom encounters, one of which is more than classic. She remembers it as more of a dream than reality, although completely vivid, as is common. It was still dark, and Kathie found herself sitting up in bed, awake, facing two small greys standing next to her. One held a black box with a glowing red light on top, and moved forward to hand it to Kathie. Again, as he moved, the second one duplicated his movements precisely, although his hands were empty. Kathie was terrified, and the experience seemed too real to be a dream. She says they spoke to her like a child, and called her by name. She narrates:

> He handed me the box. I said, "Can I have it?" He said, "No. Hold it. Look at it."
> I did. Then he took it from me gently after a minute. I said, "What is it? What's it
> for?" He said, "Look at me." Then I thought, "Do I have to?" but I did. He said,
> "When the time is right you will see it again, you will remember and you'll know how
> to use it." I said, "O.K."[23]

Upon waking, Kathie told her husband, who had slept through the visit,[24] what she had "dreamed." No subsequent information ever revealed the meaning of the cryptic statements made by the visitors regarding the box, not yet, anyway.

Underwater Joyrides

Through hypnotic retrieval Ed Walters came to believe that his dream of flying through the air and into the water was a suppressed memory of an abduction and "joyride." It is interesting to me that in my interviews of the investigators of the Gulf Breeze sightings, this dream phenomenon was largely ignored. If the abduction and "joyride" actually did occur, it is significant that Walters describes that the UFO went into the water and beneath the surface of the ocean floor into the sand.[25] One of Walters's previous missing-time

---

[23] *Intruders*, p. 14.

[24] It is common in bedroom encounters for the spouse to sleep through the incident, no matter how much conversation occurs, or how much the victim attempts to wake the spouse.

[25] *The Gulf Breeze Sightings*, p. 161.

episodes occurred while he was in a canoe on the coastline. On that occasion he saw a green glow under the surface of the water and air bubbles just off the bow of his canoe. The next thing he knew, six hours had passed and his sandwich was stale. Significantly, many abductees relate experiences of being taken beneath the water to underground or undersea complexes. Even if the explanation for UFOs lies in a realm other than reality, it is fascinating that this sort of congruency exists between the accounts of so many otherwise unrelated encounters and reports.

Many other observers in the Gulf Breeze, Florida, area reported seeing UFOs flying into the water. In fact, UFOs flying in and out of the water has been a fairly common phenomenon in UFOlogy. If these UFOs can be traced to the ocean floors, and even beneath the sandy bottoms, researchers would do well to expand their search to those areas as possible Earth bases of extraterrestrials, or places of origin for terrestrial UFOs.

9

The Extraterrestrial "Message"

Having discussed at length the scriptural teaching that human life exists in exponential quantities in our universe, it would be easy to assume that the hundreds of thousands of UFOs reported in our earthly skies are humans from any one of millions or billions of planets created by our own Savior.

Or are they from other sources? It is clear that the UFO phenomenon is not a great hoax being perpetrated on society by joy seeking liars—both UFO protagonists and debunkers agree on this. What no one seems capable of deciphering is exactly who is behind UFO appearances, and why they are appearing with such frequency at this time. Answers to these questions may be found in what contactees and abductees report they are being told by the UFO occupants themselves—the UFO "message."

Early Contactees

In the early decades of the UFO "invasion," there were those who came to the fore with tales of extraterrestrial contact, bearing messages of inter-galactic peace and Earthly holocaust if we failed to heed the UFO message. These "contactees" were generally thought to be crackpots. They still are. Their messages were so unbelievable, and their demeanor so incredible, that the public found no reason to heed their message. However, as incredible as it may seem, it could well be that these contactees were accurately reporting their perceived experiences. The most important question is, Who contacts the contactees?

George Adamski

The first of these galactic messengers was a Polish immigrant, George Adamski (1891-1965), who called himself Professor G. Adamski. He listed his address as Mount Palomar, California, where anyone would assume he was associated with the famous Hale Observatory, home of a 200-inch telescope, the largest in the world in 1944. Although it is true that Adamski lived on the southern slopes of Mount Palomar, seven miles from the Hale Observatory, his closest contact with the high tech folk was to sell them coffee from his roadside stand.

Adamski wrote science fiction space books, which undertaking was insufficient to pay his bills—hence, the coffee stand. In *Flying Saucers Have Landed* (1953), Adamski claimed to have seen his first UFO in October, 1946. He claimed he saw 184 UFOs in a single night in August of 1947, coming and going at will, streaking busily through the California night skies. Adamski wrote of flying saucer rides to the planets in our solar system, including the dark side of the moon with its rolling green hills and small villages hidden from our view. He further claimed to have encountered many Venusians who looked like humans. Interestingly, in the early 1950s it was still widely believed that the other planets of our solar system were capable of sustaining life and were the source of extraterrestrial visitation. Later, following scientific scrutiny of the surfaces and atmospheres of these nearest planets, contactees began to report that the aliens were from the nearest solar systems instead.

Adamski's Venusian friends claimed to be quite concerned about radiation leaking from Earth's atmosphere. The alien elder philosopher, The Master, discussed many galactic concerns with Adamski, the major consideration being Earth's perilous threat of destroying itself and nearby planets by its tinkering with nuclear power. The Venusians further explained that they lived among humans, and monitored us thoroughly. Aliens from most of the planets in our solar system had representatives on Earth, and because they look like us and live among us, he encountered them frequently in cafes and bars throughout greater Los Angeles.

The Aliens explained that Jesus Christ had been their spokesman at one time—now Adamski was selected to bear the Universal message of our "space brothers." This Galactic Messiah sold many books and worked the lecture circuit heavily, giving birth to an American industry. A flurry of contactees began lecturing and writing on their similar experiences of joy riding through our solar system and receiving special messages and missions from the space brethren.[1]

---

[1] *Phenomenon: Forty Years of Flying Saucers,* Avon Books (1988) pp. 121-124.

Orfeo Angelucci

Another contactee, Orfeo Angelucci, published his *Secret of the Saucers* in 1955. The message was wholly spiritual by now, containing prophecies complete with deadlines. His space brother mentor, or contact, gave him interplanetary revelation. Angelucci rode in a flying saucer, met Neptune, and received a mystical revelation, filling him with mystical knowledge. He met with Jesus once, who explained that the extraterrestrials are here to help us, announcing, that "this is the beginning of the New Age." (Remember, this was over thirty years ago.) Aliens explained to him that in a former life, he had been one of the space brethren from another planet. He prophesied of a major world catastrophe by 1986.[2]

Other Contactees

Another 1950's contactee, Howard Menger, saw his first alien, a beautiful blonde woman, in 1932, and was repeatedly contacted throughout his life. It was easy to spot the men he explained—they had long blonde hair too. He always described an overwhelming aura of love and harmony when in the presence of the aliens. These space brothers told him that many early Earth civilizations had been contacted by them and had received superior knowledge and technology from them, most of which was lost in ancient wars.[3]

In 1954, George King, a London taxi driver with a background in the occult, heard a voice while washing dishes. The voice told him, "Prepare yourself, you are to become the voice of Interplanetary Parliament." King founded the Aetherius Society, and slipped into public trances during which he acted as a medium for interplanetary communications. King revealed how he had traveled to many planets, fought a megabattle in space, and conversed with many beings on different planets—including Master Jesus, who lives on Venus.[4]

Many UFO gurus came forward in the 1970s and 1980s, most of them eventually moving to southern California with their cultish groupies. Their overt messages were generally that love and brotherhood must replace

---

[2] *Ibid.*, p. 126

[3] *Ibid.*, pp. 126-28.

[4] *The UFO Phenomenon*, pp. 78-79.

materialism, war, and nuclear power. They preached of a coming age when man would be elevated to a higher spiritual plane and enlightenment.

It would be easy to dismiss these pre-New Age contactees as mere charlatans who fabricated science fiction tales to gain a following. However, certain facts jump out of their stories that compel us to at least notice particular consistencies with both New Age doctrine and more credible UFO contact accounts. In particular, Howard Menger of the early 1950s, before the UFO literature was well-developed, spoke of his beautiful superrace of blonde men and women, describing an overwhelming feeling of love and harmony while in their presence. This is a phenomenon related by many others, including our own very credible LDS Church member, Udo Wartena. Interestingly, Howard Menger was probably the "tamest" of the early contactees, speaking little of New Age teachings of the space brothers. The remaining contactees were filled with messages closely akin to New Age doctrine. Although such beliefs were held, or at least professed by some in the "fringe" of the time, it is fascinating that most of the contactees recounted their tales in nearly mystic terms. Assuming that most of these contactees were not really in communication with extraterrestrials (a safe assumption in my opinion), we are almost compelled to accept that some of them were in contact with intelligences that fed them false, unreliable or weird information, for reasons not fully apparent at this point in our discussion. It is a safe assumption, I believe, that their contacts were the same as are had by New Age channelers.

Public Rejection Of Early Contactees

The public backlash was severe against the early contactees, generating general disdain for any person claiming to have seen an alien—or anyone claiming more than one UFO encounter of any kind. Although the public could accept that UFO sightings were truly occurring, the claim that UFOs contain alien pilots was insurmountable. Although a few self-proclaimed contactee/messengers are still to be found, preaching that they are the chosen vessels of intergalactic bulletins, most current contact with extraterrestrial entities is accomplished through New Age channelers—most of whom have at least one alien in their repertoire. The following messages from extraterrestrials to New Age channelers are representative of those published by the hundreds in New Age literature:

- I *am* one of these Advanced Spiritual Beings. I have come from a very high spiritual world called Aries; I am not an Earth Person. I am now living as an Earth Person in a physical body. I came to help the Earth people. [Uriel, through Ruth E. Norman of the Unarius Foundation]
- Will you agree to be the savior of the world? [Ashtar, to American contactee Allen-Michael Noonan]
- I, Raymere, transmit once more upon this occasion in order to speak with you about the things of the next period of time . . . you will find that you are moving into a higher frequency wherein there is a totally new dimension. [Raymere, a space being, through Alenti Francesca at the Solar Light Retreat]
- Earth's vortex is about to break because of an excess amount of hatred . . . . [The space brothers of Io, a moon of Jupiter, to "Gordon," a U.S. contactee, 1967][5]

Contactees—The Next Generation

Although the first wave of galactic gurus has come and gone, leaving in their wake a feeling that rainmakers have beat the drums, fired the cannons, and sold a little snake oil, a new breed of messengers has appeared on the horizon. They are the abductees discussed herein who have not chosen to be contacted, who do not appear to seek their contactee status, but who have been given a message for the world just the same.

Betty Andreasson Luca—An Example Of Repeated Encounters

According to Raymond Fowler, longtime UFO investigator and author, the actual events that make up a UFO abduction constitute the components of a composite UFO message. As we examine such events in greater detail, this theory becomes quite feasible. In his book, *The Watchers,* subtitled, "The Secret Design Behind UFO Abductions," Fowler documents the case of Betty Andreasson Luca,[6] who for decades was reportedly abducted by UFOs. Her case includes many of the experiences reported by others as discussed in this section, with the added dimension of being given a time-capsulized, piecemeal message to deliver to mankind. The message given to Betty Luca

---

[5] *Phenomenon: Forty Years of Flying Saucers,* pp. 365-66.

[6] Fowler has written three books chronicling this case. The first was phase one, *The Andreasson Affair,* and the second, *The Andreasson Affair: Phase Two.* Subsequent to each of the first two books the subject, Betty Andreasson (Luca), experienced surges of memory recall as "time-capsule" messages were unlocked in her programmed memory, and as she was further abducted. Fowler assumes he has written the last book on this case, believing that all has finally been revealed. I doubt it.

is being simultaneously implanted and released in the minds of others around the world. We examine Betty's experiences more closely in this chapter, however, because of the progress investigators have made on her case and the publicity given to it. The message, as gleaned from Betty's excavated subconscious, parallels the same message retrieved from the memories of others. It fits certain patterns that warrant our attention and provides important information in our search for the source of UFOs and their message.

Betty Luca is described as a woman having "a deep and exceptional beautiful Christian faith." I emphasize the "Christian" element for the dual purpose of eliminating the probability of a New Age conspiracy in which Betty may be consciously or unconsciously involved to preach a Satanic doctrine, and to alert the reader that Betty's experiences were interpreted by her as "religious" in nature—at least initially. An added dimension to the Christian aspect of Betty's experiences is that she often sought divine protection at the beginning of many of her experiences, to no avail.

Betty's first encounter with the small greys was at the age of seven, in 1944. She recounts, under hypnosis, in the persona of a seven-year-old girl what happened to her on that occasion.

> I'm sitting there eating some crackers looking at the blue flowers outside the hut, and I'm waitin' for Didi to come over and play. And then all of a sudden I see a bumblebee or something, but it's bright light and it keeps on circling my head. Maybe it's after my crackers. But it keeps on going round my head and then it stuck there . . . . It was cold and it was making me fall backwards and I felt very sleepy. I'm lying on the ground there and I hear something. There is a squiggly feeling in my head, and there is a voice speaking to me. There is a lot of them, but all talking together. And they are saying something. They have been watching me, and uh, I'm coming along fine. And they're talking to me and telling me that I'm making good progress . . . and they were getting things ready. But it won't be for awhile . . . about five years or so. I would be twelve. They would see me later.[7]
>
> [Another session covering this same experience offers a little more detail:] It's coming to a time that I will know the *One* . . . . They're going to show me something . . . that everybody will be happy about . . . that everybody will learn something from . . . . They just want to look me over *from the inside.* They tell me I'm going to be very happy soon . . . that I'm going to find the *One.* I will feel the *One.*

The phenomenon of many voices speaking in unison is quite common in telepathic UFO communication. Betty learns from the chorus that they have observed her, that they are making preparations for some great event, and that she would be ready for the event in about five years, at the age of twelve. An important component of the event is to go somewhere to *know, find,* and

---

7 *The Watchers,* pp. 7-8.

feel the *One*. Another component is to see something that will make *everyone* happy, an event instructive to everyone. The parallels to New Age beliefs as discussed elsewhere herein are obvious if these promises are taken at face value. As we shall see, the realization of these experiences is everything promised, and more.

Betty experienced a second encounter, as promised, when she was twelve, in 1949. She recounts that while playing in woods, she encountered a small grey in a high-tech-looking uniform. Having no conscious recollection of her previous encounter, and not knowing what the ugly little fellow was, she did the appropriate thing: "I took some of those stones out of my pocket. I thought it was an animal coming out. I started to throw stones at it, and, ah!—The stones hit something and *stopped in midair* and just fell down!" Betty heard the same voices say that she would not be ready for another year.[8] "They said I will learn about the *One*. They said they are preparing things for me to see."[9]

On this occasion Betty appears to have been one year premature when being checked by the beings. Premature for what? By the time of Betty's next encounter a year later, Betty had become a young woman, achieving sexual maturity. Apparently, this had something to do with an event for which things were being prepared. She would now be ready to meet the *One*.

At the age of thirteen, now 1950, following an impulse, Betty got up early one morning while her family slept and went to explore near the pond. She saw a "huge moon" coming over the hill toward her. It became "bigger and bigger" as it came toward her—she tried to run, but was paralyzed. She next found herself inside a white room feeling "very relaxed," watching as two small greys floated toward her a few inches off the floor. They said, "We're going to take you *home*." Betty responded, "I am home!" And they said, "Don't fear, don't be afraid, you're alright."

Betty was placed onto a soft "cushion-like mat on the floor of a section of the craft that was roofed by a large transparent dome. A mouthpiece was installed that kept her tongue held down." The craft accelerated at high velocity and after a time entered water and descended to an underground complex. In the complex Betty went through a museum of time with glass cases containing human replicas in the garb and natural habitat of various historical

---

8 *The Watchers*, pp. 8-9.
9 *Ibid.*, p. 331.

periods of the Earth. She next underwent a physical examination. She was then told, "You're getting closer to *home*," and was taken to a clam-shell-looking device with mirrors inside, which she was instructed to get into. It closed, and opened a moment later. She found herself in a different place made of a glass-like substance. She was shown glass-like replicas of animals and plants that were quite unusual:

> And I'm reaching out to touch a butterfly and when I did, it's fantastic! It's beautiful! There's all color coming into the butterfly now, and it's flying around and around. When I touched it, it got color and lived and it's flying . . . . Oh, it's stopped. Its color is going and it's fading into a tiny speck of light, like a tiny speck of light. Then it goes back into the ice-form of that butterfly. That was amazing! I asked him—"What's happening?" He says, "This is for you to remember so mankind will understand." And I said, "But why did it turn color and fly away when I touched it?" He told me that I will see when I get *home*. He said, "*Home* is where the *One* is." [10]

Again, Betty asked how they could do these things, and relates the response: "He told me that I will see when I get *home*. It is for me, they said, for me to go *home* to see the *One*. He said, '*Home* is where the *One* is.' He says, 'We are drawing closer to *home* where the *One* is.'" [11]

All these references to the *One* and going *home* were obvious attempts to make Betty understand that she had a close kinship to whatever awaited her—a close kinship to the place and the *One*. After being "transported" to this place called *home*, Betty was taken to a Great Door:

> We're coming up to this wall of glass and a big, big, big, big, big, door. It's made of glass. [Q. Does it have hinges?] No. It is so big and there is—I can't explain it. It is door after door after door after door. He is stopping there and telling me to stop. I'm just stopping there. He says: "Now you shall enter the door to see the *One*." And I'm standing there and I'm coming out of myself! There's two of me! There's two of me there! . . . It's like a twin. But it's still, like those people I saw in those, those ice cubes [glass cases in the museum]. [12]

This phenomenon being experienced by Betty is known as an out-of-body experience ("OBE"). It is the ultimate spiritual experience in the occult/New Age movement. What is interesting is that Betty evidently has done nothing of her own choosing to initiate her OBE. It is at this point that Betty Luca's experiences with UFOs and their occupants become uncommon—quite uncommon.

Upon entering the Great Door during this OBE Betty recounted under hypnosis what she was *able* to tell. Raymond Fowler reports that during this

---

10 *The Watchers,* p. 333.

11 *The Watchers,* p. 146

12 *The Watchers,* p. 11

portion of the hypnotic session that "a rapturous, beautific expression of pure, unrestricted happiness came over her face as she apparently met . . . the *One*." Betty would not or could not describe what happened next. She attempts:

> It's—words cannot explain it. It's wonderful. It's for everybody. I just can't tell you this. [Q. You can't? Okay, why can't you?] For one thing, it's too overwhelming and it is . . . it is undescribable. I just can't tell you. Besides it's just impossible for me to tell you. [Q. Were you told not to share it with me?] It is like even if I was able to speak it, I wouldn't be able to speak it. I can't. I'm sorry . . . .
>
> And I'm standing there and I'm coming out of myself! There's two of me there . . . and the little person is saying: "Now you shall enter the Great Door and see the glory of the *One*. I went in the door and it's very bright. I can't take you any further. [Q. Why?] Because . . . I can't take you past this door. [Q. Why are you so happy?] It's just, uh, I just can't tell you about it . . . . It's—Words cannot explain it. It's wonderful. It's for *everybody*. I just can't explain this. I understand that *everything is one*. Everything fits together. It's beautiful![13]

Whatever Betty was experiencing, it was beyond her ability to describe to investigators. The experience is very much like the mystical experiences professed by gurus and other spiritualists. It also is very much like near-death experiences ("NDE") that we read about in ever-increasing volumes. Such NDE accounts should be viewed with a discerning eye, because not every being of light is sent from God.

The "glory" of the *One* will one day be experienced by all, Betty perceives. Her encounter reminds us of the "sacred embrace" of ancient Egypt,[14] better defined for our benefit as the encounter with the gatekeeper, the Holy One of Israel.[15] She gains the ultimate spiritual insight that "everything is one," and that "everything fits together." Although this in itself is an eternal truth, it is also very much a part of the over emphasised "all is one and one is all" tenet of the New Age/occult religion.

The hypnotist made several subsequent attempts to get Betty behind the door, but she could not get past it. The "brightness" experienced during the hypnotic attempts gave her eye and head aches for several days following such undertakings. In a phase one session, Betty had mentioned the Great Door, but the investigators failed to follow up on it. When asked, "What is the *Great Door*," she responded, "It is the entrance into the *other world*. The world where light is." When asked, "Is it available to us as well as to

---

13 *The Watchers*, p. 144.

14 Hugh Nibley, *The Message of the Joseph Smith Papyri, An Egyptian Endowment*, pp. 241-53.

15 2 Nephi 9:41-42.4

you," Betty responded, "No, not yet."[16] Although these very unique and intriguing experiences had occurred before the investigation had begun more than fifteen years earlier, the investigators were unable to get to these "message" portions of the experiences until "the time was right." The messages were implanted in Betty, and others evidently, within timesensitive memory barriers. Even when the time for release of the messages arrived, investigators still encountered difficulties getting to them. They had to invent the curtains, television screens, and other mental protective devices discussed later in this chapter to get into the blocked memories.

After leaving the *One* Betty returned through a tunnel and went back through the Great Door.

> Okay, I'm outside the door and there's a tall person [human] there. He's got white hair and he's got a white nightgown on and he's motioning me to come there with him. His nightgown is, is *glowing* and his hair is white and he's got bluish eyes. And it's bright out here, and I think I see two more of them over there. [Q. Do they look like people?] Um, but tall. They are real tall and they got some ferns or something in their hands. [Q. Do you speak to them?] He's beckoning me to come over there and there's like a *shell*, an open *shell*. But it's mirrors and mirrors and mirrors.[17]

Betty was introduced through the Great Door by small greys, but received upon exiting the Door by what she considered to be angelic humans following her encounter with the *One*. In Betty's accounts, as well as those of hundreds of others, these angelic humans are often seen in close proximity to small greys, and appear to direct the small greys. Raymond Fowler suggests that Betty was welcomed back through the Great Door after having been with the *One* by these higher level beings as a sign of honor to the chosen one. Although a chosen one, it did not take long for Betty to be treated like a laboratory specimen again.

Betty was transported through the clamshell device as before, and received at the other end by the small greys. At that point Betty was taken to another examination room where she was floated up on a square table. To her horror Betty sobs in pain as she recounts how the beings removed one of her eyes and implanted a small round object behind it, and placed a long needle up her nose and implanted a BB-like object with tiny spines protruding from it up her nasal cavity in the classic membrane penetrating fashion. Although the nose implant is common in abduction literature, the object behind the eye is not. Betty describes a sophisticated procedure as the round unit is

---

16 *The Watchers,* p. 145.

17 *The Watchers,* p. 150.

implanted and tested. The implication is that all of Betty's sensory organs were wired for continuous monitoring by the beings. So much for angels communicating through the medium of the Holy Ghost.

In 1961 Betty had a "religious" encounter with the beings. She was a 24-year old mother at the time. While mopping and singing hymns, she heard a strange noise. Despite having children napping alone in the house, she walked outside and into the woods without volition. She struggled up a nearby hill, slipping on pine needles and climbing over rocks. The new message she received during this encounter warrants our attention.

> There's a strange being standing over there and I'm afraid of it. It's staring at me, and I can't move! Oh, Jesus be with me! He's telling me [telepathically] that I have been *watched* since my beginning. I shall grow naturally, and my faith in the Light will bring many others to the Light and Salvation because many will understand and see . . . .

> He has been sent and I am not to fear. The Lord is with me and not to be afraid. They are pleased because I have accepted [Christianity] on my own. I am to go through many things and that love will show me the answers because I have given my heart over to love the Son. Many things shall be revealed to me. Things that I [eyes?] have not seen . . . ears have not heard . . . . I shall suffer many things . . . but will overcome them through the Son. I have been watched since my beginning. I shall grow naturally and my faith in the Light will bring many others to the Light and Salvation because many will understand and see. The *negative voices* don't like it. [They] are against man . . . bad angels that wanted to devour man . . . hurt man . . . destroy man . . . because they are jealous . . . of the love that is upon man. Telling me strange things . . . I don't know what they're about . . . That for every place there is an existence. That every thing has been formed to unite. [He says] Jesus is with me . . . that I will understand as time goes by . . . for me not to be anxious. They want me to grow and live naturally . . . that I am blessed and that I will forget and I am now to go back to my house and I will not remember. He says, "Peace be with you as it is."[18]

It is interesting that as Betty perceives the danger of her encounter, even though she is mentally tranquillized by the small greys, her first thought, or prayer is, "Oh, Jesus be with me!" At this point, the message becomes highly religious in nature, almost like a visitation from a heavenly being. The message is compound: the beings have "watched" Betty from infancy;

---

18 *The Watchers,* pp. 334-35.

they are pleased she has accepted Christianity; her faith in the Light will bring many others to the Light and Salvation; there exist evil alien forces, "bad angels" who are jealous of mankind and seek our destruction; and, although Betty will undergo severe hardship, her faith in Jesus will pull her through.

According to the account, in January, 1967, Betty was again abducted by the beings, and taken to a distant planet. As she travelled between her two abductors along a high trestle, she entered a beautiful crystalline structure to witness a Phoenix legend enactment. There is much light and heat, and Betty cries out for help and writhes in agony. Soon the temperature drops and Betty is able to squint her eyes open. The bird is gone, and a small remaining fire dwindles into embers and ashes, from which emerges a "big fat worm." After this Betty heard a "thundering chorus of voices blended together as one mighty voice" calling her by name and asking, "You have seen and you have heard. Do you understand?" To which Betty responded, "No, I don't understand what this is all about, why I'm even here." The voice instructed, "I have chosen you." Betty again asked, "For what have you chosen me?" The voice answered, "I have chosen you to show the world."[19] Betty felt that the voice was that of God Himself. Although she did not see him, she was sure it was He. Betty professed her belief in Jesus Christ at this time, to which the voice responded that her fervent belief was the reason she had been so chosen.

Betty's encounter with this being is described as being "a profound religious experience." Raymond Fowler comments, "I have seen men with no strong religious background come to the point of tears when listening to a playback of the tape recording of this particular aspect of *The Andreasson Affair*."

As Betty was returned to her rural home where her family was tranquilized and unaware of her disappearance, Quazgaa, her escort, gave her parting paternal counsel:

> And he says, "Child, you must forget for awhile." He says my race won't believe me until much time has passed, our time . . . . They say they love the human race. And unless man will not accept, he will not be saved. He will not live. All things have been planned. Love is the greatest of all. They do not want to hurt anybody. But, because of great love . . . they cannot let man continue in the footsteps that he is going. *It is better to lose some than all.* They have technology man can use. It is through the spirit but men will not search out that portion. *Man is not made of just flesh and blood.* He keeps telling me of different things. *Of what is going to take place, what is going*

---

[19] *The Watchers*, p. 339.

to happen. They are going to come to the earth. Man is going to fear because of it.
He says that he had had others here and many others have locked within their minds,
secrets. And he is locking within my mind certain secrets. And they will be revealed
only when the time is right.[20]

During her hypnotic session to elicit this information Betty "spoke for
a time in an unintelligible tongue, interspersed with phrases like 'Signal Base
32,' and 'Star Seeso.' "[21] Whitley Strieber cites the work of a Mr. Keane,
an expert in the Gaelic language who has produced phoenetic renderings
of words of the unknown language spoken by Betty. He claims that the words
spoken by Betty corresponded nearly exactly with Gaelic equivalants. He
renders the following translation of Betty's "alien" language: "The living
descendants of the northern peoples are groping in universal darkness. Their
mother mourns. A dark occasion forbodes when weakness in high places
will revive a high cost of living; an interval of mistakes in high places; an
interval fit for distressing events.[22] The name of Betty's "Quazgaa" translates, curiously, as "One of the cross."

Betty was assured that the beings do not want to hurt anybody, but, out
of their sense of great love for humanity, they cannot let man continue in
his present course. Man is a *spiritual* being, not just flesh and blood. When
they come, man will fear it, but will benefit from their technology as it applies
to his spiritual side. How will man be diverted from his present course to
one of spiritual technology? Quazgaa explains cryptically, "It is better to
lose some than all." Somehow, the number two billion comes to mind. As
discussed in a later chapter, New Agers lament that around the year 2,000,
approximately two billion humans of lower vibrational rates will be eliminated.
After Laura, Kathie Davis's abducted sister, had overcome her difficulties
with hypnosis triggered by her UFO encounter, "she was left with one strong
thought: that by the year 2000 the world would be totally different than we
know it, but it would be only for the young and strong."[23]

Although it may seem that Betty's message has been probed, delivered,
and analyzed at this point, other lessons are to be taught to mankind. Her
next encounter is in 1973 at the age of 36. Her abductors are somewhat smaller
than the last, and are clad in silver suits instead of blue with Phoenix emblems.
Betty is kidnapped from her bedroom, unable to wake her sleeping husband,

---

[20] *The Watchers,* pp. 339-40.

[21] Paranormal Borderlands of Science, p. 183.

[22] Whitley Strieber, *Transformation: The Breakthrough,* pp. 46-47.

[23] Budd Hopkins, *Intruders,* p. 12.

screaming: "Go away! Go away! Lord Jesus! Lord Jesus! Make it go away. Whatever it is, Lord Jesus." It does not go away. At the moment Betty's blanket is pulled off of her, she becomes sedate. She feels a "pinching" sensation as the beings touch her arm.[24] She is floated through the house between two aliens, and into a light below the UFO. Suddenly, they are in the UFO.

Betty found the aliens doing something to an East Indian woman, and she attemped to calm her. To Betty's horror, the beings removed two hybrid fetuses from the woman, and placed them in a liquid-filled incubator.

After moving beyond the trauma of the recalled event, Betty was asked to describe what occurred shortly thereafter.

> They're standing in—front—of a glass case. And there's another baby there. A fetus. It's very tiny. And its just laying there inside this liquid. And—But its eyes, they've circumcised the lids. They circumcise the eyelids of those babies and their eyes look so strange. [Betty describes the interior of the "nursery"] They're telling me they have to do this. And I'm saying "Why do you have to do such a terrible thing?" And one of them is saying "We have to because as time goes by, mankind will become *sterile*. They will not be able to produce."[25]

According to the beings, this is the entire purpose behind their accelerated visitation and abduction program. Mankind will soon become sterile and unable to multiply. They, therefore, have the duty of preserving the genetic code of the race on their UFOs until after the holocaust that renders mankind sterile. This explanation is flawed, however, as demonstrated in Betty's description of what follows:

> And they're really pleased with, with this little thing because its eyes are big and black when they cut the lids—like theirs. And they said that the *splicing* took good on this one. And they're telling me that mankind gets so upset when they take the *seed*. And, really, the very first part that man and woman, when they came together, was to *bring forth*—was not for their pleasure, but to bring forth. And mankind keeps on spilling the seed of life over and over again. And they cannot understand why man gets so upset when they take the seed.[26]
>
> And they're telling me that they're doing this because the human race will become sterile by the pollution and the bacteria and the terrible things that are on the earth. They're telling me that they have extrapolated and put their protoplasma in the nucleus

---

24 It is noteworthy that many abductees report that when touched on the arm by the small greys they feel a pinching sensation. This subject arises in my mind with regard to whether or not these small greys are physical beings, or mere projected apparitions given minor, counterfeited physical qualities. The latter seems improbable because of other reports of being touched by the small greys, *e.g.*, rubbing the temples of examinees, etc. However, it is possible that even these manifestations of a physical makeup can be counterfeited, as discussed in Part III. The pinching could result from the purported fact that the little fellows only have three digits on a hand, and pinch their victims inadvertently.

25 *The Watchers,* pp. 24-25.

26 *The Watchers,* p. 28.

of the fetus and the paragenetic. [Betty stops and sounds completely frustrated.] I don't understand them. Something like the paragenetic will utilize the tissue and nutrients to—I don't know—transform the creature or something like that. I don't understand what they're saying. They're saying also about man, that he gets so upset and, and in the beginning that it was meant for bringing forth children, not for pleasure. And, they are taking the seeds so that the human *form* will not be lost—That they too are made of the *same* substance and, that some of the female fetuses don't accept the plasma very well and that they have to—I don't understand what they're saying—something about—I can't understand and I'm just trying to repeat what they're saying . . . . [Ibid.]

If they are "taking the seeds so that the human *form* will not be lost," why are they concentrating on creating a hybrid line from their own genetic stock mixed with ours? Many cases demonstrate that either small greys or hybrids are being produced from these genetic experiments—not human babies, although there is some evidence that some human children are being bred to work with the small greys.

Betty next comments that they are now working on the second fetus taken from the woman, and the hypnotist asks, "Do the beings have blood?

No. They said they utilized the blood and tissue and nutrients that are there and the *form* and the fetus for the growth of the *new creature*. And some females [alien females] just don't accept the protoplasma all together. So, they grow and use them to carry them, to carry other fetuses but they are very weak and cannot be artificially inseminated like humans. [Q. "What happens to the fetus? Do, do they keep it there, or?] The fetuses *become them*—like them. They said they're *Watchers* . . . and they keep seed from man and woman so the human *form* will not be lost.[27]

This last statement is as significant as any in constructing the extraterrestrial message: "The fetuses *become them*—like them." Although obviously significant, we can only guess at the purported meaning of this pronouncement. In its simplest interpretation, the statement indicates that female aliens have come to have difficulty reproducing, and the alien race is propagated by using human women as surrogate mothers—living incubators. But why the hybrid children instead of pure alien? Their response is that "they keep seed from man and woman so the human *form* will not be lost." Because this explanation does not fully answer the question, perhaps a more complex interpretation is in order.

A complex, yet literal interpretation of the statement is: "the highly spiritual nature of the creatures allows the transmigration of the creatures' spirits from the older, weaker bodies to the younger, genetically improved bodies." With this explanation we literally say that "the fetuses become them." Such an explanation could also account for the longevity touted by the creatures. This

---

[27] *The Watchers*, pp. 48-49.

latter explanation is quite disturbing—almost as disconcerting as the underlying, simple explanation to the entire phenomenon—they conduct their operation *to obtain bodies;* something that they cannot do without our help. This explanation is frighteningly reminiscent of "bad angels." Of course, Betty's rapid addendum "like them" could soften the impact of the assertion, but even this does not answer the question, Why hybrids instead of pure humans or pure aliens?

As Betty was readied for high velocity travel, she was placed into a simple "standup kind of seat." The aliens apologized for the inconvenience, explaining that this type of craft was not designed for human transport, and this particular type of "seat" was all they had available for her. Just before takeoff, the other being left, leaving Betty alone with one small grey. The remaining being communicated telepathically with Betty: "He's very grateful to me. [Q. Why? For what?] For being there. That I helped the lady calm down, he says. It was very beneficial for the fetus." Betty took advantage of this moment to ask some questions. We gain another piece of the message puzzle from the answers.

> Who are they? I asked. I was trying to ask him. He says that they are the *caretakers* of nature and natural forms—*The Watchers*. They love mankind. They love the planet earth and *they have been caring for it and man since man's beginning.* They watch the *spirit* in all things. Man is destroying much of nature. They are curious about the emotions of mankind. [Q. Do they have emotions?] Not like man. [Q. But, didn't he say they *love* the earth?] It is not the same emotion. It is a forever love—constant, continual. And they are the *caretakers* and are responsible. And this is why they have been taking the *form* of man. [Q. How, how long have they been taking the *form* of man?] For hundreds and hundreds of years . . . He's saying that they have *collected the seed of man* male and female. And they have been collecting *every species* and *every gender* of plant for hundreds of years.[28]

They are the Watchers, the Caretakers—they have been caring for the Earth and man since man's beginning. This is such an extraordinary assertion that it warrants some discussion. For instance, of which beginning do they refer? If they allude to an evolutionary beginning in our remote past, they have hung around for a long while. If they refer to the transplanting of Adam and Eve from another world, the period would be 6,000 years.[29] If this is their claim, it would be difficult to accept it as true without inferring that they somehow

---

[28] *The Watchers*, p. 119.

fit into the gospel plan of redemption in ways heretofore unexplained by the prophets.[30] This is true, of course, unless they are actually the Satanic spirits that were cast to the Earth in the Great War in Heaven—then the prophets would have adequately explained their role. The beings' additional assertion that they watch the *spirit* in all things only raises the ante of the prior supposition. Such could only come by way of assignment, or the Lord would certainly interfere. After all, it is they who claim that they are the caretakers and are *responsible.* If this is true, who made them responsible?

In a letter to Raymond Fowler dated July 12, 1988, Betty communicated the following information that she had obtained concerning telepathic communications between her and a being that had abducted her from her trailer.

> Although I did not see him during the sessions, I know now that another *being* was left behind in the trailer as a guard against any kind of intrusion when I was taken up.
>
> I was told, through power, they can form illusions right down to movement, heartbeat, and breathing of a person for the sake of cover. If any outsider was to approach the trailer and look in, they would have believed the moving form on the sofa was actually me. The guard would activate the power to change the thought in the intruder's mind, to turn away. An intruder would have thought it was his natural decision and will, as not to disturb me . . . .
>
> What was revealed to me again is their power can control things for miles around to a small local spot. Something can be happening right amongst the busiest activities of a host of people and yet never be seen by some except those the *beings* choose to reveal it to. The *beings'* scanners and minds pick up any and all life forms within the immediate area of a target. They said they're keepers of form. They've been entrusted with and are responsible for the care of all natural form since the beginning. They know physically all there is to know about plant, animal, and human life form with the exception of human emotions which often activates the free will to do as it pleases. Emotions make man unpredictable. That's why it is not the immediate vicinity in their

---

29 If this is their claim, we might be tempted to add to the 6,000 years of the Earth's temporal existence the time that Adam spent in the Garden of Eden, however long it may have been. However, there exist indications that the Earth was not brought to this location in space, and set in its orbit around our sun until after the fall of Adam. This assertion is supported by Abraham's comment that while Adam and Eve were in the Garden of Eden "that it was after the Lord's time, which was after the time of Kolob; for as yet the Gods had not appointed unto Adam his reckoning." (Abraham 5:13) It is quite doubtful that the Watchers would have brooded over the Earth while it was still in its place of creation, probably nearer to Kolob.

30 In making this statement I assume that the prophets would indeed know if such were the case. "Surely the Lord God will do nothing, but he revealeth his secret to his servants the prophets." (Amos 3:7)

control that concerns them, but unexpected intrusion of someone entering the vicinity. Even though they can quickly gain control of the situation, they may be too busy to detect an invasion.

These contentions of ability to control the minds and actions of many people for a radius of several miles are extraordinary. It is interesting that Udo Wartena's visitors were unable to detect his presence, and were caught off guard as he ascended from his 30 foot mine shaft. Evidently, they could not detect lifesigns through that much earth. Furthermore, if these assertions have any validity, this "intruder" difficulty could well explain how Ed Walters was able to escape abduction on the first attempt. Even he wondered if the airplane coming into the UFO's airspace didn't have a part in his narrow escape. Of course, the above statement brings to our attention another "inconsistency" or "inexplicable fact" of the Ed Walters case—other abductees (almost universally) are of the opinion that if the UFOs want to get you, there is nothing you can do to prevent abduction. Ed Walters on the other hand, evidently successfully dodged and avoided UFOs many times. Again, this may only have been a devised pretense of his abductors, as evidenced by the probability that Ed Walters was apparently abducted on two or three occasions of which he was unaware initially. Either way, it is all another example of a great cat-and-mouse game obviously being played by whoever is behind the UFO phenomenon.

Reports of "aliens" coming through the walls of the house to abduct people have become common. Betty Luca asked the beings how they did it and they replied, "By controlled vibrational levels. It is very simple, those structures are very loose." If true, then this vibrational manipulation of matter could explain how these feats are accomplished. The entire subject of "vibrational levels" is so closely connected with the New Age movement, occult spiritism, and the predicted annihilation of 2 billion humans, that we should pay special attention to these assertions. Further evidence of our need to be wary is advanced in Betty's next observation.

> I asked, "What did you mean 'too many eyes and ears watching and listening'?" He answered that—"The physical presence of eyes and ears is no concern for we control this easily. But, waves and manifestations of present energy cannot be erased. What is, is always there like grooves in the record of time. If the right tool or point is rubbed against hairlike warps and weaves, the recorded energy is artificially materialized. That is why we have to scramble the energy. When you are taken up, an excessive amount of energy will be scattered about us, masking the identity. This mask will blend and fill in any and all gaps and weaves during transition. Stay very still during the extensity of yourself," he said.[31]

---

31 *The Watchers,* pp. 181-83.

Not only do we gain insight into the nature of time (assuming that any truth exists in this statement), but we learn that what the beings are doing is being concealed from those who would look at the record inscribed in the fabric of time. This self-admitted deceit renders the acts of the "aliens" highly suspect. If, as claimed, "They've been entrusted with and are responsible for the care of all natural form since the beginning" (not that this passive contention informs us *who* has entrusted them), why is it necessary to conceal their benevolent acts from those who may check the record of time?

Speaking of the beings' prior statements about the continuum of time Fowler comments, "They insisted that our concept of time was *localized* and that time as we understood it did not really exist. The human concept of time was illusory. All is *Now*." Betty further related that: "The future and the past are the same as today to them—Time to them is not like our time, but they know about our time—They can reverse time—'Time with us is not your time. The place with you is localized. It is not with us. Cannot you see it?' "[32]

Admittedly, the beings' professed concept of time may only be true from a technological point of view (allowing for time travel), or, if they are actually fallen (or other) spirits, these principles may still hold true. It is evident that the beings exist in our temporal plane as well as in the "other self" plane simultaneously, as demonstrated during abductees' OBEs. The beings participate in the scene and interact with the OBE abductee, before, during, and after the OBE. This fact gives us much to think about in our analysis of the origin and nature of the beings.

True Experience But False Messages?

Betty Andreasson Luca's experiences are not unlike those of numerous others. Is she lying? I believe she is relating her experiences as she has perceived them. Is she hallucinating then? If she is, they are the same hallucinations being experienced by thousands, possibly millions of others— even members of the LDS Church.

I believe Betty. But does this indicate that I believe the message? No. I reject the message. Like the message as delivered to so many abductees and contactees, Betty's message is nonsensical, internally inconsistent, and at odds with similar messages delivered to the others—and, above all, it is at

---

32 *The Watchers*, p. 209.

odds with revealed truth. Consider the illogical and self-contradicting statements made to Ed Walters by his abductors. Why do UFOs seek privacy, yet adorn their hulls with bright lights? Why are no two contactees delivering exactly the same message? Why is someone going to all of this trouble to deliver an unbelievable message? Many commentators have offered their opinions. The prospects are unsettling. The possibilities are discussed in Part III.

Before analyzing the message and its source in depth, however, we take a look at the UFO/close encounter phenomenon as it affects Latter-day Saints. It does, in fact, affect LDS Church members.

10

LDS Close
Encounters

Stan Harter

Stan Harter, now a successful business attorney in Southern California, was one of the first Latter-day Saints who related his personal sighting of a UFO to me. Until that time, I had only heard of one LDS encounter, that of Udo Wartena, included below. Most of the sightings I had heard of were non-LDS, that I assumed could have found their geneses in a number of indeterminable sources. As Stan briefly narrated the details of his account, however (about a year after the occurrence), I realized that there exists a dimension to the UFO phenomenon that warrants thoughtful attention. His experience is very basic, but informative. He narrates:

When I was still in high school in mid-1970s, I was dog sitting for a family acquaintance. She was completely blind and the dog was her seeing eye dog. To keep the dog in peak performance, it was necessary for me to take the dog on a rather long walk and put it through a series of exercises each day. Demands being what they were in those days, the only time I could engage in such activities was at night. It was while I was on one of these walks that I had my UFO experience.

On that particular night we had walked to an area where there was a lot of new construction but very few occupied structures. There were no artificial lights to obstruct the view. The sky was clear and afforded quite a spectacular view. As I recall, my mind was not on the view, however. In fact, I believe I had my eyes closed at the time trying to get the full impact of being guided by a seeing eye dog. The dog came to a sudden stop which caused me to open my eyes. I followed the dog's eyes and saw a saucer-like object hovering in the air. The craft had fixed lights on the top and the bottom with rotating lights around its perimeter. In the desert air at night, sounds carry for a great distance. The craft, however, did not emit any audible sound.

The craft continued to hover in a uniform pattern for a period of about 30 seconds, then it made a very quick movement to one side, returned to what seemed to be the original location and made a very quick vertical move, disappearing from my view entirely. The dog continued to watch the sky for a moment and then continued on as though nothing had happened.[1]

---

[1] Personal letter to the author, May 8, 1992.

While pursuing my moderate interest in the UFO phenomenon, it came to my attention that many LDS Church members have experienced UFO encounters. Most are like Stan Harter's—observations from afar. Some, however, are encounters of a closer kind. Some, are too close.

LDS Encounters In The Uintah Basin

Dr. Frank B. Salisbury, an LDS scientist, documented approximately eighty UFO sightings and encounters that occurred in the Uintah Basin in the late 1960s, in his book, *The Utah UFO Display.* Joseph (Junior) Hicks, a science teacher and Priesthood leader in the Uintah Basin, had long collected data on such sightings, and made his materials available to Dr. Salisbury for the book. Junior Hicks still collects data and conducts interviews with local people who have UFO encounters. Most of the people there are LDS, and well over a hundred LDS Church members in that area reportedly have had UFO encounters.

Most of the UFO sightings related in *The Utah UFO Display* were from a distance. Many people saw alien-type craft hovering, darting, and examining the countryside with light beams. Except for a few anomalous events, the sightings were not unlike those reported in the thousands of non-LDS stories in secular UFO books. Dr. Salisbury observed that four features of the Uintah Basin sightings are essentially universal: (1) instant departure, and accelerated speed with right-angle turns; (2) pulsating lights; (3) reddish-orange coloring; and (4) noiseless craft.[2]

Dr. Salisbury notes some differences in the Utah waves of UFO sightings, however: "A few features of other sightings around the world fail to show up in the data. Except for one recent sighting Junior couldn't run down, and sighting #2, which occurred three years before the current wave of Uintah Basin sightings, no UFO occupants are mentioned. Since many of the sightings included windows or transparent domes, and since in a few cases, these were even observed for long intervals of time and with binoculars, this lack of comment on occupants could be significant . . . ."[3]

What is the significance? Dr. Salisbury did not comment in detail, but I believe that as a scientist he may have been thinking along the lines of drone

---

[2] *The Utah UFO Display,* p. 102.

[3] *The Utah UFO Display,* p. 104.

explorer ships—unmanned specimen collectors. However, this interpretation loses some weight in light of Dr. Salisbury's notation of an apparent response by the UFOs to the thoughts of witnesses.

Although no beings or occupants were seen in or near the UFOs in the Uintah Basin during the sightings of the late 1960s and early 1970s, in October of 1967, during the peak of the sightings, Jay Anderson of White Rocks, reported seeing a luminous figure in his home. He reports that it was just standing in the doorway in a metallic suit with a luminous glow about it— then it turned around and just walked away.

The Uintah Theater

Dr. Salisbury commented that there appeared to be a pattern of "theater" connected with the appearance of the UFOs in the Uintah Basin. He relates: "I, and some of the witnesses as well, couldn't help but be impressed with the idea that the UFOs *wanted* to be seen. Otherwise, why should they dive on Joe Ann Harris, follow Thyrena Daniels and many other cars, dance around in full view of dozens of witnesses for fairly long intervals of time, etc.? Why indeed should they execute the intricate and involved maneuvers? Why do their lights flash or change color? It is as though they were *putting on a display.* Often they seemed to stay around only until they could have been quite certain that they had been observed."[4]

Why indeed? It has become obvious that despite a pretense of attempting to remain unnoticed, UFOs follow a pattern designed to reveal their presence. They fly through our dark night skies looking like small cities at Christmas time. As pointed out by Ed Walters, they say "photographs are prohibited," as they pose for another. What is the purpose behind these apparent discrepancies? As we discover later in our discussion (and as we may already have deciphered), the old adage "Don't believe anything you hear and only half of what you see" should be the standard by which we measure all UFO related phenomena.

---

4 *The Utah UFO Display,* p. 108.

And In The Earth Beneath

Although we do not discuss most of the Uintah Basin sightings herein, the brief accounts of two sightings are included here because of their unusual aspects. In the first Dee Hullinger recounts that a UFO was "boiling the dust" with a light beam. He describes the beam as "something like a floodlight off the bottom of a helicopter or something, but the light, when it went out, left a big glow afterwards. And it took this glow I would say about a half hour to completely disappear."[5] Dee further says that the UFO never really left, but seemed to disappear into the ground, although he assumed that he just failed to see it leave, due to all of the dust in the air. As he and his friends were discussing the sighting later, Dee relates that an outsider had his own version of what probably happened.

> This old boy come in the saddle shop down here. He was asking questions about this stuff, because I'd been talking to some guys about it. So I told him what I saw. He said: "Well, it buried itself in the sand!" And I said: "Well, now, what gives you that idea?" And he said: "I've seen one—I've seen it do it." And he claims that he was in a pickup somewhere in Texas. He went up on this ridge and watched this outfit—it was sandy country just like we got here. He said this thing came down, and he said it blew a thrust out the bottom of it, and he said it just dug its own hole and settled right in it, and after a minute some kind of vacuum sucked it in and covered it right up.[6]

The second amazing report deals with two different witnesses in the Uintah Basin that reported shooting at UFOs. People in the Uintah Basin are much more likely to have a rifle or a pair of binoculars than a camera. This unusual fact led to some very detailed observations through binoculars or rifle scopes, a rare opportunity. It also resulted in the complete absence of any photographic evidence. The possession of high powered weapons did allow for a little good natured target practice, however. The result of shooting at the UFOs was the shooters' hearing the bullets ricochet as they bounced off the metallic-appearing hulls, after which the UFOs sped off. One shooter was followed home by the returning UFO—about seventy miles.[7]

Does the first incident necessarily indicate that UFOs hail from under the surface of the Earth, or have the ability to travel through loose soil? There are many witnesses that point to the Earth and its oceans rather than space when relating "which way they went." Does the second incident imply that

5 *The Utah UFO Display,* p. 87.

6 *The Utah UFO Display,* pp. 79-80.

7 *The Utah UFO Display,* pp. 94, 110.

UFOs are solid metallic objects, perhaps leery of small lead projectiles? That is the implication—but why the apparent apprehension of bullets?

Udo Wartena

Tim Grossnickle, a seminary instructor in Oregon, learned from his father, the Stake Patriarch, that an acquaintance of theirs had a close encounter many years before. After learning all that he could from his father about the incident, Tim interviewed Udo Wartena about the encounter while on the temple trip bus from Portland to Oakland, California, before Udo's death just a few years ago. Tim relates the pertinent portions of the interview from memory as follows:

Tim: Do you remember talking to my father about your experience while mining for gold in the remote regions of Northern Idaho in the 1920s?

Udo: Yes. Your father was the first person I ever told about it.

Tim: That was some time in the late 1960s. Why did you wait so long to share your experience?

Udo: Who would believe what I experienced? Over the years I read some of the other accounts in the newspapers and magazines and realized that some of the same things happened to others. But some of them told of strange looking creatures. I doubted them, because the people on the UFO that I saw were just like us, and very nice chaps.

Tim: What actually happened? How did you know the ship had landed?

Udo: My mine shaft was nearly vertical and was over 30 feet deep in the ground. I had built up a sluice stream nearby to wash out the gold. I heard something like a big truck, or like a jet engine, but this was before the time when I had ever heard such a sound. I came up my shaft to look, and in the meadow was a saucershaped craft supported on legs.

A man was pulling down a hose to draw water from my stream. I did not feel the least bit of fear and I walked toward the man. He came and shook my hand, apologizing that they had not known that I was in the area. It was not their custom to interrupt or allow themselves to be seen. "Why not take water from the lake," I asked. "This water is more pure and free from algae," he answered, and invited me to see his ship.

He was such a pleasant fellow. I asked his age—he was quite handsome and youthful, appearing to be middle-aged. His companion on board looked slightly older, but was also in very good health. They answered that one was about six hundred years old as we measured time, and the other was over nine hundred years old. They knew over five hundred languages and were learning ours, and improving upon them all the time.

They had come here "to monitor the progression and retrogression of our societies," he explained. They live among us from time to time.

I asked if they knew of Jesus Christ, and if they held the Priesthood. "We would like to speak of these things," he responded, "but are unable. We cannot interfere in any way."

"Where did you come from," I asked. "We live on a distant planet," he replied, giving its name and pointing in its direction.

The love, or comfort I felt in these men's presence was remarkable. I was invited to be examined with an "x-ray-like" machine, which when passed over me could record what impurities were in my system.

The ship was propelled with two rings or disks about three feet wide and a few inches thick, which circled the inside perimeter of the ship next to "battery/transformer-like" units all around the outer wall. Rods separated the disks (turned by motors), causing the disks to move in opposite directions. A force was generated which overcame the gravitational pull of the Earth, or any other planet they were on. They focused on a distant star and used its energy to draw them through space at speeds greater than the speed of light. My host specifically mentioned "skipping upon the light waves."

They invited me to accompany them on their journey, but I declined—I was driving to Portland the next day for my wedding. I didn't want to leave them though.

Upon leaving the ship and standing by a rock some distance away, I heard the same loud noise as before as the craft lifted, rotated with sort of a wobble, brought up the landing gear, and began to rise slowly. It went faster as it rose until it disappeared at great speed. An energy had permeated the area and I lost all my strength for some hours. I was unable to walk. When my strength finally returned I walked back to the base camp.

When I arrived at camp no one else mentioned the craft—I never mentioned it to anyone of them. A young man came up missing from his claim, however. Nothing there had been disturbed—he was just gone without a trace. I was never sure if it had anything to do with my experience or not.[8]

Udo returned annually to the mine for a few years following the incident, but never saw the craft or its occupants after that. He related that he always wished that he could have seen them again. Udo was so reluctant to speak of the incident that nearly five decades passed before he shared it with his wife—only after discussing it with his own Patriarch. Tim Grossnickle describes Udo as a shy, pleasant, Scandinavian immigrant—a carpenter by trade. He trusts the word of this High Priest and reports that Udo related this account to his father in a "humble and matter-of-fact way, having a relationship of friendship and trust with him."

---

[8] Personal letter to the author, January 4, 1992.

Travis Walton

In the small town of Snowflake, Arizona, a Mormon pioneer outpost, lives a community of LDS Church members. One of them, Travis Walton, has one of the most celebrated, credible tales of abduction in UFO lore. Most UFO books and "Unsolved Mystery" types of television programs include Travis's experience in their roster of top encounters. The motion picture *Fire in the Sky* is based on Travis's ordeal.

One evening Travis and a group of his friends were travelling home in their pickup through the woods after a day at work. As they talked and laughed, they suddenly saw a bright light through the trees. They thought it might be an unreported forest fire so they drove near it. As they approached, they saw that it was no fire. Travis was nearest the door so he got out and had a look. He describes how he saw a bright craft hovering off the ground. It was not obscured nor hazy, but had a "clear and distinct" form—Travis says it was so close he could have thrown a rock at it.

The thought occurred to Travis, foolishly in retrospect as he narrates, that the thing "might take off" in a movement, so he moved in to get a "closer look." As he stepped forward, there suddenly was a bright flash which knocked Travis to the ground. Travis's buddies in the pickup were already of the opinion that Travis should not have left them in the truck to wander near the strange craft. Upon seeing these otherworldly hostilities and Travis's apparently dead body lying motionless on the ground, they sped off in a panic.

Travis's best friend and future brother-in-law, Mike, was at the wheel. Within a quarter of a mile, Mike began to regain his thinking processes, and remembered that Travis was lying alone in the dirt back there. He stopped the truck and an argument about returning ensued. Soon, all were thinking clearly and they returned to the scene. Travis was nowhere to be found, however. No sign of the strange craft could be detected either.

The frightened men all held hands as they warily searched the surrounding forest for Travis. They could find no sign of him. They decided to get help from the authorities, and raced to the sheriff's office in town. The sheriff was summoned to the scene, and after a brief search, decided to continue their man hunt in the morning. Already, however, his suspicions of foul play were growing—tales of UFO abduction were new to him too. Travis's mother was notified of his disappearance.

The next morning the sheriff's office and Travis's friends conducted a thorough search of the area, finding no clues. The men recounted how they had seen the UFO and how Travis had approached it, only to be knocked to the ground by a brilliant flash. The sheriff developed serious doubts about the UFO story, and began investigating Travis's disappearance as a homicide. Mike was dating Travis's sister at the time, and the sheriff suspected that Travis had objected, Mike killed him in a dispute, and the other men helped bury Travis's body.

The group of men were questioned extensively over the next few days, and a polygraph expert was called in to check their stories. The polygraph expert had never before had so many prime witnesses to the same event. After subjecting all of the men to examinations, he concluded that they were absolutely telling the truth. So—where was Travis?

Five days after his disappearance, Travis Walton walked out of the woods. He narrates what happened in the interim:

> When I felt the numbing shock, I blacked out. And the next thing I knew, I regained consciousness—not quickly, sort of gradually. My head wasn't real clear, I was in a lot of pain. I was laying on my back—I didn't know where I was. I remembered what had happened in the woods. As I was regaining consciousness I was trying to figure out where I was and what was going on. I thought maybe I was in a hospital or something—I had been hurt.

As Travis looked around him, he discovered he was lying on a table in an examination-looking room, but that he was in no hospital—not one that accepts Blue Cross anyway. He saw two small greys at the end of the table and jumped off in a panic. He backed away from them as they stepped towards him. Travis continues:

> When I was standing in front of those things that were coming towards me—and they stopped there, and they stood there looking at me—these huge eyes, just seemed to look right through me. I didn't get any impression of emotion, it was very detached— sort of, a just observing sort of thing, but it seemed like they could see everything I was thinking of doing. It was very disturbing to me to feel so . . . *exposed.* And these huge eyes looked at me and . . . when they'd blink, and on an eye that big the eyelid just slid down and opened like a window opening and shutting—and it just had the strangest sort of feeling, and I just couldn't, I couldn't bear their gaze.

The two small greys walked toward Travis as he threatened them with a glass rod he found and shouted out "Get back! Get back!" They walked right past him and out of the room. Travis took off, running wildly through the slippery, illuminated maze of corridors.

Travis finally arrived in a room with a high-tech chair in the middle. He was alone, so he went over to look at the chair. He recounts:

> There was a lever there, and when I moved that, the star pattern [that had appeared in front of him] appeared to move. That kind of disoriented me for a minute, because I felt like I was moving, kind of, for a second, because this was—to have everything

suddenly shift like that. I figured I had better quit messing with that. I had, by that time surmised, that I was in some sort of craft—I connected it to what had happened before, and figured I might crash this thing or something.

As Travis looked around the room and wondered what might happen next, a tall, young-looking human man with long hair entered the room. Travis explains:

> This person was not like the humanoid creatures that I had seen earlier. This looked like a human being. It looked like a man, in a blue uniform. I went up to him, thinking that I was being rescued, that I was being saved—that this was a person. I started asking all kinds of questions—"Where am I? Where are we? And who were those things that I saw? Talk to me!"

The young human silently put his hand on Travis's shoulder, and led him out of the room into the corridor, and through another doorway.

> When that door opened there was an inrushing of air, and it felt fresher and cooler than where I'd been. It must have been, like—the air I was in was real heavy, moist, stifling.
>
> He just pulled me quickly on—went through some doors, down a hallway to another room.

In the other room, Travis and the young human were met by two more humans, another young man and a female. They maneuvered Travis, who was protesting and fighting, into an examination chair, something like a dental chair, and applied a "gas mask" to his face. He lost consciousness at that point, and next found himself waking in the forest, five days after his abduction. Like his friends, Travis was also subjected to a lie detector test concerning his disappearance and abduction, which he passed. However, some accounts relate that Travis's first test was inconclusive, but that subsequent polygraphs confirmed his belief in the reported experiences.

Travis has suffered a great deal of "frustration and pain" as a result of his unusual encounter—not resulting so much from the trauma inflicted by his abductors, but from that inflicted by those who accuse him of deceit. Everyone he meets fails to see him as a "person" now, he complains, but they see him as "that man," the "abductee." Travis laments, "Every contact I have with people is colored by, and filtered through the distorting lens of something that just happened to me—fifteen years ago." This is the reason that most people do not report their encounters.

Irene

On September 24, 1987, Irene (a pseudonym for the sake of relatives' privacy) was with her sister, working on her sister's trailer. They received a telephone call from their mother, asking frantically if they could look up the telephone numbers of any television or radio stations in the Salt Lake City area. She wanted the stations to photograph and cover strange objects in the sky over the northern part of the Salt Lake Valley. Her mother said that she and many other people were watching floating objects in the sky.

Irene and her sister drove to the downtown Salt Lake City area, but could see nothing because of the cloud cover. As they approached the area where their parents lived, they saw the "big cigar-shaped thing just sitting up there in the air." When they arrived, their parents were gone but the house was unlocked. They quickly went in to get their father's binoculars to better observe the object.

As they went back outside, they involved as many of the neighbors as they could find. One nineteen-year-old neighbor boy was able to get his telescope to observe the craft. To ensure that very credible witnesses were available, they got a neighbor who was a professor at the University of Utah to come and watch also. Irene attempted many times to get the television and radio stations and airport officials to look at the object, but all claimed that they were unable to see anything. Subsequent contacts with the local media indicated that they had merely dismissed the two-hour sighting as a hoax, and had failed to get any photographs. With the number of witnesses involved, the media were disappointed, and later established press liaisons with MUFON.

Irene telephoned her husband who worked in the immediate area and told him to go out and look. He and several employees went outside and watched it too. He also was fortunate to have a pair of binoculars at his disposal. While Irene was attempting to telephone people to go outside and watch, Irene's sister called to her to go outside and look. As she went out, she saw a "gold, disk-shaped craft" that flew with traditional UFO rapid, jerking motions beside and behind the larger cigar-shaped stationary object. She "assumed" that the smaller disk went behind the larger object, anyway—her initial impression was that it entered the larger object. The large object was "silvery color, with red lines around it," observers agreed. One man (whose testimony I heard) observed that although the larger object had a metallic appearance, he sometimes thought it looked more like a "window in the sky"—not in shape, but in function.

The larger object appeared to spin on its horizontal axis slowly—"It looked almost as if it were rolling as it hovered," Irene thought. It had portholes. The crowd could tell that it remained in the same place for a long period of time because they observed it over a telephone pole which served as a point of reference. The small craft finally departed with classic UFO acceleration.

MUFON investigated, and several witnesses gave statements and drew pictures. No photographs were taken at all.

Irene has learned that she has many relatives that have seen UFOs—aunts and uncles (some of whom live near Area 51), siblings, and parents. Since becoming active in the UFO phenomenon, Irene says that suddenly, lately, she feels that many things from her past have been coming out, and she has thought deeply about it all. The UFO literature has prompted her to note many incidents in her life that may have UFO roots. This is a common pattern for those exposed to UFO literature. In fact, it is often problematic because those who have no exposure to UFOs often begin to believe that normal phenomena (childhood partial memories, dreams, etc.) were UFO related, giving birth to yet another contactee.

I am not saying that this is always, or even generally the case for those with a history of anomalous phenomena. Some people seem plagued with these kinds of experiences. When I interviewed Irene, I asked her to tell me about all of the unusual or unexplained events in her life. As you read about some of those experiences below, I am sure you will note that they parallel in many ways events in the lives of abductees discussed already. I present the experiences in the order Irene recalled them.

When Irene was a little girl she was walking up a canyon (in a western state) by herself and saw a black panther up on the hill. She noticed it looking at her, but it did nothing—and she felt no fear because of it. She has always wondered why she wasn't afraid of the panther—why she didn't run. She has since encountered many LDS people with UFO beliefs who relate similar encounters with strange, docile, exotic animals like the black panther in their youth. She discussed her experience with one LDS woman who claims to have looked on one time as an animal appeared to transform from a big black bear to a big black dog. They associate these anomalous events with the UFO phenomenon. Such phenomena are often reported in Indian lore and the occult, and form the basis of the werewolf and vampire legends of Europe.

Irene's brother-in-law and his brother and buddies reported to her that while they were in Huntington Canyon (Utah) they had UFOs come right down over them, "and he could see [occupants] inside of the ship."

Irene further reports that she, her husband, her cousin, his brother, and her two sisters "saw four of them when we were coming back from fishing one night—it was on the Fourth of July. We saw four over Mt. Olympus. We watched them, and then they were gone like that." They just disappeared.

Irene's aunt and uncle (LDS), who live in Nevada, had an enormous UFO pass over their car. They report that it was so big that they couldn't see anything else when they looked out of the car. On their way to their ranch in Ely, Nevada, they saw an entire UFO fleet go over.

Irene relates, "My grandmother recalls seeing Big Foot when she was younger too—and she's the closest thing to an angel that I ever knew."

The following are what I would term demonic encounters. Irene associates them with UFOs.

> I had an experience where I woke up in the night and this tall being was standing at the bottom of the bed and said that he had come to get me and my baby. He telepathically communicated it to me. It happened when my first child was three months old—he's now twenty-seven years old. I knew it was a male, the way he communicated to me. He said he had come to get me and the baby. I was beating on my husband—I just said "no! no!" My husband finally woke up, but the being was gone. He was around seven feet tall, light colored hair, dressed in white. I did not want to go. He did not seem insistent, but only told me what he wanted.
>
> My daughter has strange things that happen to her all the time. She'll wake up at night and there will be things in her room—like a crystal she'll see. If she doesn't wake up, it will hit the bed, and then she wakes up. If she doesn't wake up, it will wake her up—it scares her to death—it will come from the foot of the bed to the top.
>
> My nineteen-year-old son has seen something that has terrorized him. His bedroom is right next to ours, and he was beating on the wall one night (18 months ago), and I jumped up and ran to the door, and he said, "turn on the light." And I asked why he wanted the light on, and he said there was this green kind of mist over in the doorway, and it came up and it came right over the top of him and it was like the pressure went right over the top of him, and scared him. He has never been scared like that, even when he was little.
>
> My son remembers seeing a UFO when he was little—laying out on the lawn at night—and he had never told me about it. He remembers seeing this thing over him, and then it went up. He had made a clay model of an alien in high school that I didn't even know about, and he said that's what an alien looked like. It has the big sunken eyes, and looks like other people's descriptions of them [small greys].

When Irene was 6, she was in bed with her mother, who kept reading a book, and waking her with nudges. "Mom was crying, saying that someone was looking through the front room window." Her father was working. She walked over to the window to see what was there. She was very frightened. She saw a light, and then all she remembers is being unusually calm. The next thing she remembers is being in her mother's bed, her mother waking her asking, "are you listening, are you listening?" It was only a short while ago that Irene's mother confided that it was aliens she was afraid of. Irene puzzles, "Why would she mention this after all of these years? Why this is all coming about now is what I would like to know. Why am I recalling different things that tie in with what other people are starting to think about—why are people starting to think about these things?—" These are very good questions.

Referring to the same house where Irene and her mother had been terrorized and had possibly experienced some missing time, she recalls, "I remember my uncle sleeping there right after he got out of the service. He had gone to sleep on the couch and woke up in the middle of the night, and something was leaning right over him, looking at him. He was terrified, and pretended to be asleep. I remember many spooky things happening in that house."

Irene relates yet another experience, a bedroom encounter, which occurred in her late teens. "I remember being terrified one night, just waking up and seeing this little dark being in the doorway. My cousin (who was married the next day), across town, saw the same little figure in her doorway that same night. It was a cloaked, hooded looking, dark silhouette—about four-and-a-half feet tall."

Without being aware of the Betty Luca telephone calls from the beings, in which they gave her posthypnotic suggestions or strange messages, Irene recalled, "I got a phone call I've often wondered about, in that same house. I remember one night the phone was ringing, and I went and answered it. She told me to stay on the line, that something important was coming through. And all I remember was, the next thing I knew, it was morning and I was in bed, and I said, 'oh, I forgot,' because I thought it was my husband's family calling from another state. I thought, 'why did I go to bed, knowing that they were calling?' " Irene later learned that no family member had called at that time.

More in the vein of Kathie Davis, Irene recounts, "I lost a baby that they never did find. I had a miscarriage when I was three months pregnant, and there was no baby." Her husband was out of town, and she was awaiting his return so he could take her to the doctor. "It was in between my other children [around 23 years ago]—I was only three months pregnant and I just started having contractions, hard labor, and when I got there the doctor checked me. They rushed me to the hospital because I was bleeding so badly. They could never find any trace of the baby. There was no fetal tissue at all they said." These experiences, of course, often have better medical explanations than abduction implications. However, the "aliens" are "telling" us that they are removing fetuses, so, we must at least keep the possibility in mind.

Irene had always wondered about an incident that had brought unknown fears to the surface. "My uncle was dying, and we drove to Las Vegas on the old highway before the freeway was built. My dad was driving, and we left around midnight. I saw this light in the sky over by the mountains, going along the mountains, and I and my right leg—now this had never happened to me before, my right leg started shaking and I thought, 'they are coming to get me—hurry, get me to the next town—if we can just make it to the next town they won't be able to get me.' Why would I think that?—because I didn't think about such things then."

Many of Irene's memories and fears, as outlined above, could possibly be explained as distorted childhood memories or dreams. However, the corroborating witnesses and similar experiences of close relatives cause Irene to doubt this explanation. And again, as Irene points out, since she has begun to read the UFO literature, these experiences appear to be common to the phenomenon. Irene has many questions. We should all have many questions about UFOs and the phenomena that seem to be manifested in association with them.

Margy Beal

Margy Beal lives in the Uintah Basin and had the following experiences in 1966 or 1967, during the peak of the UFO sighting wave chronicled by Dr. Salisbury. Sister Beal's accounts failed to make it into Dr. Salisbury's book, however, because it was later that anyone learned about them. Sister Beal is one of the active, productive Relief Society sisters in the Uintah Basin, and she has a very healthy attitude about her experiences.

> My daughter, Becky, and I were coming home from an honors banquet at the high school. We were about five miles outside of the town of Roosevelt—we lived twelve miles from Roosevelt—and as we came to the crest of a hill, we had noticed that there weren't any cars. After a banquet like that, there should be cars on the highway, but for some reason there weren't any cars following us or coming toward us. We had mentioned this, and when we came to the crest of a hill, all of a sudden, out in front of us was this saucerlike thing with all of these bright lights and it was so bright that you could see the pebbles along the side of the road.

Margy describes the craft:

> It was quite large, and it was like a saucer only it had a dome on the top. All around where the dome fit the saucer, it looked like windows. And under the edge of this saucer light came down really bright. It didn't seem to have light holes or anything, it just seemed like it was all light that came down toward the earth—very bright. And the noise was a whirring noise—a quite steady whirring noise, with a "whumpf, whumpf, whumpf," steadily, every once in a while. The whirring noise was not high pitched, it was rather low pitched.

She continues:

> There was a house there—those folks never saw it, but you could see the stems in the bushes around their house. And it gave us such a weird feeling. We don't know how long we were there but all at once I said to Becky, "I have to get out, I need to feel the ground under me." So I stepped out, she didn't want me to, but I stepped out and could feel the ground under me, then I got back in and I was oriented again. I went to start the car, and this is what was so funny, is that the key was on. The car was off—it was not in park, and I do not remember ever turning the car off or anything, and the key was still turned to the "on" position, but the motor was stopped.
>
> So I started it and we started down over the crest of the hill and that thing moved back away from us. We went about another two miles and came to the crest of another hill—we had to drop down twice—and we stopped again and we both decided we'd get out and listen to the "whir" that it made. And when we did it suddenly shot off to the east and went out of sight
>
> Then we drove through the town of Myton, and up the highway about two and a half miles. I said, "Oh, I'm sure glad we don't have that thing again," and she said "Mom, look!" And out to our right following the Duschesne river was this same thing going west as we went west. And when we arrived home, three miles from the town of Myton, Diane, an older daughter who had been watching the young children came out and was extremely agitated and worried. She thought we'd had all kinds of troubles because we were so late. It would only take about twenty minutes to drive from Roosevelt home—twelve miles. And we were two and a half hours late. Where had we been and what had happened to us?

When she had recounted their experience, I asked Margy about the "funny feeling" that she had mentioned they felt. She explained that as they came over the crest of the hill when they first saw the craft she felt as if they had been "pulled right out toward the craft." She continued, "There was no way we could hold back, we were being pulled right out toward it." The next thing she remembers was being down the hill with the car stopped, the ignition turned to the "on" position, the automatic transmission in "drive," and the engine not running. At that point she had the overwhelming feeling that "somehow or another I hadn't been touching ground—you know, that I hadn't been connected to the ground. That's why I wanted to get out of the car—to feel it under my feet."

I asked Margy how she "felt" during this experience—as a member of the Church possessing the gift of the Holy Ghost, whether there was anything "spiritual" that she had discerned about her encounter (and apparent abduction). She responded, "It didn't make me feel that there was anything sinister about it." She reiterated this feeling and then expressed, "I felt like if it was there, and it was truly a flying saucer from some other planet, that we [collectively] are supposed to know about it for some reason." I asked her again about the "obvious implications" in her story, the fact that she felt she was being pulled into the craft, that she had not been on the ground for some time, and that there was a definite period of time for which they could not account. She responded, "Well it means—I felt like I had been controlled."

I asked if she felt any kind of invasion from her experience, or if she had any spiritual insights about it. Her response was only that she "didn't have any feeling of fright." She said, "I never did feel afraid."

About six months later, Margy recounts that she was taking her mother to a Relief Society meeting one evening. Her mother had heard the girls speak of their UFO sighting and wanted to see one for herself, although she was still a little skeptical. Within about one mile of her mother's house, they came upon a UFO sitting on a little knoll about one mile away. Margy said, "Well, Mother, how about that! Take a look." Her mother was shocked as they just sat there for awhile watching it. They knew they would be a little late for Relief Society, but they thought it was worth it. Margy says, "All of a sudden it lifted straight up into the sky and took off to the right. It crossed about a mile in front of us, and went across the river and looked like it landed on a hill to the right of us, which would be north. The next morning the farmers went out to feed their cows, and they found three pod marks in the ground." Margy says that this second craft seemed somewhat smaller than the first, but attributes that to the fact that she had seen one before, and it was not so imposing on her psyche.

Some months later, in the fall of the same year, Margy and her son saw another saucer while at home. "We saw one in the sky one night and we got his rifle out and watched it through the scope. A teacher here at Roosevelt was interested, and we called him and he had a telescope, and he watched it and we watched it and we conversed over the telephone about its movements." This craft was shaped differently than the other two Margy had seen—it was the classic "cigar" shape. She later learned that it was following a young couple's car as they returned from a date.

Diane Hanson

Diane Hanson is the daughter of Margy Beal who was frantic as Margy and her other daughter returned late from their first UFO encounter. Her anomalous experience occurred in the fall of 1965, when she was 17 or 18 years old. She is not sure that she had a UFO encounter on that night, but feels that this experience early in her life is somehow related to the unusual events in the Uintah Basin at that time. Although Diane is no longer an active member of the LDS Church, she was at the time of the experience. In some ways, she says, the experience, and subsequent occurrences have alienated her from the Restored Gospel.

> My girlfriend and I, when we were teenagers, we had gone to Vernal, Utah—that's about 35 miles from Roosevelt. We had to get back to Roosevelt before it got dark because we knew we only had one headlight. Out there it's like rolling hills, and rolling hills, everywhere. As we were going along, we could see this very bright light—it wasn't dark yet, but we could see this really brilliant light. We were concerned because her brother had been doing construction work out there. He had a construction company, and they had been having a lot of trouble with the unions. They [union personnel] were going out welding the machinery all together. So when we saw this bright light we were thinking of welding—that's how bright it was.
>
> You could see this bright light coming off of the top of the hill. We knew there was a valley down there, but we couldn't see down into the valley. So we were thinking that we'd better check this out. So when we got to the valley, we turned [looked right] to look, and the next thing I knew, we were both screaming. I was the one driving, and I was screaming because I didn't know where we were—I didn't know if we were on the road—I felt like my front tires were down, but I didn't know if my back tires were.
>
> It was pitch black, and we had this God-awful fear that we were not to turn around. Finally, I was able to realize that I was on the road, and get the feel again of the car. But we still had this terrible fear—and being LDS at that time it felt so—um, let's say "unnatural" or something—the fear, I can't explain—it gives you goose bumps or something. The fear to turn around? I said, "It must be the Devil." I said, "We have got to do this Judy." And it took everything we had, and we counted "one, two, three," and we turned around to look—and there wasn't anything there.
>
> All the way from Vernal to Roosevelt we only passed one car. Judy's house was in Roosevelt, but when we went through Roosevelt, all . . . . We were getting real scared, and when we saw that one car it somehow made us feel better, like there really was civilization there. The funny thing of it was, that we were staying at Judy's house at Roosevelt—you see I don't even know what time it was, we didn't have a clock in the car or a watch on, so we didn't know what time it was—but when we got to Roosevelt the streets were quite deserted—and we were so, we just didn't even think about it. We just drove straight to Myton and up on the farm—and we were supposed to be stopping at Judy's house.
>
> We went in the house and my Mom was asleep—and we went in and were just babbling off to her, crying, and my mother asked, "What's the matter, what happened?" And we just sat realizing that we had no logical thing to tell her why we were so afraid. But it was a really late hour, so there seems to be a lapse in time.

I asked how much time seemed to be missing and she responded:

> It was getting to where the sun was going down, but we should have been able to make it to Roosevelt before it got dark, and we didn't, we weren't even to the gusher when all of this took place. It was such a really late hour when we got there to Roosevelt, so it must have been a couple of hours.

She continued:

> That's all we remembered, and then years later I started talking with [Irene, above], and I started telling her about my and Judy's experience—all of a sudden I remembered something more. And I jumped up and I picked up the phone and I called Judy, and

I said it exactly like this, I said, "Judy, do you remember when? We were driving over there, we saw the light, and when we got there we looked up the hill and what did we see?" And she said exactly the same thing as me, and both of us had forgotten it—when we looked up there had been this thing kind of like a sawhorse, kind of like the shape of a sawhorse—and like three men there, like in rubber [diving] suits. Neither one of us can really remember their faces or anything. Oh, one other thing I can remember is when we got into the valley, when we looked up the valley [to the right of the car], the light apparently must have been on the side towards Vernal, because I remember when I looked—the way it lit up the sage brush and everything, on the other side of the little valley [on the left side of the car], I remember seeing that—you know, how brilliantly it lit up everything. I mean, you could see individual leaves, branches, and everything.

I questioned Diane about the sawhorse, the light, and the men. She shared the following.

I always think of it as something like a sawhorse. It wasn't wood. Two of the men were standing behind it, side by side, and one was down toward the end, and half of his body was not behind it. It wasn't taller than the men were, it would hit around their thighs. Their suits were something like frogmen's suits, but I don't think that . . . they were black, but at that time I didn't think of frogmen's suits as being black [Mike Nelson, on *Sea Hunt* wore a light colored suit]. I had assumed that they were construction workers, and I tried to think of everything I was experiencing in terms of construction workers. The suits were black, and they were glistening—it wasn't metalliclike glistening, it was just like wet, and very formfitting. I remember the shapes—I guess I just went through this big jolt of trying to reconcile—I was trying to make sense, I was trying to understand—because I was trying to make sense, I didn't notice as many details.

Their heads were covered with the suits, so I couldn't see any hair. The bright light was behind them, so I couldn't see their facial features—the front part was vague. Their hands were covered, but their faces weren't, I know there was lots of whiteness in their faces.

The one on the end was beginning to move, and I was concerned about that. I was still thinking construction, and thought that maybe we had happened onto some kind of illegal activity, and when that guy started to move—maybe they were going to do something to us. I just remembered that he was moving, and I just wanted to get the hell out of there! We had slowed down tremendously to see what was happening—but I don't even remember hurrying after that, I just remember that I thought we should get the hell out of there.

The next thing I remember is . . . , I don't remember where we were at—it was pitch dark—I don't even remember my headlights—they must have been there, but I don't remember them. Then the next thing I do remember then, and I could find myself on the road, but first, I don't think I had headlights—because I didn't know where I was. I didn't know how to drive because I didn't know where I was, and I didn't think that my back tires were on the road. I was just screaming for Judy to help me because I didn't know where I was going or where I was. We both just kind of came to, and both of us were just screaming.

It's funny, but Judy and I never talked about this. Never again. [Q. Why, do you think?] I don't know! I thought that was strange—but we had never talked about it. So, after all of these years I called her up—and it's so strange that both of us would remember after all that time, the three men, after never remembering them before. It was that

that made me think that maybe it was a UFO experience—I had never thought of that before. The fact that we were so afraid—the fact that we had forgotten and then suddenly remembered that one part—is the one thing that made me first start thinking that very likely it was. We never talked about it after that—I don't think we ever did, not even the next day. Normally we would have discussed it a lot—that night we blubbered about it to Mamma, and then we never talked about it again. I wasn't afraid to talk about it, I just never thought about talking about it. The only time I was ever afraid was when we were not supposed to turn around, we were not supposed to look, you know, when we first came to in the car—we were not supposed to look back. We were just terrified for some reason—and we tried to understand what it was, and we thought surely it must be of the Devil. It was horrible, evil, and unnatural.

I include Diane's account here not only because of the missing time aspects of her experience, but because I recognized some similarities between her encounter and two reported by Jacques Vallee. The first encounter occurred in Abbiate, Buazzone, near Varese, Italy, on April 24, 1950:

At about 10:00 p.m., Bruno Facchini heard and saw sparks which he attributed to a storm, but he soon discovered a dark mass hovering between a pole and a tree 200 yards from his house. A man dressed in tight-fitting clothes and wearing a helmet appeared to be making repairs. There were three other figures working around a huge craft. This work being over, a trap through which light had been shining was closed and the thing took off. Other details were as follows: The object made a sound similar to that of a giant beehive and the air seemed strangely warm around it. Two of the men were standing on the ground near a ladder; the third was on a telescopic elevator, the base of which touched the ground, and was holding something near a group of pipes: this produced the sparks seen by Facchini. They were about five feet nine inches tall, dressed in grey diving suits with an oval transparent glass in front of their faces, which were concealed behind grey masks. From the fore portion of the masks a flexible pipe emerged at the level of the mouth. They wore earphones. Inside the craft could be seen a series of oxygen-type containers and many dials."[9]

Welding instruments, flashes of bright light, sparks, men in diving suits—the similarities are marked. The next account merely reinforces the man in a "diving suit" with a "bright light device in his hand" scene witnessed by Diane, as well as Bruno Facchini, although there is no mention of welding or sparks.

On October 9, 1954, in Lavoux, Vienne, France, a farmer who was riding his bicycle suddenly stopped as he saw a figure, dressed in a sort of "diving suit," aiming a double light beam at him. The individual, who seemed to have "boots without heels," very bright eyes, and a very hairy chest, carried two "headlights," one below the other, on the front of his suit.[10]

Diane reports incidents of paranormal activity in her life. The first felt as though the veil was parted and a spiritual being had entered the room.

9 *Dimensions,* pp. 161-62.

10 *Ibid.,* p. 108.

She felt these impressions unmistakably. On two occasions she reports being visited by dead relatives, witnessed by coworkers on one occasion and by her children on another. She was not particularly close to the departed relatives, and had never even met the female. Neither apparition spoke a word.

Paul P.

Paul, who requests anonymity for privacy reasons, says he did not believe in UFOs, despite his own brother's testimony of having seen one while traveling on a commercial airliner. In June of 1964, Paul became a believer.

Paul and his wife had moved up Emigration Canyon, just east of Salt Lake City, and were visiting at their neighbor's home. Paul's wife had to go to work the next morning so she excused herself and went home around 11:30 p.m. He stayed until around 1:30 a.m. His hosts were completely exhausted from their fun, so he showed himself out the side door of the house. There was no light on that side and the sky was perfectly clear. He began to "feel" a noise or vibration that pulsed through him like an electronic signal or hum. In that part of the canyon one could not make any sound at night without setting off the entire neighborhood dog population—but as he listened and the pulsating tone became louder, there was no barking. A power transformer had burned out not long before, so his first thought was that it was going out again. He looked, but saw no sign of fire up or down the lines.

"Then this object came over the ridge behind our home, blocking out the stars" where it passed, as if an opaque silhouette was between him and the starry sky. He could see no details, only the opaque outline where the stars had disappeared. He estimates the length of the object as being the width of a football field, approximately 150 feet. He says, "It looked like a dirigible," but insists that it was not. It seemed to be travelling about 30 or 40 m.p.h. as it crested the ridge, then slowed down. It "floated" toward him, to within a very short distance and completely stopped, just above their driveway. It was very close—30 feet away, possibly. It had round windows like portholes. He describes it as something between a "skinny football or a fat cigar." There was a pale green light inside.

"I had a frightened feeling—I felt like a rabbit hiding behind a bush." He wondered how they could see him in the perfect darkness, "yet they stopped and they came to the portholes, and they stood there, and I could make out shoulders and the forms of heads, but I couldn't make out any hair or anything like that." As the "people" came to the portholes to look, he noticed lights underneath that had the appearance of "welding torches." The lights were bright and filled with different colors.

At that time Paul received what he felt was a "telepathic suggestion" from the "people" in the UFO. He could not make out discernable words, but "felt" an invitation to come with them. The thought of his "pretty young wife and children" coupled with his immediate fear caused him to reject their offer, attempting to convey his feelings of responsibility toward his family. They just "continued on," much as if a helium balloon had been released.

He believes the entire encounter lasted just a few minutes. He ran into the house, shook his wife to wake her up, to which she responded, "You're dreaming, go back to sleep." All of the animals remained silent and out of sight following the encounter—he felt that they were aware of what was happening, and had been too frightened to come out after that.

Paul worked for the Utah State Department of Highways at the time, so he telephoned the Civil Air Patrol and asked if there were any dirigibles in the area. They informed him that there was nothing like that within several states, and assumed that there were no lighter-than-air vehicles being used anywhere in the United States around that time. He proposed many possible scenarios and explanations to the Civil Air Patrol that may have explained what he had seen, but they knocked them down one at a time, finally becoming irate, and demanding his name. With that, he hung up the telephone.

Paul says, "I felt extremely inferior to whatever it was that was up there observing me." He adds that there are various levels of apprehension that he feels in different situations—in this case he says, "I would say that I had a greater level of apprehension concerning this than I would about finding a rattle snake under my seat." However, he is adamant that he feels that the UFO occupants were completely benevolent and meant no harm.

Carl

In the mid-1960s, Carl, who was eleven year old, was in the alfalfa fields of his family's farm with his seventeen-year-old sister, doing the watering. Carl's family lived in Howell, Utah, about fifteen miles northwest of Tremonton, and their 350-acre farm was set in a valley, about five miles wide and eight miles long, running north to south. The family farm lay in the middle of the valley, and in the south end of the valley was Thiokol plant number 78.

Carl and his sister were doing the watering at about 2:00 a.m., admiring the clear sky with its bright moon and stars. They were struck by the sudden appearance of a craft in the north end of the valley as it came over the mountains, about three or four miles away from them. It was enormous, filling almost one-third of the valley from side to side. Carl and his sister believe the UFO was about a mile in diameter. The craft was flying low—between 70 to 100 feet from the ground, they recall. It moved slowly and steadily from the north end of the valley. It made no noise at all. The two youths did their best to duck down in the alfalfa, but it was only a foot tall at that time. They jumped into an irrigation ditch that had not yet been flooded. Carl's sister reports that she prayed the entire fifteen to twenty minutes it took the craft to travel the length of the valley—prayed that it wouldn't notice them, or if it did, that it would not molest them in any way.

Carl's only memory about what he was thinking at the time was how big the craft was, how silent, how overwhelming—and, how scared he was. Carl and his sister describe the craft similarly—a double convex ("like two curved plates stuck together") with a ten-foot-high mid-section separating the plates. The belt-like section around the middle had evenly spaced lights around the entire perimeter, like large holes in a belt. Carl's sister recalls that these round lights were as large as the mid-section, ten feet in diameter, and yellowish-orange in color. The lights were so bright that as the UFO came over the mountains it lit up the entire valley. Although the craft took nearly twenty minutes to pass the eight miles through the valley, and was only a mile or so from them as it passed, Carl and his sister had difficulty making out any distinguishing characteristics other than the basic shape. It was more of a silhouette surrounded by the bright yellowish-orange lights, although it appeared to be completely solid and tangible in every respect. They could see that the craft was "smooth, curved with a dome," but could see no other appendages or irregular shapes attached.

The craft "floated" from north to south, making no noise at all, and continued without any deviation from its course or speed. Carl could not believe the silence associated with such a gargantuan structure. There was no wobble, no wind—nothing. It just floated in a straight course, very slowly. Carl's sister says it was "eerie."

The only change occurred when the UFO reached the south end of the valley. When it arrived at the Thiokol plant, it stopped, and hovered over it. After that, the yellowish-orange lights changed their hue to a bright red, and the craft drifted up over the mountains at the south end of the valley.

This was Carl's only close sighting. It was not his sister's only sighting, however. When she was younger, she and her brother (between her and Carl in age), and some neighbor children were walking outside late one evening. They were near each other, and suddenly saw three strange lights in the cloudy night sky. One light separated from the others and approached the children. As they watched, they could see that it was a saucer-shaped UFO. When the craft was only twenty feet from them, directly overhead, the children saw a panel slide open. From the open panel they saw a tubular light beam telescope its way to the ground. They instantly found themselves surrounded by bright light as they huddled together, seeing how they were lit up. The light flooded them for three to five minutes as they feared that they were being examined or that their thoughts were being read. Carl's sister was especially concerned that because she was the oldest of the children, it was her responsibility to protect them. She assumed that although her father was working in an outbuilding on the farm, he was over a mile away, and would not hear their cries if they called for help.

As the children stood there huddled in the light beam, it never occurred to them to run. Carl's sister reports that her thought processes seemed to function normally, although she was terribly frightened, but she never thought to run the entire time. She says that there was no apparent physical abnormality about the light beam. It was not hot or cold, and she did not feel paralyzed or controlled. They just assumed they were being watched by someone with a much higher capacity than we have.

After three to five minutes in the light beam, the children saw it begin to retract. It telescoped up a ways—again, as though it were a solid conduit of something—then it "gathered itself and retracted into the UFO." When the light beam had reentered the UFO, the panel slid closed and the UFO joined the other two, and together they flew off into the clouds. This was another no-noise encounter.

This was not Carl's sister's first sighting. Years before she had spied a "shiny basketball-looking" sphere above a neighbor's house. She watched it for twenty minutes as it floated around the house. Although she kept calling for her mother or someone else to come and look at the shiny sphere, her mother could not get away from a chore and no one else was old enough to care. It took off in a great hurry, disappearing in the distance in a second or two.

Carl's older brothers had observed UFOs with their father on several occasions while working the farm at night. The family spoke often and openly about the UFOs that were visiting their area. Carl's father also worked at Thiokol for 28 years. This interested me. It is widely reported throughout the world that UFOs are often seen in the vicinity of aerospace facilities. I asked Carl if his father had ever reported these UFO sightings to his superiors, or if Thiokol had a policy requiring the reporting of such anomalous encounters or observations. Carl did not know, and his father died a few years ago. Carl's sister, however, says that she knew several Thiokol employees who had seen UFOs in the area, and knew that they had reported them.

Carl's sister relates the story of her friend who had an unusually close encounter in the valley. She was driving along in a pickup and watched a UFO come right down over her. She was especially surprised when the UFO landed right on the roof of the cab. With that, the pickup's engine died and all of the electronics went out. She experienced a blackout of her own, and when she regained consciousness the UFO was gone.

We see in Carl's account many of the classic UFO themes: an area frequented by UFOs; a family with multiple encounters; the classic double-convex craft with yellowish-red lights around the circumference of the hull; the UFOs moved without any sound, floating along in quiet observation; and rapid acceleration at unfathomable speed. What was different about the sighting, of course, was the mammoth size of the craft. Many observers report UFOs the size of football fields, or three times that size. These are thought to be very large by UFOlogists. A UFO approximately one mile in diameter, however, is a very rare sighting indeed. One staggers at the principles of science that allow such a craft to hover silently in Earth's atmosphere, disturbing nothing, creating no wind or other interference. Even more incredible is the propulsion system that propels such a monstrosity from 200 feet above the ground to high orbit in a brief second or two without a whisper of a sound, without a rush of displaced air, without a sonic boom, and without overheating the craft's hull.

Yet, the only difference between Carl's sighting and those of tens of thousands of others is the size of the UFO. Whatever principle is at work here fails to differentiate between ten-foot wide craft and those a mile wide.

Mary M.

Mary[11] is an active LDS Church member, and the grandmother of nine. She describes her husband as being quite active also (the finance clerk of

---

[11] I do not use Mary's full name herein, although she permitted me to use it. I base this decision on those issues raised in the main text below.

their ward) and very supportive of her throughout her many difficulties. I have reserved her experiences for the last for a couple of reasons. First, Mary is concerned that her experiences not be analyzed in Part III, wherein we discuss the various possible sources of UFO encounters. Second, Mary's more complex experiences are in the Betty Luca "high strangeness" range, and frankly, an abductee is never accepted in her own land—or in other words, her experiences push the very limits of believability.

This is not to say that Mary's experiences are anything but what they are represented to be. Frankly, however, due to the high strangeness of her encounters, I feel that much more inquiry is warranted. Therefore, I reproduce here only the more "common" aspects of Mary's experiences, leaving the complex issues to others. In my opinion, Mary has suffered criminally at the hands of an evil, unknown personage—not unlike many who report entity encounters—but in a way that warrants some kind of intervention. My full meaning manifests itself in Part III—I fear for Mary, and have told her as much.

In 1965, during the Watts Riots, is when I saw my first ship, that I remember seeing. At that time I was in Kernville, California, on vacation. My mother and I were stuck out at the park in Kernville [high mountains] all night, waiting for my dad to come out and pick us up. We packed up to leave because of people in the camp throwing firecrackers and shooting. We had five kids with us. We sat there from 7:00 o'clock at night until 7:00 o'clock in the morning. There wasn't room in the car for the kids and us, so my mother and I sat out on the curb.

At one point I looked up and I saw this star, and it looked like it was moving. I was watching it with binoculars. It looked like it was jumping up and down, moving back and forth. So I handed the binoculars to my mother and I said, "Look at that star and tell me what you see." She said, "If I wasn't so tired, I'd swear it was moving." We both figured we were tired, so we put the binoculars down and we didn't watch any more.

We were watching the road and counting the cars, and I looked over my left shoulder at one point to see if there were any cars coming, and it looked like the moon had gone out of orbit—it was a big, huge, white, moving object, and it was moving so fast that I didn't have time to say "Hey Mom, look!" I got "Hey Mom" out of my mouth, and the thing was gone. And it had to travel a distance of about 35 miles in that time. It went behind two mountain peaks, turned around, and came back, and went out of sight. I thought that was very strange, but I thought it must be a meteor. The Los Angeles Examiner carried a column that had talked about the new moon, and meteors going through, and comets, and when to expect them, so I thought it must be a meteor as big as that was, but it was never in the paper.

About a month later, a friend from Navy Intelligence came to me and said, "I know that you and your husband go camping a lot. What's up in the mountains that would scare a man half to death?" I said that there really was nothing that wouldn't kill him at the same time.

The Navy Intelligence officer told Mary that the Navy had taken a group of men up to Miracle Hot Springs that night a month before for a survival training course. She told him what she had seen that night, and he took the information back with him. He returned in one week and said that he "would play a guessing game" with her. He was not allowed to tell her what he knew, but in return for her help he would let her guess in three questions what he had learned about the traumatized enlisted man and the streaking moon. For every right answer he would go on talking to her husband, and if she was wrong, he would just answer no. At the conclusion of their guessing game, Mary had properly surmised that a crashed spaceship was involved. Beings were burned in it according to the traumatized Navy man, and had attempted to get help. She does not know if the military found or recovered the craft. Two years later the young man was still confined to the psychiatric unit at the Balboa Naval Hospital.

On June 28, 1970, Mary was travelling from California to Colorado. She watched a star move over Las Vegas headed toward Mesquite, Arizona. It got bigger, but she wasn't worried. Without filling in the informational gaps, Mary says that they eventually got under the "star," which was only 50 to 100 feet above the road at that time. "It was shaped like a flying wing in the front and was open in the back." It had protruding square things with black holes in the middle, coming from the bottom. It also had 10 to 15 lights in the front. The one-and-a-half-hour drive took four hours. They had two hours of missing time.

In 1985, Mary was in bed alone in a basement bedroom. She had not fallen asleep yet, and lay listening to a clicking noise in the kitchen just above her room. She assumed that it was her daughter, who was recovering from knee surgery, getting a drink. The noise continued and Mary finally got up (about 1:30 a.m.), thinking her daughter needed help with the drink of water.

Mary went upstairs. She stopped to check the front door as she passed. She also stopped in front of her daughter's bedroom as she went by, and saw no light under the door. She called through the door softly, but there was no answer from her daughter. She checked the back door, because they had found it open before, after locking it and going to bed. It was locked tight, with a leaded bat positioned against it to keep it closed.

When she turned around to go back, "there was this face peering around the corner from the hallway" at her. She was perplexed, thinking that someone had entered the locked house. She decided to turn on the light, and go through the dining area to the living room to try to catch the intruder—but there was someone blocking her path in that direction too. She woke up two hours later in bed, with no memory of what had happened after that. She weighed 180 pounds at the time, and her children could not have put her to bed.

Mary describes the "people" she saw as being small and hairless, with light or pale complexions. She had no thought of aliens at the time because she had not been exposed to the phenomenon or literature. Like many others, Mary complains that the above experiences were only disjointed memories, and none of them made any sense to her until she read *Communion*. "Then," she says, "it all hit me." After seeing the picture of the "small grey" faces on *Communion* and in other UFO books, she knows they are the same as her own intruders.

Beginning about two years ago, Mary began to experience the "high strangeness" encounters with UFO entities. I relate this aspect of these encounters here because it is fairly well documented that a "Big Foot" entity is associated with many UFO/entity encounters. I feel it prudent to add that the apparent association of Big Foot with UFOs does not necessarily exclude any other explanation of the Big Foot phenomenon. I feel that Big Foot could be exactly what it appears to be—a species of mammal that hides itself well in the forests of the world. Other explanations could be true. For example, because we know that at least one Big Foot creature presented itself to Apostle David W. Patten and introduced itself as Cain, there exists the possibility that the Big Foot species is, in fact, the race of Cain.[12] Whatever the true nature of the Big Foot, whatever is creating the UFO phenomenon could also be creating the Big Foot phenomenon as it relates to UFOs—that is, if the UFO phenomenon is merely a false "presentation" based on the true principle of interplanetary intercourse, the Big Foot/UFO phenomenon could be such a counterfeit of a true principle as well.

On the first occasion, Mary woke up from a sound sleep feeling someone holding her hand, very gently. She thought it was her husband until she saw his back turned toward her. She opened her eyes and saw "this big, hairy thing sitting beside me on the bed, holding my hand. I'm not usually a screamer, but that night I decided to scream!" It scared him, and he ran down the hallway and into the family room. Her husband did not wake up.

---

12 Lycurgus A. Wilson, *The Life of David W. Patten*, (Salt Lake City: Deseret News, 1900), pp. 46-47.

She lay there the rest of the night watching for the thing to return through the hallway—to come back to the bedroom or exit the house—but it never returned. When it became light outside, she went down the hallway to see, but nothing was in the family room.

Two weeks later Mary had some surgery, and woke up to find her hand being held again—the same gigantic hand as before. Due to her soreness, she decided not to risk being jolted by a fleeing creature, so she lay quietly.

Around the first of December she woke up to use the bathroom. It was cold, so she cuddled up behind her husband when she returned to bed. Within five minutes she felt something moving across the bed, and two large hands moving beneath her. She was lifted out of bed, and figuring it was this same Big Foot creature, she peeked just enough to confirm it. He lifted her gently, stepped back a few feet, and they rose right up through the floors and ceiling. She closed her eyes, and although she felt herself "moving up," she did not feel anything as they moved through the floors or ceiling.

Mary remarks, "When he picked me up I decided it was a good time to pray. I didn't know whether Satan had me, which was a distinct possibility." However, she felt that she was in no danger, and did not struggle. She remembers nothing between going up and coming down, but she remembers going up and coming down. When he returned her he put her back into bed, and held her hand again. She thought it wrong for a married woman to have her hand held like this, so she gently pulled it away—nicely enough, or so she thought. "But he evidently took it the wrong way, and he had to prove a point—that he was capable of hurting me if he wanted to, but didn't want to—and he jumped on top of me, and I have never seen anything move that fast. And when he did he didn't hurt me. He was on his knees on top of me."

At this point I pointed out that Big Foot reportedly weighs up to a half ton, and she responded that "He didn't put his weight on me, he just pinned me to the bed. When he did so his front teeth, whether it was in a mask or whether it was his own I don't know, but the teeth hit me in the forehead and my head hurt for three days afterwards where the teeth had hit."

These Big Foot apparitions continue, and Mary perceives that she has been repeatedly carried to a UFO, where she is given tasks to accomplish. Her experiences are filled with vivid detail—again, not unlike those of other percipients of the UFO phenomenon.

Mary and I discussed many possible sources of her experiences, including dream sequencing, hallucinations, mental disorders or diseases, and spiritual abuse. She is cognizant of these possibilities, and has considered them in turn many times. She says that she has discussed her experiences with her husband and Priesthood leaders. She relates their support, and general acceptance of the phenomenon. Although this surprises me somewhat, I am not privy to such counsel. I suggested that some kind of surreptitious monitoring might help her to establish what is occurring. Mary responds that it would not work, and anyone who attempted such a thing would risk serious harm. She says this, however, believing her abductors to be essentially benevolent, although she knows some are "evil."

Because of the concerns I raise in the remaining portion of this work, I hesitate to go further into Mary's experiences. As I said earlier—I fear for Sister Mary, and all who face her nightmare—whatever its source.

LDS Encounters Are Similar To Others'

The LDS close encounters included herein are representative of those being experienced by hundreds of Church members. From distant sightings of zig-zag lights in the night sky, to personal encounters with UFO beings bearing messages, the experiences of LDS Church members are no different than those of non-LDS individuals. Does this reveal anything about the origin or nature of the UFOs or their occupants? It could. Nothing conclusive comes to mind, however. The oddness is the same. The gaps in memory, likewise. Cruel abductions and examinations seem universal. In short, no UFO questions are answered by examining LDS encounters and comparing them with those experienced by non-LDS witnesses. Can such questions be answered? We make the attempt in the remaining chapters.

Part III
UFOs In
The
New Age

In Part I it was concluded that this universe is a vast cradle of human life, and that there is no limit to the number of Heavenly Father's children that inhabit it. We also discussed the very real possiblility that although there may be some slight deviation, people throughout the universe are more or less like we are in appearance and temporal conditions, including their religious and philosophical orientation. This is because they are set upon their individual planets to fulfill the same Plan of Salvation as ours. Then, in Part II we looked at the stark reality of the visitor phenomenon and its attendant message to mankind. Now, in Part III we analyze and synthesize the data, comparing them with revealed truth—weighing them in the balance. The nature of the visitors and their message give us clues about their origins. Can we learn the true idendity and purpose of the "aliens" with the information we have? We try in the remaining pages.

11

What Is The New Age?

A Brief History Of The New Age

To the uninitiated person the term "New Age" may hold little meaning—denominating a form of easy listening jazz music, perhaps, or indicating an "enlightened" viewpoint on complex social issues. The New Age is a movement of astronomical proportions and consequence, however, and it is incumbent upon every Latter-day Saint to understand the message and import of the New Age movement. Why we must gain this understanding and how it relates to the subject of extraterrestrial visitations to Earth will become apparent as we survey the beliefs and goals of the New Age movement and as we explore the purported purpose and message behind the wave of UFO visitations to Earth.

None of us can forget the decade of the 1960s. It saw, among other things, the birth of the free speech movement with its attendant mass protestation and denunciation of everything of traditional value. Lasting into the 1970s, vocal leaders, entertainers, and educators decried the avarice and savagery of the contemporary "establishment," demanding that love, peace, and global harmony supplant the evil cultural and governmental systems that oppressed the world. Traditional social and religious institutions were condemned as sponsors and advocates of the evil *status quo* and an entire generation of western civilization was instructed to "tune in, turn on, and drop out." The parts about turning on and dropping out were in reference to drugs and society, respectively—but the tuning-in portion of the mandate is of special interest to us here.

A new way of life was preached during this time of social and cultural revolution. Free expression, free love, and free lunch became the Holy Trinity of a new generation. The greed and guilt of the Picean Age were obsolete—the (precarious) Age of Aquarius was dawning. Its adherents looked to the East for direction. Zen Buddhism, Hinduism, astrology, astral projection,

168

transcendental meditation, Yoga, spiritualism, psychic surgery, globalism, holism, humanism, mysticism, numerology, iridology, and reincarnation became the elements of a new faith—the religion of Self.

Who Makes Up The New Age Movement?

The Aquarian Age of the 1970s went "main stream" in the 1980s, allowing traditionalists an opportunity to clean up after the "party" of the prior decades. The Aquarians did not die or fade away during this resurgence of conservatitism, they simply blended into the traditionalist landscape. They became the leaders of political movements and parties, education, and the media. They are comfortable wearing silk ties and pinstripes or blue jeans. They drive European sports cars and monitor the airwaves with Japanese electronics—there are no easily distinguishable delineations of wealth or preference. What the Aquarians have in common is their belief in, and devotion to, the New Age.

What Do New Agers Believe?

The New Age movement is a coalition of distinct, yet compatible, belief systems centered in the task of taking humankind from what it perceives is its current tier of evolution to the next. The next level of human evolution, according to New Agers, is not the imperceptible next rung of advancement that one would expect of natural evolution—it is a quantum leap in human ability and enlightenment. The seeming incongruity of this belief by those who so whole-heartedly embrace theories of natural evolution is resolved by an understanding that humankind will be catapulted into this next evolutionary phase through external assistance. The espoused source and means of this external aid constitutes the delineating distinctions among the various New Age groups,[1] but certain adhesive constants are shared by them all.

---

[1] The term "cults" would be more suitable in many instances.

New Agers accept man[2] as a spiritual being whose spirit is self-existent[3] and self-realizing.[4] They believe that Man's spirit is individually progressing through several successive episodes of mortality,[5] but is simultaneously a component of a universal psychic entity. According to New Agers, there are those, on this planet and others, who are currently at low levels of spiritual evolution, and those who are at higher levels. Some have acquired *very* high levels of spiritual attainment, and an elite handful have reached the very zenith of man's spiritual quest. And they believe that in order to progress spiritually, we must look within ourselves, not to another being (God). We are our own savior. Man must get in touch with the true person within him, then call on the abilities of that person to help him gain further enlightenment. Although this is an individual effort and quest, no one can find the way without guidance. Therefore, a spiritual guide (a spirit on a higher level of progress), acts as a guide on one's path to greater spiritual enlightenment. An initiate seeks to attain a state of spiritual openness by clearing his mind of worldly matters and concentrating inwardly. The initiate believes that when he reaches a point of "accommodation," wherein he can be "overshadowed" by a guiding spirit, he receives direct spiritual communication, knowledge, and enlightenment from his spirit guide.

New Age Gurus And God

To aid the millions of New Age practitioners in their quest for spiritual progress and enlightenment, a billion-dollar industry has arisen in the last decade. Miscellaneous Human Potential and Human Transformational organizations offering seminars and instructional cassette tapes have helped

---

2 The term "man" is, of course, used in a gender-neutral manner. This practice is generally unacceptable to New Agers because it fails to pay homage to their feminist branch, which desires to return to the glory days of goddess worship and matriarchal societies.

3 New Agers perceive themselves individually as "I am," or "I am that I am."

4 Self-realization is the journey and the end, culminating in personal deification—"god-realization."

5 Most New Agers believe that this progressive course is common reincarnation, the transmigration of one's spirit from a dying body to a birthing body.

millions to see the light of New Age techniques and practices.[6] They teach meditation and visualization, and they sell pyramids and crystals, complete with instructions on overcoming poor health or non-believers whose bad vibrations interfere with personal progress.

Although concepts like God and Jesus are often spoken of in New Age literature and practice, it is the universal consciousness or psychic organ to which New Agers refer when speaking of God. It is of their own individual spirits that New Agers refer to as God—they do not accept God, our Heavenly Father, as their God. Jesus, although accepted as an individual human, was not *the* Son of God. He was an important spiritual figure, however, an Ascended Master of spiritual enlightenment, teaching global peace and inner spiritualism. New Age gurus teach that Jesus spent a number of years in the East gaining spiritual enlightenment and mastering spiritual practices before beginning his ministry as recorded in the New Testament. They teach that He was not *the* Christ nor was he any more deified than anyone else of his advanced spiritual level. When he died, he reported to the more advanced Ones before continuing his journey in another body in another life. "Christ," to New Agers, is the Christ Consciousness that we each are, unrealized until we attain our Ultimate Consciousness.

The Christ "office" was held temporarily by Jesus of Nazareth according to New Age leaders, but no longer. It is now filled by those who are able to embody the consciousness of the true Messiah through spiritual enlightenment. The new Master, often referred to with names such as the One or the Universal Mind, directs the great global work of transforming humanity into a more highly evolved being. To reach "godrealization" or this ultimate consciousness sought by New Agers, gurus worldwide offer instruction and guidance. For example, one New Age yoga instructor offers a course entitled "Contacting the Tree of Life and the Tree of Knowledge." His brochure claims, "While meditating with another person, you die and enter the Garden of Eden. You see the Tree of Life and the Tree of Knowledge, surrendering to the great evolutionary intelligence to give you what you need."[7]

---

6 Many *Fortune 500* corporations have employed New Age firms to teach their techniques to employees. It is thought by New Age watchdogs that New Age "moles" have been planted in corporate human resource departments to proselytize converts by inviting New Age firms in to teach stress reduction and self-awareness clinics.

7 Bob Larson, *Straight Answers on the New Age,* p. 46.

When And How Will The New Age Arrive?

The New Age message is that this great evolutionary change will occur
in the year 2,000,[8] facilitating a "quantum leap in elevated brain power" that
will "result in an upward alteration in mankind's vibrational rate."[9] As Bob
Larson, one New Age observer explains:

> Many New Agers refer to our day as the Aquarian era—a time when a mass visitation
> of angels and Ascended Masters is occurring. Incidental intervention of higher beings
> in the past has become an invasion of elevated energies. Our brothers in the beyond
> want only to lead us to unlimited freedom and joy. If we heed the call, we can avoid
> annihilation and experience the "playground of existence," guided by the "life-force"
> of the universe.[10]

Of course, even New Agers realize that not all people are spiritually attuned
enough to make the evolutionary quantum leap. This group is made up of
what they refer to as Millennialists—those who hold tenaciously to the outdated
Jesus the Christ/Messiah belief, who believe that He will usher in the
Millennium as foretold in the Bible. In the New Age point of view, those
persons with such lower "vibratory rates" will not escape the great
annihilation, and approximately two billion of Earth's children will be
"eliminated" during the ushering in of this global harmonic period.[11] New
Age guru Ruth Montgomery is told by her spirit Guides that the cleansing
will be precipitated by "the coming shift of the earth on its axis, which they
say will occur near the close of this century, after a devastating war."[12]
Montgomery explains that UFOs will play a part in preserving the "enlightened
ones" to repopulate the Earth with good seed after the coming catastrophes.
"Although most Earthlings will lose their physical lives when the earth shifts

---

8 Interestingly, New Age idol Nostradamus, born in 1503, predicted in his work *Centuries:*
"In the year 1999 and 7 months, there will come from heaven the great king of terror,
to raise again the great king of the Mongols, before and after Mars shall reign at will."
New Agers see this as an opportunity for "The Plan" of the New Age to save mankind,
while occult observers see it as the One's attempt to put The Plan into effect.

9 *Straight Answers on the New Age*, p. 119. Speaking of the specific eating habits of some
New Agers, Bob Larson quotes "one macrobiotic proponent" as explaining: "Planet Earth
is surrounded by and immersed in a vibrational body of energy, which is conscious."
According to this New Age culinary guru proper diet places one in harmony with this
"etheric web of consciousness." At 83, *citing* "Michio Kushi's New Deal," *East West
Journal*, January 1976, p. 22.

10 *Ibid.*, pp. 104-05.

11 John Randolph Price, *Practical Spirituality*, (Austin, Texas: Quartus Books, 1985), pp.
18-19.

12 Ruth Montgomery, *Strangers Among Us*, p. 15.

on its axis at the close of this century, a good number of enlightened ones will be evacuated by the galactic fleets and returned to Earth for its rehabilitation."[13]

New Ager Barbara Marx Hubbard, in an unpublished work titled *New Age Commentary on the Book of Revelation,* terms those of a lower vibrational rate "the bad seed." Hubbard's spirit contact explains that the bad seed must be eliminated before the "paradigm shift" can occur. The paradigm shift is something of a code name for the coming shift in world-view, or the quantum leap in human evolution. More benevolent New Age writers explain that this purging will occur in a natural way—that a series of cataclysms will scourge the Earth, eliminating most of the unready. In the New Age view, these natural purgings will send the unprepared on to other lives wherein they may raise their innate vibrational levels and participate in the New Age after all, in another life. One less generous spirit contact declares:

> We have proven that all old religions are based on falsehood. Man is deity! Man is divine. When you bow and worship me you are worshipping the essential deity of all mankind. All who oppose this new unity are a cancer in the flesh of humanity and must be put to death for the greater good of all who remain.[14]

The supplanting of the *status quo* with the age of enlightenment is to be implemented through "The Plan." The Plan, according to New Age watch-dogs,[15] is a global secret combination led by powerful persons[16] dedicated to

---

[13] *Strangers Among Us,* p. 43.

[14] David Allen Lewis & Robert Shreckhise, UFO: *End-Time Delusion,* New Leaf Press, p. 172, *citing Tribulation.*

[15] Unfortunately, most of the information being disseminated to expose the New Age movement comes from fundamentalist Christian writers who are little more enlightened than lower-level New Age participants. These writers often lump the restored Gospel with New Age beliefs on the supposition that any belief that differs from their own is necessarily founded in the occult. One LDS writer, Derrick T. Evenson, has published a New Age whistle-blowing book under the pseudonym Troy Lawrence, titled *Lord Maitreya— The New Age Christ Identified.* He evidently used a pseudonym to enable the publication of his book in "Christian" markets, but has recently been challenged as a "closet Mormon" by Texe Marrs, the Fundamentalist New Age watchdog. (*Flashpoint,* May 1992.) Lord Maitreya is reported by many to be the great Ascended Master who will take the reigns of world governments and religions pursuant to The Plan.

[16] Not only are these men said to be wealthy and politically well-connected, but are self proclaimed to be of superior makeup—mentally and spiritually. They are worshipped as "supermen" by the New Age elite insiders who are aware of the full import of The Plan. This belief in a race of supermen that will lead the world into the Aquarian Age is of great importance in light of the New Age message of UFOs, as discussed below.

Antichrist and his world reign, who are carefully orchestrating global implementation of New Age dogma and practices. The Plan holds no place for the traditional family, free enterprise, nationalism, or Christianity—all relics of the Picean Age.

The New Age Movement Is Pervasive

The New Age movement is not limited to those who indulge in ouija boards and crystal balls. All of those who believe that the planets have an influence on their lives and daily examine their horoscopes, a large percentage of the American population,[17] make up a branch of the New Age. Of course, most New Age participants are unaware of the ultimate designs of the New Age elite. It would be truly paranoid to think that hundreds of millions of people are "in" on a global plot to usher in Antichrist. However, hundreds of millions do follow people whose designs are to facilitate the New Age advent of a "new race" of humanity. Only the New Age elite insiders know who is at the helm. Although lower level participants have little knowledge of The Plan, they enthusiastically proselytize new converts to the movement. Tarot readings and dial-a-psychic services have proliferated exponentially, while trance channeling has empowered New Agers with the ability to reach out and touch *everyone.*[18]

Most Eastern religions already fit nicely into the New Age movement, they being the source of most of its beliefs and practices, and their leaders are often its leaders. Satanic cults, much more widespread than commonly thought, have moved from their traditional South American stronghold into

---

[17] More than 50 million according to a recent Gallup poll.

[18] Trance-channelling, acting as a medium for a disembodied spirit, now allows each New Ager to speak with anyone, anywhere, to gain the spiritual enlightenment sought. Although famous spiritual leaders of the past (and future) are always popular contactees through channelers, extraterrestrials, Atlanteans, and ocean mammals are chic. Approximately 15% of Americans in 1987 believed in trance mediums according to a *USA Today* poll. (Monica Collins, "Not Some Spaced-Out California Concept," *USA Today,* 16 January 1987, p. 1A.) Channelers have received wide recognition by the media since 1987, and anyone with a telephone can be in contact with a dolphin from a distant planet in only a minute for a channeling fee of $25 to $100. A University of Chicago poll shows that 67% of Americans believe they have had a psychic experience. (Art Levine, "Mystics on Main Street," *U.S. News & World Report,* 9 February 1987, vol. 102, no. 5, p. 67.) A Gallup poll of students 16 to 18 years old showed that they too are believers: 51% believe in astrology; 62% in ESP; 24% in witchcraft; and 21% in ghosts.

North America with surprising speed and potency. Because New Age ideologies are generally intertwined with references to God or Jesus, or at least the Supreme Creator, many liberal Protestant churches or their members have been enticed into the fold. Never has the concept of "the doctrines of men, mingled with scripture" had such practical application as in the New Age movement.

The New Age pervades Western culture nearly as potently as its Eastern counterpart has dominated that hemisphere's religious sects for millennia. From film and television stars to top political leaders, the New Age receives widespread endorsements daily around the world. The Plan is progressing as planned, and the One, or the Universal Mind, or whatever name is given to the implementing persona of the New Age movement, is poised to step in as soon as the opportunity presents itself. According to New Age beliefs, the opportunity will come in the form of a global cataclysm, either natural or manmade.[19] At that time, only the One and his New Age elite will be able to offer mankind the helping hand required to get us through the colossal difficulties imposed by the catastrophe. Those who resist will be adjudged incompatible, even obstructive, and will have to be eliminated for the good of the whole, because in the New Age, "All is One, and One is All." There is no room for dissension—that would not be harmonious.

Earth Spirit

Many New Agers believe that the Earth is a living being—the goddess Gaia.[20] According to them, Gaia is communicating with "Ascended Masters of the Hierarchy of the universe."[21] "They believe that soon our 'space brothers' will raise a human leader from our midst whom they will endow with supernormal powers and wisdom. This man will lead the world to global government and world peace." Many at this time will be imbued with super-human, paranormal abilities for the purpose of facilitating the ushering in

---

[19] Trance channeling and other forms of participation in the occult traditionally peak during times of crisis and uncertainty.

[20] It is, of course, our understanding that the Earth is indeed a living creature of God, possessing a spirit. The "Green Goddess" belief of the New Age, however, holds that the Earth is more than a living creature, it is a goddess—having power, being self-willed, and is anxious to facilitate the transformation of humans into the New Age.

[21] *UFO: End-Time Delusion,* p. 16.

of the Aquarian era. Those of a more cultic bent believe that Gaia will be
impregnated by the Sun, giving birth to the superhuman manchild. This
superhuman leader will help us solve all of our worldly problems—hunger,
poverty, crime, pollution, war, and nuclear and industrial contamination.
He will lead the world from its present course of self destruction and from
the ecological and economic siege it will soon be under, into the New Age,
the Aquarian Age of peace and prosperity. But first, the Earth will experience
a "cleansing" of those who are incompatible with the New Age, in which
cleansing Gaia will willingly cooperate.

Is the New Age and its goals something that Latter-day Saints should take
seriously? New Age author Brad Steiger, quotes Constable, a New Age Guide,
as stating:

> Man will win or lose the battle for Earth itself, for he is at once the goal of the battle
> and the battleground . . . . The stakes in this battle are not the territory, commercial
> advantages, or political leverage of ordinary wars, but the mind, soul, and destiny of
> man.[22]

A survey of modern television programming and motion picture themes
demonstrates that New Age dogma is indeed saturating our culture. Morbidity
is fast becoming a favorite theme—vampires, the current craze, are said to
fulfill our spiritual, sexual, and violence needs all at once.[23] *The Psychology
Today* article that speaks to this subject bills its article, "Pop Culture's Occult
Boom: The Sudden, Curious Allure of Vampires." The article was published
in 1989 and things have worsened since then. The 1992 motion picture release
schedule was likewise filled with death, occult violence, and the fulfillment
of abnormal passions and appetites. Ready or not, the New Age is coming.

A UFO/New Age Connection

It is not too difficult to perceive a very close tie between the apparent message
of the space brothers, as revealed through early contactees and channelers,
and the message of the New Age movement. At this point, the New Age is
so inextricably intertwined with the UFO phenomenon that it is impossible
to distinguish where one ends and the other begins. Shirley MacLaine, the
formerly popular actress who has become a well-known New Age spokes-

---

22 *The UFO Abductors,* p. 212.

23 *Psychology Today,* "Hunger for the Marvelous: The Vampire Craze in the Computer
Age," Katherine Ramsland, November 1989.

person predicted, as did spiritual guides, that during the filming of the television movie based on her book *Out On a Limb,* UFOs would appear. They failed to materialize, leaving MacLaine and the Masters of the Universe to explain that the failure resulted from the low vibrational rates of nonbelievers associated with the project.

For two decades a melding of the New Age, UFOlogy, and western culture has been occurring—even our pop music has been lighting the galactic way to help our youth discover for themselves how to be ready when we are finally contacted and enlightened, as directed in a popular song that instructs:

> *With your mind you have ability*
> *you know*
> *To transmit thought messages*
> *through the vast unknown,*
> *Just close your eyes, and concentrate,*
> *that's the way, you see,*
> *Upon this recitation we're about to sing*
>
> *(Chorus)*
> *Calling occupants, of interplanetary craft*
> *Calling occupants, of interplanetary craft*
> *Calling occupants, of interplanetary,*
> *most extraordinary craft*
>
> *(Alien Response)*
> *We've been observing your Earth*
> *And one day we'll make contact with you,*
> *We are your friends.*

12

A Gospel View
Of The New Age

Discerning The New Age

The prior chapter presented an overview of what New Age writers and critics alike consider to be the salient tenets and goals of the New Age movement. The reader will certainly recognize the disturbing similarities between these New Age beliefs and aims and the predicted pre-Second Coming prophecies concerning Antichrist's conquest and rule over the Earth. Because many good books are currently in print outlining the predicted events precursing the Second Coming, I will not attempt here to detail most of those events. However, because of the exceptional subtlety and cunning with which many of the premillennial events and operations will be implemented, even numerous of the elite of the Kingdom (five of the ten virgins) will be deceived by Antichrist.[1] Therefore, some discussion regarding the prophets' teachings concerning the latter days is appropriate before continuing with the New Age/UFO connection.

Reincarnation—A Doctrine Of The Devil

First, the doctrine of reincarnation constitutes the very foundation of New Age philosophy. As with all false doctrines, that of reincarnation, or the transmigration of the spirit from one body to another in successive life-

---

[1] For in those days there shall also arise false Christs, and false prophets, and shall show great signs and wonders, insomuch, that, if possible, they shall deceive the very elect, who are the elect according to the covenant." (*Joseph Smith* Matthew 1:22)

episodes, is a Satanic counterfeit of the true principle of "eternal progress."[2] The Prophet Joseph Smith taught this doctrine in connection with a man to whom he had offered lodging, who called himself Matthias. As Joseph discerned the man's spirit, he became concerned and questioned him:

> I resumed conversation with Matthias, and desired him to enlighten my mind more on his views respecting the resurrection.
>
> He said that he possessed the spirit of his fathers, that he was a literal descendant of Matthias, the Apostle, who was chosen in the place of Judas that fell; that his spirit was resurrected in him; and that this was the way or scheme of eternal life" this transmigration of soul or spirit from father to son. [*Teachings of the Prophet Joseph Smith*, p. 105]

Having heard this, Joseph quickly discerned the problem:

> I told him that his doctrine was of the devil, that he was in reality in possession of a wicked and depraved spirit, although he professed to be the Spirit of truth itself; and he said also that he possessed the soul of Christ.
>
> He tarried until Wednesday, 11th, when, after breakfast, I told him, that my God told me, that his god was the devil, and I could not keep him any longer, and he must depart . . . . (Nov. 9, 1835.) *History of the Church*, vol. 2, pp. 304-07. [*Ibid.*]

It is significant that although Joseph had properly diagnosed the spiritual problem, he sought Heavenly Father's counsel concerning what to do with this misguided fellow. The answer was direct—his god was the devil, and Joseph must cast him out.

Joseph's response to Matthias also clarifies the nature of the second controlling substructure of the New Age—guidence from spirits on a higher level of existence. New Agers say that without the helping hand of more exalted spirits reaching down to guide and enlighten, man cannot progress to higher spiritual planes—the essential element of eternal progress. Through meditation, chanting, and focusing, practitioners claim to receive spiritual communications, knowledge, and ultimate truth from ascended spirits. If the direct connection is too difficult initially, beginners seek the aid of channelers who bring the spirit to them, thereby opening the channels of communication.

Channelers and practitioners all claim that they are merely "overshadowed" by these Ascended Masters, but deny that they are "possessed" by them. Again, Joseph instructs that those who consort with these extramortal

---

[2] Caution is urged at the use of the term "eternal progress" due to misguided attempts to demonstrate that God is not perfect because progress is eternal, and He is, therefore, still progressing. We are to understand that personal development ceases at some point after the resurrection, although the proliferation of one's personal kingdom, or stewardship, continues forever—hence, "eternal" progress.

providers of such mystical knowledge are "in possession of a wicked and depraved spirit." True to the New Age conviction, Matthias retorted that he was not possessed by an evil spirit, but in fact, professed to be "the Spirit of truth itself." He added to this claim of personal supernatural status that he "possessed the soul of Christ," which is also one of the most familiar assertions of the New Age. God instructed the Prophet Joseph Smith that Satan was the purveyor of such doctrines, and to cast out such that accept them.

Satan's Influence And Deception Have Flanked The Restoration

The similarities of Matthias's claims and beliefs to those of the New Age movement are almost uncanny. However, all it demonstrates is that Satan's tactics change very little over time. Matthias was not unique in his day. The occult existed then as it does now. Even in the early Church, Joseph was obliged on several occasions to correct many who were deceived by evil spirits. He records the difficulty himself:

> Soon after the Gospel was established in Kirtland, and during the absence of the authorities of the Church, many false spirits were introduced, many strange visions were seen, and wild, enthusiastic notions were entertained; men ran out of doors under the influence of this spirit, and some of them got upon the stumps of trees and shouted, and all kinds of extravagances were entered into by them . . . .
>
> There have also been ministering angels in the Church which were of Satan appearing as an angel of light. A sister in the state of New York had a vision, who said it was told her that if she would go to a certain place in the woods, an angel would appear to her. She went at the appointed time, and saw a glorious personage descending, arrayed in white, with sandy colored hair; he commenced and *told her to fear God,* and said that her husband was called to do great things, but that he must not go more than one hundred miles from home, or he would not return; whereas God had called him to go to the ends of the earth, and he has since been more than one thousand miles from home, and is yet alive. Many true things were spoken by this personage, and many things that were false. [*Teachings of the Prophet Joseph Smith,* p. 214]

Satan maneuvers men with subtle deception, filled with half-truths and half-lies, designed to lead them far enough astray to make them lose sight of the light of truth. Then, when darkness surrounds them, it is almost impossible for men to find their way back. The deceived Korihor confessed:

> But behold, the devil hath deceived me; for he appeared unto me in the form of an angel, and said unto me: Go reclaim this people, for they have all gone astray after an unknown God. And he said unto me: There is no God; yea, and he taught me that which I should say. And I have taught his words; and I taught them because they were pleasing unto the carnal mind; and I taught them, even until I had much success,

insomuch that I verily believed that they were true; and for this cause I withstood the truth, even until I have brought this great curse upon me. [Alma 30:53]

Korihor would have felt very comfortable as an agent of the New Age movement. The message and tactics of his time are the very same that we find escalating today.

Satan's Tactics Have Not Changed

Joseph Smith further instructs us that these same New Age/Satanic machinations have existed throughout the history of the Earth:

> It is evident from the Apostles' writings, that many false spirits existed in their day, and had "gone forth into the world," and that it needed intelligence which God alone could impart to detect false spirits, and to prove what spirits were of God. The world in general have been grossly ignorant in regard to this one thing, and why should they be otherwise—for "the things of God knoweth no man, but the Spirit of God."
>
> The Egyptians were not able to discover the difference between the miracles of Moses and those of the magicians until they came to be tested together; and if Moses had not appeared in their midst, they would unquestionably have thought that the miracles of the magicians were performed through the mighty power of God, for they were great miracles that were performed by them—a supernatural agency was developed, and great power manifested . . . .
>
> There always did, in every age, seem to be a lack of intelligence pertaining to this subject. Spirits of all kinds have been manifested, in every age, and almost among all people. If we go among the pagans, they have their spirits; the Mohammedans, the Jews, the Christians, the Indians—all have their spirits, all have a supernatural agency, and all contend that their spirits are of God . . . .
>
> One great evil is, that men are ignorant of the nature of spirits; their power, laws, government, intelligence, etc., and imagine that when there is anything like power, revelation, or vision manifested, that it must be of God. [*Teachings of the Prophet Joseph Smith*, pp. 202-203]

In reality, every false teaching and incorrect precept in the world is a product of Satan's attempt to lead men astray. He does not tell big lies to lead us to error, not initially anyway—they are too easily detected. Satan takes Gospel truth, and changes it just enough to convey an untruth. Why does he carry on this incessant campaign of deception? His entire design is to trick humanity into worshipping him as the Universal Master, thereby owning their souls: "And he became Satan, yea, even the devil, the father of all lies, to deceive and to blind men, and to lead them captive at his will, even as many as would not hearken unto my voice." (Moses 4:4.) The insightful book *Commentary on the Pearl of Great Price* remarks on this scripture:

> But, after all exegetical comments have been made; after a critical explanation of this portion of scripture we are forced to say: "It does not matter to Satan, who is the

devil, what we believe or what we do not, as long as we do not believe in Jesus Christ, Whose adversary the devil was from the beginning."

Ever since he rebelled against divine authority and therefore was cast out of heaven, Satan has carried on a ruthless, yet abortive attempt to thwart the purposes of the Lord God. [At pp. 133-34]

Satan Will Succeed For A Time

The latter-day deception of Satan will be successful—for a time, in any case. Satan will indeed take the reigns of world government and religions because precious few will be capable of discerning his methods or withstanding his power. Of Satan's special latter-day representative, Antichrist, Bruce R. McConkie wrote: "This great antichrist which is to stand as the antagonist of Christ in the last days, and which is to be overthrown when he comes to cleanse the earth and usher in millennial righteousness, is the church of the devil (Rev. 13; 17), with the man of sin at its head. (2 Thess. 2:1-12)" (*Mormon Doctrine,* p. 40) To counter the latter-day outpouring of the Lord's Spirit upon His people Zion, as prophesied by the prophet Joel,[3] Satan will counterfeit the phenomenon with an escalation of his own spiritualism, to show the world that he is indeed the god of this world.

And I beheld another beast coming up out of the earth; and he had two horns like a lamb, and he spake as a dragon. And he exerciseth all the power of the first beast before him, and causeth the earth and them which dwell therein to worship the first beast, whose deadly wound was healed. And he doeth great wonders, so that he maketh fire come down from heaven on the earth in the sight of men, And deceiveth them that dwell on the earth by *the means of* those miracles which he had power to do in the sight of the beast; saying to them that dwell on the earth, that they should make an image to the beast, which had the wound by a sword, and did live. And he had power to give life unto the image of the beast, that the image of the beast should both speak, and cause that as many as would not worship the image of the beast should be killed. [Revelation 13:11-15]

And I saw three unclean spirits like frogs *come* out of the mouth of the dragon, and out of the mouth of the beast, and out of the mouth of the false prophet. For they are the spirits of devils, working miracles, *which* go forth unto the kings of the earth and of the whole world, to gather them to the battle of that great day of God Almighty. [Revelation 16:13-14]

Fundamentalist writers believe that the "amphibious" appearance of these spirits and the fire from Earth's orbit will indicate "alien" origins.

---

[3] "And it shall come to pass afterward, *that* I will pour out my spirit upon all flesh; and your sons and your daughters shall prophesy, your old men shall dream dreams, your young men shall see visions: And also upon the servants and upon the handmaids in those days will I pour out my spirit." (Joel 2:28-29)

Billions Are "Anxiously Engaged"

The scriptures tell us that one third of the hosts of heaven were cast out, down to the Earth with their master Satan. Assuming that a proportionate number of these evil spirits are assigned (or confined) to this planet, at any given moment there are approximately 35 billion[4] Satanic spirits on Earth carrying out the will of their evil master (six or seven per mortal person);" a staggering consideration indeed. Their task is to lead men's souls into the spiritual captivity of their master, Satan. Their method is to trick men through deceit into following after false gods and foresaking their own Heavenly Father—rejecting Him by rejecting His gospel, His commandments, and thereby rejecting His promised reward of exaltation and eternal life. To ancient Israel the Lord commanded that anyone who communed with such spirits was to be avoided by the people of Israel, and was to be "put to death."

> When thou art come into the land which the Lord thy God giveth thee, thou shall not learn to do after the abominations of those nations. There shall not be found among you *any one* that maketh his son or his daughter to pass through the fire, *or* that useth divination, or an observer of times, or an enchanter, or a witch. Or a charmer, or a consulter with familiar spirits, or a wizard, or a necromancer.[5] For all that do these things *are* an abomination unto the Lord: and because of these abominations the Lord thy God doth drive them out from before thee. [Deuteronomy 18:9-12]

> A man also or a woman that hath a familiar spirit, or that is a wizard, shall surely be put to death: they shall stone them with stones: their blood *shall be* upon them. [Leviticus 20:27; Exodus 22:18]

Some visionaries of the Restoration have been permitted to look through the veil into the regions of the spirit world. Although they describe the beautiful spiritual planet that occupies the same physical space (or parallel space) as the Earth and the wonders and exalted personages that are present there, they

---

4 This number represents one half of the estimated 70 billion that have lived on Earth in mortality thus far, equaling one third of the total 105 billion (70 billion + 35 billion). Granted, this line of reasoning assumes that we are dealing with fixed numbers when referring to the two thirds and the one third of preexistent spirits. That is, we assume that in the Grand Council in Heaven wherein Jehovah and Lucifer presented their opposing plans, leading to rebellion and war, that only the population of this Earth was represented at that particular Council. If this is true, the numbers are fixed. If, however, all of God's spiritual offspring were there present, the numbers would not necessarily be fixed, although the percentages probably would be. The latter scenario is probably not the case, however, due to the evergrowing numbers of God's spiritual offspring, e.g., tomorrow's offspring, to be assigned to a future planet, were not present at the Council.

5 Each of these forbidden professions is very much a part of the New Age movement, and is professed to be necessary to bring one to a higher plane of enlightenment and elevated spirituality.

also describe the malicious, hateful demons that occupy that plane in great numbers, entirely devoted to our personal destruction. These are the spirits that answer the call of mediums and trance channelers, who teach men that there is no God and no devil—no good and no evil. They are "anxiously engaged" in their great cause to destroy the Plan of Salvation and Exaltation, supplanting it with their own master's Plan—to overthrow God and His Son, by thwarting their work and glory, "to bring to pass the immortality and eternal life of man." (Moses 1:39)

Brigham Young warned the Saints that the power of Satan was expanding in the world. In his unique way, he explained that only the power of the priesthood could keep such spirits at bay.

> Why do we lay hands on the sick? Is there virtue in doing so? There is, and the wicked world as well as the Saints prove this. Since Joseph Smith received revelations from God, Spiritualism has taken its rise, and has spread with unprecedented rapidity; and they will lay hands on each other—one system proving another—spiritualism demonstrating the reality of animal magnetism? Is there virtue in one person more than another? Power in one more than another? Spirit in one more than another? Yes, there is. I will tell you how much I have. You may assemble together every spiritualist on the face of the earth, and I will defy them to make a table move or get a communication from hell or any other place while I am present. [*Journal of Discourses,* vol. 14, p. 72]

The Priesthood—Man's Only Protection

Joseph Smith was quite concerned for those who would be on the Earth during this time of temporal and spiritual upheaval. His mandate to preach the Gospel to everyone in an effort to bring them to Zion was imperative in his time, and is the only means of sparing men a portion of the ravages of Antichrist in our time. Joseph relates that Satan's deception will be so clever, so sophisticated, that only those who possess the Priesthood will be able to detect him.

> Or who can drag into daylight and develop the hidden mysteries of the false spirits that so frequently are made manifest among the Latter-Day Saints? We answer that *no man can do this without the Priesthood, and having a knowledge of the laws by which spirits are governed;* for as no man knows the things of God, but by the Spirit of God, so no man knows the spirit of the devil, and his power and intelligence, which is more than human, and having unfolded through the medium of the Priesthood the mysterious operations of his devices; without viewing the angelic form, the sanctified look and gesture, and the zeal that is frequently manifested by him for the glory of God, together with the prophetic spirit, the gracious influence, the godly appearance, and the holy garb, which are so characteristic of his proceedings and his mysterious windings.

A man must have the discerning of spirits before he can drag into daylight this hellish influence and unfold it unto the world in all its soul-destroying, diabolical, and horrid colors; *for nothing is a greater injury to the children of men than to be under the influence of a false spirit when they think they have the Spirit of God.* Thousands have felt the influence of its terrible power and baneful effects. Long pilgrimages have been undertaken, penances endured, and pain, misery and ruin have followed in their train; nations have been convulsed, kingdoms overthrown, provinces laid waste, and blood, carnage and desolation are habiliments in which it has been clothed. [*Teachings of the Prophet Joseph Smith,* pp. 204-05, emphasis supplied]

Although portions of the Church *may* escape some of the ill-effects of this premillennial black cauldron, most of the world will be under Satan's power as foretold by the scriptures: "for by [Satan's] sorceries were all nations deceived." (Revelation 18:23) Speaking prospectively of the time when Satan's premillennial kingdom would be overthrown, the Apostle John prophesied that Christ would eventually deliver the world from Satan's grasp: "And [Christ] cast him into the bottomless pit, and shut him up, and set a seal upon him, that he should deceive the nations no more, till the thousand years should be fulfilled: and after that he must be loosed a little season." (Revelation 20:3)

The New Age Will Bring Antichrist To Power

The scriptures, ancient and modern, speak of these events with great clarity. Numerous are the verses that detail the rise of Satan to power. Explicit are the details outlining the conditions that will enable his rise to world dominion, and the state of the people of the Earth during his reign. Although not fully explored herein, the reader is exhorted to pursue knowledge concerning these late Sixth Seal and early Seventh Seal events which will preceed the Second Coming.[6] So doing, he or she will be better prepared to withstand the tremendous pressures which will be exerted to force all people to participate in Satan's premillennial kingdom.

The New Age movement appears to be the vehicle, or a preeminent component at least, by which Satan will establish his premillenial kingdom. The "Network," as New Agers call it, is being put into place even now, awaiting a natural or economic, or some other kind of international catastrophe that will

---

6 In the Revelation, Chapter 6, John witnesses Christ opening the first six seals attached to the book containing the complete history of the 7,000 year temporal existence of this Earth. (*D & C* 77:6.) Each of the seven seals represents important events pertaining to each of the seven thousand year periods making up the Earth's temporal existence. (*D & C* 77:7)

render the world's sovereign nations vulnerable to takeover. The scriptures are quite clear that the premillenial difficulties enumerated in the Sixth Seal portion of the Book of Revelation will supply just such a worldwide crisis.[7] When this occurs, family, religion, and life as we know them will become relics of the Picean Age—that outdated time when Jesus was thought to be the only Christ—the Savior of this broken world.

What does all of this have to do with UFOs? Although it is not yet clear, the occupants of the UFOs, whoever they really are, together with their earthly agents have been sending us a strong message that they may be very much involved with the coming Aquarian Age.

---

[7] We now live near the very end of the sixth period, whose events are contained in the sixth seal of the book, which events have not yet occurred (although some commentators feel that *some* may have occurred out of sequence). A thorough study of the sixth seal events leads us to understand that a devastating worldwide earthquake (and resulting related cataclysmic events) will trigger many of the premillennial catastrophes outlined therein, and will certainly facilitate the breakdown of current social, political, and economic systems.

13
Paranormal Properties
Of UFOs

UFOs Are Not What They Appear To Be

As quoted above, New Age author Brad Steiger has observed, "A historical survey reveals that reports of strange objects in the skies are laced through documents of the ancient and recent past. Interestingly, the records seem to indicate that UFOs have adapted themselves to the cultural milieu and the technological capacities of the observers."[1] Steiger's commentary correctly establishes not only the longterm status of the UFO phenomenon, but also its ephemeral, transitory nature. UFOs and their occupants are thought by many to be chameleons—apparitions of something else—something capable of producing supernatural effects in our environment and hallucinatory images in our minds. We discuss these properties in this chapter, and analyze them in the remaining two chapters.

Concerning the ephemeral, or paranormal nature of UFOs, Dr. Jacques Vallee concludes after 30 years of UFO research: "I believe that a UFO is both a physical entity with mass, inertia, volume, and physical parameters that we can measure, and a window into another reality. Is this why witnesses can give us at the same time a consistent factual narrative and a description of contact with forms of life that fit no acceptable framework? These forms of life, such as the small grey men seen by Kathie, may be real, yet a product of our dreams. Like our dreams, we can look into their hidden meaning, or we can ignore them."[2] This conclusion is significant, and seemingly grandiose for a mystery that most people feel was solved decades ago. Although important and exciting, the extraterrestrial nuts-and-bolts origin of UFOs is widely accepted and offers an explanation that most people have come to accept as "comfortable." Dr. Vallee's conclusion, however, appears to place

---

[1] *The UFO Abductors*, p. 212.

[2] *Dimensions*, p. 224.

the enigma into an unfamiliar paradigm, one with which the masses are uncomfortable—for good reason.

Dr. J. Allen Hynek was originally a scientific skeptic working for the American military, and set out to debunk UFO stories. After much exposure to the UFO phenomenon he became a leading advocate of the extraterrestrial spacecraft theory. However, after reviewing facts like those presented herein, he finally came to think that UFOs may have a paranormal or supernatural origin:

> I would have to say that the extraterrestrial theory is a naive one. It's the simplest of all hypotheses, but not a very likely explanation for the phenomenon we have seen manifesting itself for centuries. In Toronto, Canada, not too long ago, I spoke before a group of liberalthinking scientists who had gathered for a serious discussion on the latest discoveries in the field of parapsychology. The conference was sponsored by the New Horizons Research Foundation that is ably presided over by Dr. George Owen, a former fellow of Trinity College, Cambridge, England. I told these astute men of learning—including a respected Nobel Prize winner in physics—that we should consider the various factors that strongly suggest a linkage, or at least a parallelism, with the occurrences of a paranormal nature. Among the factors that belie the interplanetary theory is the proneness of certain individuals to have repeated UFO experiences. Another peculiarity is the alleged ability of certain UFOs to dematerialize. A plasma is said to envelope the object in many cases. Then the "cloud" becomes more and more opaque until it completely obscures the UFO. Finally the whole cloud vanishes as though going into another dimension . . . . There are quite a few reported instances where two distinctly different UFOs hovering in a clear sky will converge and eventually merge into one object. These are the types of psychic phenomena that are confronting us in the UFO mystery.[3]

The following account helps to illustrate just how far from "explainable" the UFO phenomenon remains.

The Healing Of Dr. "X"

The fast-paced evolution of the paranormal aspects of UFO sightings and encounters was noticeable as early as the 1960s. One case, reported by LDS UFO researcher Dr. Frank B. Salisbury in his book *The Utah UFO Display*,[4] relates just how metaphysical the phenomenon is becoming. This particular

---

[3] J. Allen Hynek interview, *UFO Report Magazine*, August 1976, p. 61.

[4] *The Utah UFO Display: A Biologist's Report*, pp. 211-18. The full report of the incident is published in the *Flying Saucer Review:* Aime Michel, 1969, Special Issue No. 3, September, "UFO Percipients," *Flying Saucer Review;* and *Flying Saucer Review,* November-December, 1971, No. 17, (6):39.

encounter was especially intriguing because it was the best investigated of its era. The witness was a political figure and Ph.D. in his town in the southeast of France, and the physical evidence was well documented as well as overwhelming. The witness, known as Dr. "X" in UFO literature, chose to remain anonymous at the time because of his political standing, but he was personally known to some of the best scientific investigators in UFO research, and was perceived to be completely credible. Salisbury relates the experience as follows:

During the Algerian War, he was caught in a mine blast (May 13, 1958), and after several months of recuperation was left with a hemiparesis on the whole of his right side. He could not stand on his right foot unassisted, and he lost much of the use of his right arm, making it nearly impossible for him to play the piano, which he had formerly done very well—and, as we shall see, was able to do again.

On October 29th, 1968, as he was chopping a stump on his property, a slip caused the stump to strike the front edge of the left tibia, producing a superficial wound with a broken vein that led to enough swelling to deform the trouser leg and to cause intense pain. In spite of antibiotics and drugs administered to reduce the inflammation, the wound was extremely painful and the swelling extensive. This was on the night of November first just before the sighting.

Some time before four in the morning of November 2nd, the doctor's fourteen-month-old child calls out. He is expressing the onomatopoeic sounds by which he designates everything shining—a sort of *rho! rho!* The doctor arises (his wife remains asleep), fills the empty feeding bottle, and gives it to the baby. The baby is pointing at the window where periodic flashes of light are showing around the edges of the shutters. The doctor is preoccupied with the pain in his leg and pays little attention to this phenomenon. He hears a shutter banging on an upstairs window and, after painfully making his way up the stairs, gets his first look at the countryside. It is being illuminated by flashes of pale light about the color and intensity of the full moon. The wind is blowing and a storm is brewing, so he at first thinks of lightning, but the flashes are coming at intervals of about a second in a manner quite atypical of lightning. He cannot see the source of the light from this window, so he returns to the kitchen, pours himself half a glass of cold water from the refrigerator (indicating how low his level of excitement remains at this point!), and then makes his way onto the terrace. The clock in the kitchen reads 3:55 a.m.

As he steps onto the terrace, he finally sees the source of the flashing light: it is coming from two luminous objects hovering at some distance to his right. The objects have the double convex form reported by several Uintah Basin witnesses. The top half is a luminous silvery white, but not as brilliant as the full moon; the bottom half is a deep sunset red, brighter at the top than at the bottom. Two "antennas" extend out horizontally, one from each edge of each object. A third antenna on each object is located at top center and is perfectly vertical . . . .

A vertical, cylindrical, white shaft of light is coming from the lower center point of each object. It illuminates the thin mist hanging in the valley below his home. As soon as the doctor steps on to his terrace and notices the objects, they begin to move to the left and toward him. In a moment or two, the points where the two light beams strike the ground can be seen at the top of a small hill. From then on as the objects flash on and off with their one-second periodicity, illuminating the surrounding country side (up to a distance of a few kilometers), with the weak white light, the doctor is forming almost photographic images in his memory. Later, when Michel[5] investigates, the doctor can draw the objects on photographs taken from his terrace, indicating at each point in time their size and the positions of the beams of light on the ground below. White light is also emanating from around the antennas, and the doctor has the impression that these objects were "sucking in the atmospheric electricity and that I could see it entering through the antennas and then exploding between the two objects, the whole thing producing one single glow of light." It is this glow that is lighting up the countryside more than the narrow vertical beams.

The objects continue to make their broad sweep to the left, at the same time approaching each other. As they nearly touch, light seems to jump between the approaching antenna. It is bright, but not so brilliant that the doctor cannot observe it directly (e.g., the way one can observe a fluorescent lamp). When the objects are nearly in front of the house, an amazing thing happens. They continue to come together until they actually touch and then begin to interpenetrate each other. This continues for a moment or two until the interpenetration is complete, and only one object identical in its structure to the previous two is now visible . . . .

Just before the interpenetration, the flashing lights on the antennas cease, and the countryside becomes dark again. (The vertical beams of light illuminate it only for a short distance.) After the two objects become one, this object swings closer to the witness. When it is directly in front of the house (on a line at right angles to the face of the house), it begins to move directly toward the doctor. As it approaches, it appears to grow in size until it is enormous. At its closest approach, the doctor is able to accurately estimate its size in relation to the houses and trees below. Michel later measures the diameter at about sixty-five meters (about two hundred feet, exclusive of the antennas, which were estimated at about seventeen meters each, equal to the thickness of the object at its center).

At this point, the doctor, who was first astonished and then perplexed, begins to experience considerable fear. With the object so close, he is able to observe it in detail. He can see a protrusion on the bottom from which the beam of light is being emitted. The bottom half has sections, and there is a dark line that appears to move from the middle toward the bottom much as interference lines sometimes drift across a television screen. This phenomenon holds him transfixed, so that he is unable to run inside and get his movie or still camera.

The object remains stationary for what seems like a long interval of time, then suddenly the doctor notices the beam of light moving toward him. This is not because the object is moving, but because it is beginning to tip or rotate on an axis through the two protruding antennae, so that the top antenna is moving away from him. Finally, the object must have tipped almost ninety degrees, for the light beam illuminates the doctor and presumably all of the front of his house. He instinctively raises his arms to cover his face.

All of a sudden there is a sort of a "bang," the first sound during the entire encounter. Then, according to the witness, the object dematerializes, leaving nothing behind but its cloudy, whitish, fleecy shape, which at once disintegrates and is borne away eastward by the wind. A very luminous, fine, white thread shoots out vertically in a fraction of a

---

[5] Aime Michel is the chief investigator of this case, and was personally acquainted with Dr. Salisbury. He related the details of the incident as Dr. Salisbury drove him to the Salt Lake airport in early 1972.

second toward the sky and vanishes there into a small white shining dot, which then vanishes with the sound of an explosion like an aerial bomb on the 4th of July.

The doctor experiences considerable shock. He goes indoors and notes that it is 4:05 a.m. He gets a note pad and writes down the details of his sighting along with sketches (thereby qualifying himself as one of the best UFO witnesses on record). He awakens his wife and tells her all that he has seen. Both are deeply moved. Suddenly she cries, "Your leg!" The doctor, who is walking to and fro talking excitedly, has lost his limp. He pulls up his pajama trouser leg, and the wound is healed, both the swelling and the pain completely gone. They do not return. Michel visits five days later and is able to ascertain the facts in relation to the healing of the wound, not only from the doctor and his wife, but from others including the doctor's physician.

The doctor falls asleep and remains in a sound sleep until two o'clock the following afternoon (his wife awakens at ten that morning). When he awakens, he remembers nothing of his experience until he suffers a fall on the living room stairs, which produces a bump on his head and the full memory of the previous night's events!

For a few days, the doctor experiences further shock, and this produces certain physical symptoms of illness. During this time, he becomes aware that the symptoms of his Algerian War wound seem to be no longer with him. Finally, as the symptoms of shock disappear, it becomes apparent that this is indeed true. And once again he is able to perform expertly on the piano.

The investigators brought in many experts in various fields to help establish the truth or deceit in the doctor's story. Within a few days, the doctor began experiencing discomfort in the area of his navel. The skin became red, forming a perfect isosceles triangle. The researchers were really stumped when the fourteen-month-old baby developed an identical triangle on his navel. The triangles come and go periodically, in tandem evidently. As a follow up to this account, the investigators relate that the doctor complains of continued paranormal activity in his life following this close encounter. He has experienced telepathic and poltergeist phenomena, as well as levitating. Electrical circuits and appliances are also known to malfunction in the doctor's presence. The investigators believed at the time that these subsequent claims of paranormal activity diminished the doctor's credibility concerning the initial encounter. However, as we examine herein, such paranormal phenomena following close encounters have become common.

UFOs And OBEs

Many commentators are beginning to accept as routine the out-of-body experience phenomenon in connection with UFO encounters. In an effort to demonstrate that Betty Andreasson Luca's UFO/OBE episodes are not as atypical as a newcomer would assume, Raymond Fowler cites a 1973 case in which an Army Reserve helicopter was approached by a UFO, and tractored from 1,700 feet in altitude to 3,800 feet.

Captain (now Lt. Colonel) Lawrence J. Coyne, the helicopter commander, was contacted by the Department of the Army, Surgeon General's Office, and asked if he or any other crew member had experienced any unusual incidents or dreams subsequent to the UFO encounter. The "number one" question concerned dreams of body separation. Coyne reported that he had experienced an out-of-body episode in which he got out of bed during the night, only to find he had left his body in the bed. After a brief moment of amazement, he lay back down where his body was, feeling as though he were sinking into something, and woke up. Additionally, Coyne was quite disturbed by a very vivid second dream in which he heard an authoritative voice say, "The answer is in the circle. He looked down to see he was holding a clear, bluish-white sphere in his hand.[6]

Crewman Sgt. John Healy also reported out-of-body experiences following the UFO encounter, that might be better described as near-death experiences. The Pentagon's interest in these specific areas of OBEs following UFO contact appear to support numerous similar OBE reports by nonmilitary witnesses.

UFOs And ESP

Along these same lines, civilian reports indicate that frequently, paranormal activity follows the UFO experience participant. Heightened extra sensory perception (ESP) and poltergeist-like phenomena are often reported. Uncontrollable levitating and electrical disturbances also occur. Some investigators claim that the U.S. government is (or has been) especially interested in following up on UFO sightings to learn of the existence of such post-experience occurrences.

In many cases, contactees, or even those who only witness UFOs come away with expanded enlightenment, spiritual and/or scientific. Nearly a full one third of UFO encounters are said to include a psychic experience. This is often manifested as telepathic communication with the UFO occupants. Interestingly, those who claim psychic tendencies are more likely to experience UFO encounters. Not surprisingly, self-proclaimed psychics nearly always claim contact with UFOs and their occupants.

---

6 *The Watchers*, pp. 188-90.

Whitley Strieber, the famed fiction writer whose book *Communion* informed the world that he was plagued by "visitors" closely akin to "aliens," reports that he has a great deal of interest in the occult, including astral projection, a self-induced form of travelling out of one's body. Which comes first, paranormal experiences or interest in paranormal activities? It is hard to tell. One may be inclined to believe that the experiences lead to personal investigation. However, those who feel "compelled" to investigate UFO-related paranormal phenomena often discover that they have latent experiences buried in the subconscious realms of their minds—evidently, anyway.

Strieber, as well as many other contactees has discovered the presence of ongoing "alien" contact and paranormal experiences throughout his life. He rejects the idea that the "visitors" are extraterrestrial. He feels that they are interdimensional beings, who have visited our "phase" of the world throughout human history, communicating with us through demonstration and theater.

Strieber describes having his interest in "ancient nature religions and shamanism" piqued by his childhood memory of sitting at a table and working out an anagram the result of which was, "We work by ancient laws." Whoever the visitors are, Strieber believes that they gave him this anagram, and therein revealed something about themselves to him. I agree.

The Entity Enigma

Respected journalist Ed Conroy, has published a work that goes behind Strieber's *Communion*, analyzing the data and interviewing witnesses. He writes concerning Strieber's conclusion:

> In actuality, Strieber's line of thinking is reflective of the vast array of experiences connected with and explanations offered for what some investigators have come to call the "entity enigma." At first glance, it would seem that the content of Strieber's story is no different from hundreds of cases on record of people reporting terrifying experiences with "bedroom visitors," ghosts, poltergeists, apparitions, religious visions, and what have been regarded as demons. The entire array of such phenomena is beginning to be studied by serious UFOlogists with training in the psychological and social sciences, most notably by Hillary Evans, whose *Visions, Apparitions, Alien Visitors: A Comparative Study of the Entity Enigma*, makes an attempt to thoroughly survey the colorful panoply of anomalous phenomena concerning strange, human beings.[7]

---

[7] Ed Conroy, *Report on Communion*, William Morrow Company. Inc., New York (1989), p. 261.

Many guests at Strieber's upstate New York cabin were exposed to the "visitor" phenomenon, including Ed Conroy. One such weekend guest, Philippe Mora, director of *Death of a Soldier* and *The Howling III: The Marsupials,* was hired to direct the motion picture *Communion.* In his interview with Conroy, Mora related the following:

> Then we all went to bed, and I still believe—I had one of these nightmares, quite vivid dreams. Now, you've got to bear in mind that I had been working with Whitley on the script, and was psyched up, although I can't say when I went to bed I was. I was relaxing. I had the experience of lights blasting through the bedroom window, lights blasting under the crack under the door of the bedroom—I tried to turn the light on in my room, and I couldn't turn it on and I was pushed back into the bed. All the while I was consciously saying to myself, "This is a hell of a nightmare."
>
> Then I remember being outside the guestroom door, in the kitchen area, and the whole cabin lit up—every opening, every exterior opening, the whole thing was lit up with moving lights. And I looked through Andrew's bedroom. The door was open, and he was asleep, lit up. I remember Anne [Mrs. Strieber] rushing up to me and saying, "Whatever you do, don't wake Andrew." And then I woke up the next morning, . . . very scared.

Reality Testing

Like Strieber and many others, Mora relates that the experience occurred while in a semiconscious state. The inability to perceive whether or not the percipient is dreaming the experience or living it is a classic characteristic of such experiences. This is true, again, of both UFO occupant encounters and poltergeist and related paranormal phenomena. Strieber relates that on one occasion when the visitors abducted him, he was being floated helplessly through his house, when he decided to perform a "reality testing" experiment—he grabbed the family cat on the way through.

Upon arriving at the quite plain looking "office" of some rather ordinary human-appearing persons (one woman even had her hair in a bun and glasses on her nose), Strieber was chastised for bringing the cat along. When asked why he had done it he replied that he just wanted the company. After some quiet discussion among the entities, they told him that he had made a serious mistake, but that they would remedy it. With that, one of them touched the cat's leg with a small triangular object, and the cat went limp immediately. The day following the abduction experience the cat slept for most of the day and that night. It slept through most of the days that followed, and did not regain its normal strength and habits for several months afterward.

Historical Parallels

A great deal of research is currently underway comparing the behavior of the UFO phenomenon with that found in historic myth, legend, and fairy tales. Initially, this seems like a long shot, even childish. However, the parallels are striking, and research appears to be bearing enlightening fruit.

Jacques Vallee has compared much of the pertinent literature and shares the following legend as being typical of one type of parallel experience:

> According to the Paiute Indians, California was once populated by a superior civilization, the *Hav-Masuvs*. Among other interesting devices, they used "flying canoes," which were silvery and had wings. They flew in the manner of eagles and made a whirring noise. They were also using a very strange weapon: a small tube that could be held in one hand and would stun their enemies, producing lasting paralysis and a feeling similar to a shower of cactus needles.[8]

These descriptions are common in the folklore of native tribes and ancient civilizations. So, who are these airborne, stun-gun toting tribes that are reported worldwide throughout recorded history? We generally assume that they are mere tribal embellishments of feared enemies. Of course, the fact that they are recorded in similar terms throughout the ancient world tends to lend weight to the veracity of the legends.

Are there tribes of humans, or other beings, hidden from our view, living incognito on our globe? We know that there are Israelites who have been separated out—where they are now, we cannot know. We also know that the Lord will someday reveal "the hidden things of his economy concerning this earth during the seven thousand years of its continuance, or its temporal existence." (*D & C* 77:6) This informs us that there are hidden aspects of things on Earth of which we have no knowledge. The Lord reiterates this in Section 101:32-34, wherein He says: "Yea, verily I say unto you, in that day when the Lord shall come, he shall reveal all things— Things which have passed, and hidden things which no man knew, things of the earth, by which it was made, and the purpose and the end thereof—Things most precious, things that are above, and things that are beneath, things that are in the earth, and upon the earth, and in heaven." Whatever these many things are, it is clear that we live in substantial ignorance of things of which we have come to assume we have a great deal of knowledge.

---

[8] *Dimensions*, p. 86.

The Secret Commonwealth

For hundreds of years European scholars have attempted to document and piece together the legends of nonhuman beings in their region, historical and contemporary. A wonderful synthesis of the phenomenon was authored by Reverend Kirk of Aberfoyle.

In the last half of the seventeenth century, a Scottish scholar gathered all the accounts he could find about the *Sleaghmaith,* and, in 1691, wrote an amazing manuscript entitled *The Secret Commonwealth of Elves, Fauns, and Fairies.* It was the first systematic attempt to describe the methods and organization of the strange creatures that plagued the farmers of Scotland. The author, Reverend Kirk, of Aberfoyle, studied theology at Saint Andrews and took his degree of professor at Edinburgh. Later he served as minister for the parishes of Balquedder and Aberfoyle and died in 1692.

Kirk invented the name "The Secret Commonwealth" to describe the organization of the elves. It is impossible to quote the entire text of his treatise, but we can summarize his findings about elves and other aerial creatures in the following way:

1. They have a nature that is intermediate between man and the angels.

2. Physically, they have very light and fluid bodies, which are comparable to a condensed cloud. They are particularly visible at dusk. They can appear and vanish at will.

3. Intellectually, they are intelligent and curious.

4. They have the power to carry away anything they like.

5. They live inside the earth in caves, which they can reach through any crevice or opening where air passes.

. . .

8. Their chameleon-like bodies allow them to swim through the air with all their household.

9. They are divided into tribes. Like us, they have children, nurses, marriages, burials, etc., unless they just do this to mock our own customs or to predict terrestrial events.

10. Their houses are said to be wonderfully large and beautiful, but under most circumstances they are invisible to human eyes. Kirk compares them to enchanted islands. The houses are equipped with lamps that burn forever and fire that needs no fuel.

11. They speak very little. When they do talk among themselves, the language is a kind of whistling sound.

12. Their habits and their language when they talk to humans are similar to those of local people.

13. Their philosophical system is based on the following ideas: nothing dies; all things evolve cyclically in such a way that at every cycle they are renewed and improved. Motion is the universal law.

14. They are said to have a hierarchy of leaders, but they have no visible devotion to God, no religion.

15. They have many pleasant light books, but also serious and complex books dealing with abstract matters.

16. They can be made to appear at will before us through magic.[9]

---

[9] *Dimensions,* pp. 87-89.

Following is another example typifying the parallels between legendary abduction accounts and those found in modern UFO literature.

> A Swedish book published in 1775 contains a legal statement, solemnly sworn on April 12, 1671, by the husband of a midwife who was taken to fairyland to assist a troll's wife who was giving birth to a child. The author of the statement seems to have been a clergyman. "On the authority of this declaration we are called on to believe that the event recorded actually happened in the year 1660. Peter Rahm alleges that he and his wife were at their farm one evening late when there came a little man, swart of face and clad in grey, who begged the declarant's wife to come and help his wife then in labor. The declarant, seeing that they had to do with a Troll, prayed over his wife, blessed her, and bade her in God's name go with the stranger. She seemed to be borne along by the wind.
>
> In another tale, the midwife's husband accompanies her through the forest. They are guided by the "earthman"—the gnome who has requested their help. They go through a moss door, then a wooden door, and later through a door of shining metal. A stairway leads them inside the earth, to a magnificent chamber where the "earthwife" is resting. Kirk reports that in a case whose principals he personally knew the abducted woman found the home of the Little People filled with light, although they could not see any lamp or fire. [10]

Magonia, or fairyland, is thought to be a remote country or invisible island reached after a long journey, aerial or otherwise. Vallee observes, "But a second—and equally widespread—theory, is that Magonia constitutes a sort of parallel universe, which coexists with our own. It is made visible and tangible only to selected people, and the doors that lead to it are tangential points, known only to the elves and a few of their initiates."

Vallee cites Hartland, who offers tales that illustrate the latter theory, such as the following:

> In Nithsdale a fairy rewards the kindness of a young mother, to whom she had committed her baby to suckle, by taking her on a visit to Fairyland. A door opened in a green hillside, disclosing a porch which the nurse and her conductor entered. There the lady dropped three drops of precious dew on the nurse's left eyelid, and they were admitted to a beautiful land watered with meandering rivulets and yellow with corn, where the trees were laden with fruits which dropped honey. The nurse was here presented with magical gifts, and when a green dew had baptized her right eye she was able to behold further wonders. On returning the fairy passed her hand over the woman's eye and restored its natural powers. [11]

The parallels with modern descriptions of UFO occupants and related entities are remarkable. Strieber describes an abduction in which he was made to think he was on a strange airplane. He then relates how the stewardess gave him some eye drops for motion sickness (yes, he noted the strangeness of this remedy), after which he was taken to exotic places.

---

10 *Dimensions*, p. 127.

11 *Dimensions*, p. 128.

Vallee cites many cases wherein the historical beings are described as having glowing eyes and many other characteristics identical to those ascribed to many UFO occupants, and Kirk documents humans' ability to make pacts with the beings for personal gain or for protection from them.

Magic Wands

Ed Walters, like many other UFO witnesses, describes certain wandlike instruments carried by the "aliens." These silver wands or rods are apparently the same as that carried by the single small grey on the night it attempted to lure Ed Walters out of the house into the clutches of the blue beam. Although we can assume that such a glowing silver rod was nothing more than a stun gun, or communication device, the presence of the silver rods that "glowed" is worth noting from a traditional, or paranormal viewpoint. Betty Luca, as well as others, describes how such devices are used to manipulate the environment, ambiance, or technological appliances in the vicinity of the encounter.

Certain ancient religious texts occasionally refer to superior beings, or those sent with ecclesiastical authority, as possessing various types of rods, holding them in their hands as though they conveyed authority. For instance, from the *Apocalypse of Abraham* we read: "And I rose up and saw him who had grasped me by the right hand and set me upon my feet: and the appearance of his body was like sapphire, and the look of his countenance like chrysolite, and the hair of his head like snow, etc. and a *golden sceptre* was in his right hand. (Section X.)" Also, from the Iliad we read: " 'And the Elders were seated upon shining stones [stones of truth] in a holy circle,' with scepters of inspired utterance in their hands . . . ." (Hugh Nibley, *Abraham in Egypt, quoting Iliad,* XVIII, 497-508) Besides these, our scriptures, as well as our secular monarchies, are replete with examples of the possession of such rods or scepters as symbols of authority or power.

Why rods that appear like scepters? Why not, for instance, small handheld spheres or cubes—why always scepters? No other analogy is suggested here except for the universality of the principle. It is, however, reminiscent of the unauthorized wearing of Priestly apparel and emblems or the invocation of holy names in an attempt to feign claim to Priesthood or other authority.

Crossing The Time Zone

Another characteristic of fairyland that is also common in UFO abduction cases is what I term the "Rip Van Winkle effect." When visiting with the elves or fairies or Gentry, humans are said to be missing for days, months, or years, when to them the time passed as though it were only minutes or hours. In fact, it is based on this rich folklore that Washington Irving wrote *Rip Van Winkle.* The reverse is true also—the abductee often feels that he or she was in fairyland for weeks or longer, only to find that no time has passed in our world.

> This is our fourth point, and quite a remarkable one. Time does not pass there as it does here. And we have in such stories the first idea of the relativity of time. How did this idea come to the storytellers ages ago? What inspired them? No one can answer such questions. But it is a fact that the nonsymmetry of the time element between Magonia and our world is present in tales from all countries. [12]

In many UFO abduction cases the victim's absence went unnoticed because no time had passed. In others more time had passed than was realized by the victim. Of course, there exist other plausible explanations for such phenomena—drugs, for example. These are plausible, but not generally probable. In one case, a military watch in South America approached a landed UFO, and one of the men went over the knoll to get a closer look. A few minutes later he was found by his colleagues, disoriented, with several days growth of beard.

Elves And Fairies

Describing the UFO entities Vallee says:

> Entities human witnesses report to have seen, heard, and touched fall into various biological types . . . . Most of the so-called pilots, however, are dwarfs and fit into two main groups: (1) dark, hairy beings—identical to the gnomes of medieval theory— with small, bright eyes and deep, rugged, "old" voices; and (2) beings—who answer the description of the sylphs of the middle ages or the elves of the fairy-faith—with human complexions, oversized heads, and silvery voices. All of the beings have been described with and without breathing apparatus. Beings of various categories have been reported together. The overwhelming majority are humanoid.

In describing the entities' behavior Vallee adds:

> The entities' reported behavior is as consistently absurd as the appearance of their craft is ludicrous. In numerous instances of verbal communications with them, their

---

12 *Dimensions,* p. 131.

assertions have been systematically misleading. This is true for all cases on record, from encounters with the Gentry in the British Isles to conversations with airship engineers during the 1897 midwest flap and discussions with the alleged martians in Europe, North and South America, and elsewhere. This absurd behavior has had the effect of keeping professional scientists away from the area where the activity was taking place. It has also served to give the saucer myth its religious and mystical overtones.[13]

Vallee feels that the entities and their UFOs, whoever they are, "are paranormal in nature and a modern space age manifestation of a phenomenon that assumes different guises in different historical contexts."[14] In an interview with *Fate Magazine*[15] Vallee said, "We have evidence that the phenomenon can create a distortion of the sense of reality or to substitute artificial sensations for the real ones."

Pursuing his paranormal activity theory, Vallee suggests, "It is conceivable that there is one phenomenon that is visual and another that creates the physical traces. What I am saying is that a strange kind of deception may be involved."[16] He also notes, "It seems as if an external force takes control of people. In the close encounters people may lose their ability to move or speak; in the abduction cases, which are the most extreme example, they gradually enter into a series of experiences during which they lose control of their senses."[17] John Keel, a well respected UFO researcher similarly relates that "over and over again, witnesses have told me in hushed tones, 'you know, I don't think that thing I saw was mechanical at all. I got the distinct impression it was alive.'"

Vallee concludes his study of similarities between UFO occupants and the Gentry of the past stating: "The UFO occupants, like the elves of old, are not extraterrestrials. They are the denizens of another reality." What does this tell us? Nothing, yet. However, our underlying theory that UFOs and their occupants are nothing more than modern versions of historical manifestations of spirit entities appears to be accepted by the top scientists in UFO research.

---

13 *Dimensions,* p. 166.

14 *Dimensions,* p. 213.

15 "Vallee Discusses UFO Control System," p. 65.

16 *Fate Magazine, (Ibid).* p. 63.

17 *Ibid.,* p. 64.

Modern Gentry

Raymond Fowler was contacted by a young man who saw a UFO. He said that a "few years later he woke up to see a *beam of light* entering his bedroom. It contained an entity with long blond hair. Like [Fowler, as a child], he could not tell whether it was male or female. Like [Fowler], he was filled with an indescribable feeling of love." These encounters with angelic appearing humans are perceived almost as religious experiences by the witnesses—for good reason I might add—this is clearly the intent of the entities.

Fowler relates that his father had been hit by "lightning" while stationed at a U.S. Naval Radio Compass Station. The lightning came through the equipment and hit him, lodging behind his solar plexus, "where it remained and revolved like a fiery sun" inside of him. He sat baffled wondering why he wasn't dead, watching as the eight-inch ball of energy whirled inside him, pulsating to the beat of his heart.

Fowler's father looked up to see a beam of light coming through the station roof, going up to a "radiant star." The light also went down deep into the rock beneath the station. He sat for a long time, feeling outside of time and space. Then the light expanded, from which three entities sprang. He described them as "majestic-looking smiling men in shining robes of light," who communicated with him telepathically. He formed questions concerning the startling events that were occurring, but his visitors did not answer them.

His father further described the three as "fine-featured" and having "light cream-textured complexions. Their eyes were so bright it was difficult to see the color but [he] thought they were blue." He said they wore odd hats that were the same shining blue as their robes. One of the beings pointed at him and the ball of energy leaped from his body into the being's hands. The three of them tossed it between them until it disappeared. The three smiled, bowed, and disappeared into three flashes of light. The Radio equipment was incinerated.

Although there is no direct relationship to UFOs in this account, the fact that the Fowler family was generally involved in UFO sightings is illustrative of the phenomenon—those who have UFO encounters often have other, similar anomalous experiences. I believe it is obvious that this was no lightning strike incident. From beginning to end the account is better described in spiritual terms.

Many years after Fowler's father had the above experience, he related a very vivid dream he had to Fowler and his wife. He dreamed he went into a large movie theater, sat down, and watched as the lights dimmed, the curtains opened, and a large silver screen was revealed. Trumpets blew as a date appeared on the screen: "October 4, 1957." He heard a loud voice declare, "On this day the Cosmic Age will be ushered in!" The date faded, the curtains closed, and he left the theater. Fowler relates that although he and his wife rolled their eyes at each other in the usual incredulous fashion, he did write the date on a scrap of paper. It was years later when the predicted date arrived—the headlines that morning announced that Sputnik had launched mankind into the Space age. Fowler remembered the date and ran to fetch the scrap of paper. The date was the same. It is interesting that Fowler's father made another prediction that came true also—the fascinating part is that it dealt with a UFO sighting.

Catholic UFOs

Throughout history there have been thousands of anomalous encounters with the unknown that have the appearance of religious manifestations. Many of these meetings contain components characteristic of UFO encounters. Many researchers of the UFO phenomenon have noted the well attended and well documented case of the "Miracle of Fatima." Dr. Salisbury offers the following condensed account.

> For six months beginning in May of 1917, three children near Fatima, Portugal, were visited on the thirteenth of each month by an apparition that identified itself as the Virgin Mary. The transparent little blue lady with her hands in an attitude of prayer was seen by Lucia de Santos (age ten), Jacinta (age nine), and Francisco (age seven), but she was heard only by the two girls. She gave them messages quite appropriate to Catholics in the Portugal of 1917. Each time she appeared, a larger crowd of people was on hand, but only the children were able to see her. Finally she said that on October 13th, a sign would be given that would convince everybody. It is estimated that some 70,000 people were milling around in a muddy field during a light rain storm waiting for the sign. Suddenly the clouds parted, the rain stopped, and the "sun" came through the clouds—that is, it *flew* through the clouds, being not really a fiery ball too brilliant to look at, but rather a flattened disc shining like a pearl. It maneuvered around in the sky for a few minutes while all of the witnesses looked on—including some who were as far away as fifteen miles, having been unable to make the pilgrimage to Fatima itself. Finally, it became a brilliant, blood-red color, not unlike numerous red spheres described in the Uintah Basin. It began to move rapidly toward the crowd below, appearing much larger and more fiery at each instant. The crowd, dried by the heat given off from the object, fell on their knees and cried for mercy, convinced that this was the end of the world. At the last moment, the Fatima sun halted its terrifying descent and retreated back through the clouds from whence it came. It was never seen again.[19]

---

[19] *The Utah UFO Display,* pp. 198-99.

Jacques Vallee explains that in the initial conversations with the Madonna, she gave enlightening information and instruction to the children. "It is also remarkable that the children were shown a vision of hell that terrified them and were given a specific prophecy announcing more apparitions of unknown lights in the sky." The little blue lady (Blessed Virgin Mary) made further prophecies concerning the coming major wars and calamities of the twentieth century. This was as much a series of religious apparitions as any Catholic Saint had ever produced. Vallee is not convinced, however:

> The final "miracle" had come to the culmination of a precise series of apparitions combined with contacts and messages that place it very clearly, in my opinion, in the perspective of UFO phenomena. Not only was a flying disk or globe consistently involved, but its motion, its falling-leaf trajectory, its light effects, the thunder claps, the buzzing sounds, the strange fragrance, the fall of "angel hair" that dissolves upon reaching the ground, the heat wave associated with the close approach of the disk—all of these are frequent parameters of UFO sightings everywhere. And so are the paralysis, the amnesia, the conversions, and the healings.[20]

Hundreds of similar experiences have been reported from around the world. Either departed Catholic Saints have nothing better to do than put on sophisticated light shows for the faithful, or UFO occupants are counterfeiting Saintly apparitions. If this was a Saintly manifestation, what was the children's role in it and why could only they see the Madonna, while only the two girls could hear her? Another obvious question is, Was this a spiritual or extraterrestrial event? As with the major contactee encounters of today, it appears that the encounters of yesterday were extraterrestrial with religious overtones or vice versa. Remember the Miracle of Fatima as we analyze the data in Chapter 15.

Blessed UFOs

Ed Conroy comments on the religious nature of UFO apparitions:

> An alternate hypothesis about the apparent connection between UFO phenomena and apparitions of the Blessed Virgin Mary holds that the majority of such cases are examples of the manipulation of mass human consciousness by entities capable of producing visual and auditory displays that are specifically designed to lead worshipers of the Virgin to believe that the displays are, in fact, the Virgin herself. The motivation for this deception, according to Salvador Freixedo, a Spanish ex-Jesuit priest, who does not blush at proposing hypotheses that would give the tabloid press a field day, is the entities' desire to psychically feed upon the mass emotions of agony and ecstacy that

---
[20] *Dimensions*, p. 200.

are only observed in miraculous shrines. Freixedo goes so far as to hypothesize that we are literally preyed upon by certain classes of entities who create UFO phenomena in the interest of feeding off of our religious emotions, in a manner analogous to the way in which blood has been found entirely removed from cattle that had been strangely mutilated in UFO related events throughout the world.[21]

Agreeing, Vallee attempts to focus in on what the phenomenon is: "The system I am speaking of, a system with mastery of space and time dimensions, will be able to locate itself in outer space. Nonetheless, its manifestations cannot be *spacecraft* in the ordinary nuts-and-bolts sense. The UFOs are physical manifestations that simply cannot be understood apart from their psychic and symbolic reality. What we see here is not an alien invasion. It is a spiritual system that acts on humans and uses humans."[22] UFO researcher John A. Keel likewise agrees that these paranormal apparitions, what he terms "soft objects," or "sightings of transparent or translucent objects seemingly capable of altering their size and shape dramatically," are "temporary manipulations of matter and energy."

But what are they? No one seems capable (or willing) of proposing a tangible theory. The only thing that these UFO researchers appear to agree on is that UFOs are *not* spaceships.

Ouija Boards And Seance Rappings

One of the most bizarre UFO contacts on record was experienced in the Uintah Basin, by LDS Church members. Again, we have Dr. Salisbury to thank for publishing the account.

Sighting #41 is well calculated to frustrate the careful objective approach of a scientific UFO investigator. The Clyde McDonald family was informed by one of its members, a fourth grader, that a flying saucer was going to appear above the Roosevelt Hospital at eight o'clock on the evening of February 23, 1967. How did the young lady know that the flying saucer was going to appear? Why, some of the students in the other fourth grade class had been playing with a ouija board, and the ouija board had informed them that this event would take place. Mother and father chuckled properly and sat down to watch television. They were relaxing in their bare feet when the children began to bundle up and go out to meet their eight o'clock appointment with the UFO. Mother said, "You'd better hurry. It will be gone before you get there." Then, as Mrs. McDonald says: "Tim looked up, and he hollered, 'Oh, run, Tammy, There it is!', and they about broke that door off getting in. So we all ran, the three of us, jumped up and ran to

---

21 *Report on Communion*, p. 337.

22 *Dimensions*, pp. 284-85.

the door, and, of course, then we could see that big light right out there by the Jennings' yard. Boy, they were behind us and they wouldn't go out then. And we saw that light, and, of course, we just stood out there then and watched it, and we about froze,—we were barefoot and everything, but we didn't want to come back in and lose it! It was kind of an orange ball, orange to red, kind of in a circle, bigger than an ordinary light." How big was it compared to a full moon?" I asked her. "Well, it wasn't that big. I'd say probably a third, wouldn't it be?"[23]

At least five other witnesses saw this same UFO from another location at the same time in the same place. Others claimed to have seen the object at slightly different times, moving, rather than stationary. Another witness claims that the object flew alongside his car for about a mile, then flashed vertically until it was out of sight.

What do we make of a UFO that announces an appearance at a certain time and place via a ouija board? When Dr. Salisbury first reported the case, his scientific approach seemed somewhat impotent to him.

Whitley Strieber speaks of nine distinct taps on the upper side of his cabin, in three groups of three, followed by two light taps. He ascribes much importance to the incident because he knows that the rappings were made by the visitors, while he was in full consciousness. Strieber devotes an entire chapter to the rappings, convincing the reader that no person could have slipped by his security system to reach that portion of the house, describing his cats' unprecedented reaction, and depicting the rappings as so precise that there was a hidden message in them for him. The point that Strieber fails to appreciate is that such rappings and related phenomena have long characterized paranormal contact. There is no meaning or message—there is only rapping.

Photographing The Unknown

Joanne Wilson and her business companion, as reported in the book *UFO: End-Time Delusion*,[24] were followed by a UFO early in the morning as they drove to a swap meet. When asked if the UFO had a definable form she responded as follows: "It was like a cloud of gas or fog or something like that. Very dense though. But the light did not shine out. It didn't light the trees or the ground or anything. It was all contained within itself . . . . And there were big columns of light. They were white, white lights that came

---

[23] *The Utah UFO Display,* p. 38.

[24] David Allen Lewis and Robert Shrechise, *UFO: End-Time Delusion,* New Leaf Press, Arkansas (1991).

on inside it. They were so far from the bottom and so far from the top. They didn't touch the top or the bottom."[25]

Joanne and her friend stopped the truck, locked the doors, rolled down the window and attempted to take photographs of the UFO: "She took a couple of pictures there, and that's the two that turned out. And when we took the pictures, it dissolved, almost completely. It just dissolved itself. I thought to myself, *Whatever it is doesn't want its picture made.*"[26]

The photographs came out blurry, with white streaks instead of the clearly visible forms and columns seen distinctly by the two women.

This result is quite common in attempts to photograph other paranormal phenomena such as poltergeist manifestations. The photographer will see a clearly outlined manifestation, but the photograph will reflect only streaks of light. Additionally, the description of a brightly lit craft that fails to shed its light on surrounding objects is not only common in UFO reports, but also in other paranormal encounters. In the Gulf Breeze case, photographic analysis of the "UFO just above the road" photograph reveals that the light source was very bright at the point of departure —the UFO— but experts were puzzled that the light appeared to be confined to that specific area, and did not light up more of the road and surroundings. This is not to say that it failed to light the surroundings up at all, as in the case of superimposition of an image onto the film—but the radiated light is less than one would normally expect to view in the photograph. Personal LDS friends have recounted spiritual experiences wherein a true visitation would be precursed by a sphere of light in a dark room. As you might predict, the light is contained, and does not radiate to light up the darkened surroundings.

New Age guru Ruth Montgomery quotes a New Age channeler in contact with an alien who explains such phenomena, saying that "the photograph was really an illusion; that it was not a photograph of physical matter, and humans were wrong in perceiving it as physical matter."[27]

Ghostly Apparitions

The ability of the Gulf Breeze UFOs, as well as many others, to suddenly "wink out," or completely disappear fits into this paranormal occurrence

---

25 *UFO*, p. 32.

26 *UFO*, p. 33.

27 *Strangers Among Us*, p. 144.

parameter. Other UFOs similarly appear to oscillate between this plane and another—seeming at first solid, then transparent. Betty Luca's opulating and deopulating UFOs appear to be more than interplanetary industrial products. Is the ability to shrink a solid craft and its alien and human passengers superior science, or paranormal projecting activity? Why shrink such a craft and its occupants?—fuel economy? Hardly.

In the chapters that follow the famous Men In Black phenomenon as it relates to paranormal activity will be discussed. It suffices to say here that the MIB are quite ephemeral in nature, almost supernatural, and that they are every bit as anomalous as any aspect of UFOs and their occupants.

Panoply Of The Paranormal

Ed Walters and others hear telepathic voices and see vivid pictures within their minds; light beams are used to lift, immobilize, and transport; those who encounter UFOs have their will taken over by an external force; UFOs disappear and reappear as though outfitted with *Star Trek* cloaking devices; UFOs dash through our skies at tens of thousands of miles per hour, causing no wind or sonic booms; UFOs can see, hear, and control remotely; people who encounter UFOs are compelled to act; contactees are taken to strange new worlds, shown wonderful architecture and technology, and are floated over valleys and through walls; UFO occupants deliver religious and prophetic messages that are untrue; and, UFOs are able to change their size, shape, and appearance at will, as are their occupants.

If these same characteristics common to UFO encounters were referenced in a mystical or spiritual context—say, we merely eliminated the spacecraft itself from the equation, there would be no doubt that they properly fit into the paranormal classification. I believe that the fact that they are "presented" in a superior science context fails to remove them from the paranormal realm. Furthermore, the historical presence of the phenomena only supports their paranormal underpinnings. In short, whatever UFOs are, they have always been with us and they exist outside of our everyday space-time continuum—in many cases, anyway.

14

Who Is Sending
The Message

Isn't It Obvious?

The overriding question behind the UFO phenomenon is Who is sending them, complete with a message to mankind? The apparent response is that they are piloted by humans or humanoids from another planet. Yet, as we examine the nature of the UFOs themselves, as well as the "message" that they appear to be sending, the apparent answer becomes less evident.

A Paradigm For A Plethora

In this chapter we reexamine the possible sources of UFOs, weighing the supporting evidence for each such source against revealed truth. In this, we have a great advantage over most UFO researchers. For example, Christian Fundamentalist researchers believe that this Earth is the only planet created by God for the purpose of human habitation. Therefore, their answer to the UFO enigma cannot be extraterrestrial life—and hence they conclude that UFOs must be demonic in origin. On the other hand, the UFO debunkers believe in nothing that cannot be fully documented on the network evening news, especially extraterrestrial life or spiritual entities. They, therefore, accept only natural phenomena (meteorological, electromagnetic, psychological) as possible explanations of UFO sightings and encounters.

New Agers believe that UFOs are piloted by, or are manifestations of, more highly advanced spirits that have come to Earth to usher in its next step in evolution—the Aquarian quantum leap. Other observers have come to believe that UFOs and their occupants are extradimensional—hailing from parallel universes or other time periods in our own universe, fading in and out at will. However, most UFO researchers and "fans" fall into the "extraterrestrial explorer" category, accepting at face value that we are indeed being visited by beings from other planets. They appear to accept the practical aspects of the UFO message—that Earth is becoming polluted and will require alien help to overcome an impending cataclysm, and that they are performing genetic research to preserve our race and/or theirs.

The Latter-day Saints, however, through latter-day revelation and the restoration of many lost scriptural texts know certain truths about the universe and its population—human, animal, spiritual, and otherwise, that shed light on the phenomenon. Many of these fundamental truths were discussed in Part I. Armed with this greater abundance of truth, we should be able to better discern the origin and nature of UFOs and decide how we should respond to them. We shall see.

Theory 1: Extraterrestrial Explorers

The extraterrestrial explanation is the most widely accepted in our society. Indeed, UFO occupants declare themselves to be humanoid inhabitants of other planets, arriving in nuts-and-bolts flying machines built with engineering capabilities acquired over tens of thousands, or even millions of years of scientific inquiry. In support of this hypothesis we have millions of independent witnesses telling believable stories of sighting solid, reflective craft that maneuver at incredible speeds, performing feats that are deemed impossible by the standards of our current level of technological understanding.

Hard Evidence

In addition to the numerous sightings, we have evidence of the physical presence of UFOs. This evidence, however, when considered in tandem with other reported properties of UFOs, leaves experts unsure about their nature. Scientific inquiry is almost impossible under present circumstances, and mere analysis of the available data sheds little light on the problem, as observed by James McCampbell as recorded in the *SCP Journal*.

Physicist James McCampbell, speaking to a UFO symposium in 1975, rendered a succinct analysis of the problems encountered in a scientific study of UFO characteristics: "Evidence left at landing sites leaves little room for doubt that UFOs are heavy, ponderous objects when at rest. Yet in flight, their startling departures, sudden stops, and right angle turns at high speed require them to be virtually massless."[1]

This seeming contradiction is explained away by "extraterrestrial theory" adherents as merely superior science. The fact exists that there have been many well-documented landing sites throughout the world. Although insufficient to convince debunkers of the reality of UFOs, the physical evidence of their presence is mounting. In addition to these material signs of the physical reality of UFOs, we have numerous photographs. All of this, however, can be counterfeited at one level or another.

Photographs

Ed Walters's photographs are among the most convincing that UFOs are actual, solid, real objects. There exist many others as well. In addition to those mentioned above who have taken movies and videos of UFOs, television News and "Mystery" program film crews have photographed what they believe to be UFOs on high quality motion picture film as well as commercial-grade video tape. The weekly television program *Sightings,* which covers subjects in the realm of the paranormal, documented a research crew's efforts to film UFOs in one of the latest UFO "hotspots," Anza, California. Citizens of that town report an escalating number of close encounters, including abductions and breeding experiments. The film crew set up its cameras in a place well known for sightings, and within two days was able to film a UFO moving through the sky. Of course, no attendant documentation or investigation was available at the time of airing the program, so it was only assumed that no other explanations existed for the presence of the strange flying craft. The effort does demonstrate, however, that UFOs are becoming bolder with each passing year. Similar efforts reaped comparable results in Gulf Breeze, Florida. *Sightings* receives enough videos depicting UFOs that its audience is treated to weekly displays accompanied by experts analyzing the videos.

---

[1] *SCP Journal,* August 1977, Vol. 1 No. 2, "UFOs—Is Science Fiction Coming True?", p. 14.

Prime Time Videos

One late night "news" program (frankly, not known for its journalistic professionalism) aired in late May, 1992, a video sent back live from the space shuttle that was indeed intriguing. A UFO researcher was analyzing the video as it was replayed again and again. On the screen we saw a view of the Earth, toward the edge so that we saw the horizon to the right, and outer space beyond that. Travelling over the Earth from the bottom of the screen to the top within a few inches (on the television screen) of the right horizon was what appeared to be an unanimated object. NASA had just commented that the object looked much like an orbiting hunk of ice (very large), expelled from this or another mission. This particular object appeared to be orbiting at several times the speed of the rotation of the Earth, which is approximately 1,000 miles per hour—my layman's guess would be that the object was travelling at 40,000 to 50,000 m.p.h., possibly much faster. Just as this object was about two-thirds of the way up the screen, still travelling at the same high velocity, it made a perfect right angle turn toward the right of the screen, moving toward outer space. This it did without any interruption or hesitation—it changed direction instantly at 90 degrees as though it had been a billiard ball rebounding off of a table cushion.

If this maneuver were not exhilarating enough, within one or two seconds of the object executing its amazing right angle turn, a second object shot up from the direction of the Earth's surface through the point of intersection where the first object would have been had it not made its seemingly "evasive" maneuver. The second object quickly shot off the screen toward the top, while the first continued on its course to the right of the screen into outer space, quickly fading from view. The second object was moving even more rapidly than the first, and because of its "streaking" appearance, it seemed that it could have been some kind of energy burst rather than a solid object.

The scene was extraordinary as it replayed over and over on television. The UFO analyst shared obvious observations about the speed, trajectory, and apparent tactical implications of the display as we watched it repeatedly. It was an amazing display, and does much to support the nuts-and-bolts UFO theory—after all, as far as we know, we have no such vehicles flying around out there that can maneuver in such an incomprehensible manner.

In this space shuttle spectacle, the second object is of almost greater interest than the first. If, as it appeared, the second object was "fired" at the first— who launched it and what was it? Did our government shoot something at an unknown object, so close to our own space shuttle? It does not seem likely. Neither does it seem plausible that one of the few foreign governments with sufficient technology to fire such a projectile would do so with the shuttle so near. If so, does this imply that governments of the Earth are in active combat with UFOs? If this is true, then we are being kept in the dark about a serious enemy and technology well beyond our current understanding. If not governments of the Earth, is someone else in active combat with UFOs? Who? Could it be "good" and "bad" UFOs fighting over the Earth? Could it be hidden Earth civilizations locked in combat to protect us all? Although this entire discussion will seem quite sophomoric to some, these scenarios are precisely appropriate if the space shuttle video accurately recorded what appears to be a high-velocity right-angle turn to avoid an incoming projectile.

Target Practice

Whether or not world governments are locked in combat with UFOs, another apparent piece of evidence that UFOs are solid objects comes from the projectile-launching deer hunters of the Uintah Basin of eastern Utah. At least two hunters report taking shots at UFOs with their rifles and hearing the ricochet as the bullet glanced off the seemingly metallic object. In both cases the UFO left immediately, and in at least one case, returned and followed at a distance.

Personal Testimony

In addition to the millions of sighting witnesses and mounting physical evidence of the tangible presence of UFOs, we have the testimonies of thousands, including members of the Church, who claim direct, personal contact with UFO occupants. Not only do these contactees and abductees convincingly relate the spiritual or emotional feelings (horror or overwhelming love) that they felt during their ordeal, but they are able to describe with great clarity the features of the beings they encounter and the nature and properties of the craft, and their means of operation. These abductees are absolutely convinced of the reality of their encounters with strange beings in foreign craft, and relate many physical aspects of their experiences.

The Personal Touch

For example, many claim to be physically touched, moved about manually, or examined or operated upon by their abductors. The material aspects of such personal encounters tend to place them in the real, physical realm. Our own Udo Wartena recounts how he shook hands with those whom he encountered who professed to be from another planet. Because of this act, our temptation to write the entire phenomenon off as a demonic hoax is somewhat tempered by Joseph Smith's "three grand keys" to discerning the nature and origin of unearthly visitors:

> When a messenger comes saying he has a message from God, offer him your hand and request him to shake hands with you. If he be an angel he will do so, and you will feel his hand. If he be the spirit of a just man made perfect he will come in his glory; for that is the only way he can appear—Ask him to shake hands with you, but he will not move, because it is contrary to the order of heaven for a just man to deceive; but he will still deliver his message. If it be the devil as an angel of light, when you ask him to shake your hands he will offer you his hand, and you will not feel anything; you may therefore detect him. These are three grand keys whereby you may know whether any administration is from God. [*D & C* 129:4-9]

Although our fact situation is not precisely on point (Udo's aliens did not claim to be messengers from God), the circumstances seem sufficiently analogous to fulfill the requirements of the test. The visitors did claim to be from another planet, they indeed responded to Udo's outstretched hand, and he did feel their hands as he shook them. Of the volumes that fill library shelves and researchers' notebooks around the world concerning the reality of encounters with beings from foreign worlds, this single act of a Priesthood bearer shaking the hand of a self-proclaimed alien in 1920 is the most convincing evidence of the physical existence of legitimate explorers of Earth from another planet. If we accept this as a true, non-Satanic[2] visitation of humans from another planet, it may serve as an invaluable guide to discerning the physical reality of other reported encounters.

If we can use Udo Wartena's encounter as a standard by which to measure close encounters generally, there appears to be a clear division of encounter types. The first is the kind in which the contactee is fully conscious during the entire encounter (although Udo reports becoming unconscious upon the craft's departure) and reports many physical aspects about the encounter. The second would be the semiconscious bedroom visitor type. The distinction

---

2 We address the possibility of a Satanic deception in Chapter 15. There exists the real possibility that Satan employs physical beings to carry out a physical deception.

becomes muddled, however, because percipients of both groups, often are convinced of the physical reality of their respective experiences.

A Standard

From Udo Wartena's encounter we learn that handsome and youthful appearing humans ranging in age from 600 to 900+ years travelled here from other planets in a saucer-shaped craft supported on retractable legs. The age of the human visitors and shape of the craft are similar to the reports of others. As also related by others, Udo's visitors were here to gather water through hoses for their craft and to do research on cultural progress and pollution levels of the Earth. Udo likewise felt overwhelming love in the presence of his visitors, and was told of their "noninterference" policy, as are related by many other contactees. Finally, Udo's extraordinary description of the craft and its technology and means of propulsion are very similar to many other accounts. His explanation of the craft focusing on the energy of a distant star and skipping upon the light waves at ultralight speeds was given decades before most people had ever heard of Einstein or his pertinent theories.

There are a few ways in which Udo's experience differs from those of others. For instance, although some report hearing loud noises at landing and takeoff as did Udo, the majority relate a stillness that falls over everything, with the possible exception of a "hum." Again, although many report encountering completely human occupants of UFOs (generally benign), the majority identify the occupants as the "small grey" variety, or some other variation of the gnome or humanoid forms. Udo specifically queried his visitors concerning their knowledge of the Savior and the Priesthood, to which they merely responded that they were not at liberty to discuss such matters pursuant to their noninterference directive, despite their desire to do so.

Unlike these, Betty Luca's visitors, as well as others', talk extensively about the spiritual or religious aspects of their missions—in seeming violation of their self-declared policy of noninterference. Although others have recounted cordiality between them and their visitors, as does Udo, most of those claiming to have such intimate contact with UFO occupants relate nonpermissive experiences with tranquilizing mind control and physical examinations or operations. No genetic samples such as blood, tissue, or semen specimens were removed from Udo. And finally, although Udo's visitors invited him to continue their journey with them, an offer not unprecedented in the literature, most receive no such proposition. Generally, "spokespersons" selected by the Space Brothers claim a UFO ride or two in our solar system, but rarely do we find such a *bona fide* offer of long distance journeying. Finally, and perhaps most significantly, Udo was not a "repeater"—he never saw his extraterrestrial friends again.

Technological Dispensations

These evidences of visitation to our planet by aliens are somewhat augmented by our understanding that Heavenly Father has created millions of planets like Earth and populated them with his children. As in our own history, He has assuredly meted out mechanical and engineering knowledge at times to these planets—possibly in greater abundance than on Earth. We are without knowledge concerning his purposes in dispensing such technological information, so we cannot tell from history or from the Gospel if it is done in any particular phase of temporal existence. We cannot deduce whether or not Heavenly Father may apportion technology earlier and in greater abundance in other worlds, enabling the kind of technology that we see in UFOs during the normal temporal existence of planets like Earth. From all appearances, the great technological advances on Earth of the past few centuries have had two basic objectives—to enable the worldwide spread of the Gospel and to enable the eventual destruction of the Earth. Assuredly, peripheral benefits to His children such as medicines and comforts have been allowed, but they are not essential in the overall purpose of the creation of this Earth as evidenced by the lack of such amenities in the lives of most of his children.

If, then, significant technological advancement is generally reserved for the end of a planet's temporal existence, as on Earth, it would be difficult to imagine that the technology displayed in UFOs is possible. However, estimating the technological advancement of UFOs at one to two hundred-years ahead of our current levels, it is not difficult to believe that planets in their sixth thousand-year period of temporal existence could have received technology one to two hundred years earlier, and are visiting us regularly therewith.

The Quarantine

Of course, the question arises, Would Heavenly Father allow such interplanetary visitations? We do not know, and can only speculate. Our discussion in Part I includes nothing that would exclude this possibility. I have heard Church philosophers conjecture that because of the Earth's uniqueness in having reared and crucified the universal Savior, and in possessing the most wicked as well as the most righteous of Heavenly Father's children, there may exist a "quarantine" of this planet that does not necessarily exist with others. This theory was discussed earlier, and could be accurate—we do not know. The concept is somewhat bolstered by the reported "noninterference" policy declared by some humanlike aliens (although practiced by few overall). However, the fact that we are visited by those from other planets would tend to negate the fact of quarantine. We have received no published revelation on this matter and do not know.

Exploration Or Conquest?

We know that on our own planet the more advanced cultures are allowed to visit the less advanced, leaving an impression of magical abilities and awe. Are such visitations always conducted in a benign culturaloutreach style? Certainly not. We remember well the fate of the Lamanites who extended the hand of friendship to the cross wielding representatives of European governments and churches. Therefore, if we assume that interplanetary visitation is allowed at any level, because of our own example, we cannot decisively conclude that conquest at some level is disallowed. For the same reasons we cannot completely rule out genetic experimentation, or any other source of inflicted human trauma—our history is saturated with it. Because Heavenly Father gives us full reign to love or abuse one another on Earth, there is no reason to believe that another standard exists if He allows interplanetary visitation.

An Intergalactic War Zone?

What about the good vs. bad aliens that are reportedly locked into battle around Earth? For the same reasons discussed above, there is no cause to believe that foreign wars cannot be fought on our Earth's soil or in its skies. Assuming also that interplanetary visitation is permitted, the question arises whether or not God would allow our alien brethren, good or evil, to play a significant role in the winding up scene of the last days. We discuss this possibility at greater length below. At this point in our discussion, based on the assumptions we have made, there is no reason to believe it is not *possible*.

Anything Is Possible

Even though we have ignored some glaring red flags in our discussion of the possibility that UFOs are actually of extraterrestrial origin, there is nothing revealed at this time in the Gospel that precludes such a conclusion. Indeed, we know they are out there on their own planets, in great numbers. The only questions are, Do they visit us? and if so, Are they in the UFOs reportedly seen by millions worldwide? Is there some unknown logic or hidden meaning behind their apparently nonsensical message? Certainly, millions of trust-worthy witnesses bear most solemn testimony that the craft and occupants are real, physical objects. We would like to think that all of the UFOs reported are piloted by benign human brethren from fellow telestial spheres, here to extend a warm hand of fellowship. This is *possible*—but not probable.

Theory 2: Returning Earthlings

As discussed elsewhere above, there are those who speculate that UFOs are the flying machines of those who have (or will have) departed from this Earth, and who have returned for some unknown purpose. The dominant theories are: an ancient, advanced Earth civilization that once left the Earth is now sending back scouts, much as King Limhi sent scouts to find his root society of Zarahemla; a translated or otherwise disengaged society like Zion, Salem, or the Ten Tribes is visiting the Earth preparatory to returning; and, time travellers, from our past or future are here on a mission to observe us or to save the planet and mankind from certain self-destruction.

The Time Traveler

The easiest of these theories to deal with is probably the last, the time traveller. We have progressed in our scientific thinking to a point where we acknowledge that at some distant time, travel through time *may* become a possibility. Accepting this, the question is, Does the Gospel indicate any details about the past or future of the Earth that would limit the application of this principle?

The Gospel gives us information regarding at least the future of *this* planet that would tend to preclude the possibility of future Earthlings returning to lend assistance. The scriptures are quite clear that (1) the Earth enjoys a seven-thousand-year temporal existence, after which it will become a celestial globe, at which time all of Earth's "temporal existence works" will have been accomplished; (2) the last, or seventh thousand-year period is the Millennium, which will follow severe devastation to the surface of the Earth, during which time technological advancement will play a lesser role in the works that are performed, and will be centered in the spiritual salvation of mankind, not the physical salvation of the planet through time travel; and (3) our Lord and Savior controls the destiny of the Earth and its inhabitants and at no time does He lose control, necessitating time travel to repair mistakes.

In short, the Earth's future does not include continued scientific progress for the purpose of time exploration. It will be wholly devoted to the fulfilling of the Gospel Plan of Salvation for each of Heavenly Father's children—ensuring that no opportunity fails to be tendered. The known future of the Earth, except for the next half century, is sufficiently at odds with the theories of those that surmise a long future with scientific discovery and progress, that the future time traveller hypothesis is moot.

As for the time traveller from our past, we cannot say for sure. Although it is possible that technology was given in the past to some prophet (or other person in communication with superhuman or supernatural beings) sufficient to enable him to transport himself to our time, the other problems mentioned above remain. The greatest question that would arise from such a scenario is Why would a prophet (or anyone else) from the past be required to skip through the centuries to perform some mission now? Most of those of our past who were given superior knowledge were translated. Certainly, the existence of translated beings provides for whatever purposes may be realized through time travel from our past. And again, Heavenly Father does not have "emergencies" of time that would require the immediate travel of a person from our past to our present—and He certainly would not accomplish such a mission through the use of Time Machines/UFOs flying around in our skies. Never would such a mission include the kinds of genetic experimentation and other trauma that are much a part of the UFO phenomenon. The possibility of a remote time traveler receiving technology and a mission from sources other than Deity is also discussed below.

Translated Societies Visiting

Moving backwards in our list of possible theories, we come to translated disengaged societies like Zion or Salem visiting the Earth preparatory to returning. This theory is not as easily dismissed as the earlier although it has its problems. As we discussed at length in Part I, we know that the inhabitants of Zion live on another planet, and that at times, members of their society minister to people on the Earth. The two questions that naturally arise are Do they travel in protective craft when they come? and if so, Do these visitations account for the millions of UFO sightings reported worldwide?

The first question raises a related, and even more interesting consideration—Do angels, or does God, travel in any kind of craft when personally visiting the various planets of our universe? Indeed, does Heavenly Father employ the use of any technology or machinery in His administration of His immense kingdom? Returning for a moment to our *Extraterrestrial Life Survey,* only two percent of LDS Church members that responded believed that angels travel in space vehicles to visit the Earth, and the same two percent believed that God does. As discussed below, there are many nonmembers who believe that the UFOs are piloted by angels that minister to the Earth, and some writers in the Church who advance the theory as being scripturally supported.

Although we do not know what means of interstellar transportation is employed in the eternities, we can assume that omnipotent God and his agents do not *require* the physical protection or propulsion of a spacecraft. It is also safe to assume that God is not hindered by the time-space considerations that beset mortals. We know that our universe is multidimensional and that God and angels have access to at least two dimensions that occupy the same space. This is clear from our understanding of the spirit world—that it occupies a parallel plane to this Earth. Human spirits, in the form of angels or other beings, as well as resurrected beings, are able to act within both worlds. Although in our limited understanding of such principles it is difficult to fully grasp these concepts. Knowing that they are verities, however, informs us that God does not travel or interact in the same spacial and temporal limits as we.

As to whether or not translated societies are returning to the Earth preparatory to their mass arrival, we have no information. If so, whether they travel in protective craft when they come is also an unknown. What little knowledge we have regarding translated beings is that they cannot die or feel pain or sorrow due to their elevation to a quasiresurrected, terrestrial state. (3 Nephi 28:15, 37-38) Does this imply that their bodies are impervious to the ravages of space's harsh environment? Probably. We read of the translated John the Revelator being boiled in a pot of oil without any adverse effects. Does it indicate that they transcend the physical laws that apply to a temporal existence—that they are no longer subject to time-space constraints? Presumably so. (3 Nephi 28:13-15) From these assumptions we can infer that translated beings have no *need* of protective, propulsive craft. Whether or not this is true, or if without the need, the craft might be employed for another unknown purpose, we have no indication.

The question has been raised, Was the translation and removal of the City of Zion and its surrounding countryside accomplished with the aid of any devices or craft? For the same reasons that we do not know the truth of the prior questions without divine revelation, we cannot know the answer to this question. Again, we can only surmise that because God is omnipotent, He *can* accomplish such feats without the aid of technology. However, our knowledge that He employs "devices" and follows predetermined methods (*e.g.* physical creation) in accomplishing His works fails to eliminate any of these possibilities.

Assuming then, the possibility that translated beings from our past could be visiting the Earth in spacecraft, could these visitations account for the millions of UFO sightings reported worldwide or the thousands of encounters with "alien" beings? I believe that the sheer number of such sightings indicates that the answer to this question is "No." Surely, discretion has always been a hallmark of such visitations. Furthermore, these visitations would not include the kinds of genetic experimentation, abduction trauma, and psychic activity that *are* so much a part of the UFO phenomenon. The "visitors" themselves would all have the appearance of normal humans, which they do not. And finally, the "message" of UFO occupants is not harmonious with a message that we would expect from a translated being sent from God. To cite a favorite fundamentalist scripture, "But though we, or an angel from heaven, preach any other gospel unto you than that which we have preached unto you, let him be accursed." (Galatians 1:8) The entire scenario bypasses the latter-day ecclesiastical structure painstakingly put in place by Heavenly Father, and for this reason alone, I would reject the theory.

Returning Emigrant Societies

The final "returning earthling" theory is that an ancient, advanced Earth civilization that once left the Earth is now sending back scouts for some unknown purpose—presumably, according to the message, to avert impending disaster here or to reintroduce themselves as our departed brethren. Many of the possibilities relative to this theory have been covered in the prior two: was there sufficient technology revealed at some time in the past six thousand years to enable such an exodus?, and if so, who revealed the information and why?; and, most UFO occupants appear significantly different from us.

Other than these two problems, I cannot think of a limitation enunciated in the Gospel that would prohibit such emigration. In fact, branching to foreign lands is a hallmark of the Gospel. Branching to other worlds is part and parcel of translation. A middle position, branching to other worlds by certain telestial tribes, appears to be plausible, although unorthodox. Christ's declaration to the Hebrews that He had other sheep not of their fold whom He had to visit was only partially fulfilled in His visit to the Nephites. Of course, this does not necessarily support the hypothesis that hidden telestial branches emigrated to other planets, but our limited knowledge does not foreclose the possibility.

One potential difficulty with this theory is made evident in the question, Where would such a branch have been taken? To another probationary planet peopled with telestial beings? Is this mixing of world families allowed? If so—What about the chain of Earth's human family stretching from Adam to the last born? Perhaps then to an uninhabited (no homogenous tribes) planet, prepared for such hidden branches? As unlikely as these prospects seem, we have the unresolved questions in Church history concerning the possibility that untranslated beings, such as the Lost Ten Tribes of Israel, may have been whisked away in just such a manner.

Again, because of the numbers of sightings and encounters, the hostility, and the message, I believe that the possibility of UFOs belonging to an ancient, departed Earth civilization is remote. However, this does not preclude the possibility. There is no limitation that we know of on the existence of numerous, hostile encounters with departed tribes that deliver nonsensical messages. Certainly, analogous circumstances exist among Earthbound peoples.

Theory 3: Natural Phenomena

The Debunkers' theory that all UFO sightings and encounters (as well as scriptural encounters with Deity and angels) are explainable by naturally occurring phenomena fail to address the hard physical evidence or the abduction phenomenon. Debunkers can blindly attempt to convince the world that millions have been mistaken (including thousands of Church members) in thinking that they saw silvery disks flying erratically in the sky, but this position is purely untenable at this point in the phenomenon. Too many trained observers have carefully watched UFOs perform their stunts from close range to be fooled by flocks of geese, meteors, or swamp gas. Mass hallucination is itself a pipe dream.

Debunkers proffer theories that Jungian archetypes common to all humans, or possibly birth trauma memories, are responsible for psychological ordeals like these that are similar, yet experienced by persons with little else in common. The range of witnesses is far too wide to draw any cultural or psychological boundaries around those who see UFOs and those who do not. Clearly, the Debunkers do not have the answers.

Because of the interrelated nature and complexity of the remaining theories—that the UFOs and their occupants are demonic, extradimensional, or spiritually evolved entities—we discuss them together in a separate chapter below. As for those theories treated in this chapter that attempt to explain the nature and origin of UFOs and their occupants, our only conclusion can be that they are *possible, but not probable.* This is not to say that some of the encounters cannot be fully explained by the extraterrestrial theory or some other theory discussed here—it merely indicates that none of these theories is inclusive enough to accommodate the wide range of behavior of the UFO phenomenon. This may indicate that different phenomena are being manifested—perhaps, a mixture of theories we are discussing is the answer. It is possible that many witnesses see robotic craft from other worlds in our skies, while others encounter true extraterrestrial explorers. Yet, I do not believe that many of the encounters we discuss are answered by these explanations. I suspect that many "alien" encounters may be better explained by the theory we explore in the next chapter.

15

Are UFOs And Their Message
A Satanic Deception?

In this chapter we discuss the possibility that UFOs and their related phenomena originate from spiritual sources—more specifically, whether they are of Satanic origins. This is the least flattering of all of the possible sources that are discussed herein, yet the most pregnant with opportunities for analysis. As I have said from the outset, Christian Fundamentalist writers dismiss the entire UFO phenomenon as a demonic device *ab initio.* This is due not to their thorough analysis of the facts, or to divine inspiration, but to their mistaken belief that Earth is God's only creation on which he has placed his finite number of spiritual/physical creations—man. With this understanding, Fundamentalists have no place in their theorizing for extraterrestrial humans; their reasoning is that the UFOs, if not built by Earth humans, must necessarily originate from the only other available source of intelligence in the universe—Satan.

Counterfeits Are Patterned After True Principles

Although we are not restricted in our theorizing as are the Fundamentalists, we must genuinely consider the real possibility that UFO phenomena are demonic in origin. The evidence of such is great. However, this is not to say that the Earth is not visited occasionally by our extraterrestrial brethren even if the bulk of UFO encounters turns out to have Satanic origins. We well know that if Satan sets out to deceive, he does so by manipulating truth. If the majority of UFO sightings are a Satanic device employed for a purpose that we discuss at length below, or some other unknown purpose, Satan having selected it as a deceptive device supports the proposition that his manifestations are counterfeits of true occurrences.

This "counterfeit" principle is borne out in the scriptures and our own Church history. As cited earlier Joseph Smith recorded:

223

> Soon after the Gospel was established in Kirtland, and during the absence of the
> authorities of the Church, many false spirits were introduced, many strange visions
> were seen, and wild, enthusiastic notions were entertained; men ran out of doors under
> the influence of this spirit, and some of them got upon the stumps of trees and shouted,
> and all kinds of extravagances were entered into by them; *one man pursued a ball that*
> *he said he saw flying in the air,* until he came to a precipice, when he jumped into
> the top of a tree, which saved his life; . . . [*Teachings of the Prophet Joseph Smith,*
> p. 214; emphasis supplied]

Satan's *modus operandi* in his efforts to undermine God's work has always been to confuse, divide, and distract God's children, as is demonstrated in this chronicle. His tactics are like those of the famed courtroom attorney, Perry Mason. If a witness saw Mason's accused client at the murder scene, Mason does not directly attempt to convince the witness that he does not "know" what he saw. Instead, Mason employs an "Acme Models girl" to dress like the client, and stage a second appearance before the witness to "implant" a new memory of the original witnessing. When the witness identifies Mason's client as the one seen on both occasions, Mason puts the counterfeit on the witness stand, who swears that it was she who encountered the witness on the second occasion. This confusion technique, of course, confuses the witness and has the effect of rendering the witness's testimony invalid as to both events.

Satan sends counterfeit messengers—glorious, radiant beings, praising God and commanding the percipient to worship God the Father and His Son Jesus Christ, and none other. The messenger of light then proceeds to deliver a message that is 95% true. The five percent portion of the message, however, is generally deadly in terms of God's will in the matter. Some examples of false spirits appearing as angels of light, bearing messages from God were presented in Chapter 12. Others are prevalent in Church History. Still more are found worldwide, throughout the past two millennia as "Blessed Virgin Mary" apparitions. Satan sends these counterfeits for the same reason Perry Mason does—to confuse what we innately know to be the truth. They appear and act like the real thing, yet their message is distorted just enough to make the truth a lie.

It is curious that Joseph Smith chose to include in his enumeration of the activities of false spirits the account of the man who "pursued a ball that he said he saw flying in the air," which attempted to take his life by leading him over a precipice. The description of the flying sphere is more than reminiscent of the spheres, globes, and other disks that occupy a great portion of UFO-encounter literature. Did Joseph believe that such apparitions were necessarily Satanic, or was his discernment derived from the attempt on the brother's life? This much we know—the only recorded flying sphere incident in early LDS Church History was a Satanic attempt to destroy a Church member.

Power Of The Air

Joseph Smith may have known something about Satan's power that we do not, as alluded to in the following:

> It would seem also, that wicked spirits have their bounds, limits, and laws by which they are governed or controlled, and know their future destiny; . . . and when Satan presented himself before the Lord, among the sons of God, he said that he came "from going to and fro in the earth, and from wandering up and down in it;" and he is emphatically called *the prince of the power of the air;* and, it is very evident that they possess a power that none but those that have the Priesthood can control, as we have before averted to, in the case of the sons of Sceva. [*Teachings of the Prophet Joseph Smith,* p. 208; emphasis supplied]

Joseph's reference to Satan as the "the prince of the power of the air" is taken from the New Testament wherein the Apostle Paul called him by that appellation. (Ephesians 2:2) What does it imply to call Satan "the prince of the power of the air"? We are nowhere given the answer to this question. However, Joseph Smith referred to the title in association with the fact that Satanic spirits "possess a power that none but those that have the Priesthood can control."

Remember that in our discussion in Chapter 12 Joseph Smith and Brigham Young both referred specifically to the overwhelming latter-day power of Satan and warned us that only through the power of the Holy Priesthood could we combat him. The admonition bears repeating here:

> Or who can drag into daylight and develop the hidden mysteries of the false spirits that so frequently are made manifest among the Latter-day Saints? We answer that *no man can do this without the Priesthood, and having a knowledge of the laws by which spirits are governed;* for as no man knows the things of God, but by the Spirit of God, so no man knows the spirit of the devil, and his power and intelligence, which is more than human, and having unfolded through the medium of the Priesthood the mysterious operations of his devices . . . . *A man must have the discerning of spirits before he can drag into daylight this hellish influence and unfold it unto the world* in all its soul-destroying, diabolical, and horrid colors . . . . [*Teachings of the Prophet Joseph Smith,* pp. 204-05; emphasis supplied]

It seems certain that Satan will demonstrate his powers in the air in the last days. How will he do this? Moreover, *how can* he do it? We discuss some possibilities below.

Deceptive Devices

I raise the devices of "theater," "counterfeits," and "*knowledge* distracting implants" above because as we analyze the UFO phenomenon from the demonic origin viewpoint, we should view each aspect of the UFO encounter in light of how it could be the implementation or employment of one of these devices. We are not the first to raise these issues. Many observers of the UFO phenomenon have remarked how closely related it appears to be to phenomena associated with demonic hauntings, apparitions, and possessions. Even Dr. Salisbury, in the early 1970s, noted how the UFOs seemed to be putting on a "display," something that a scientist was hard-pressed to explain. Of course, a UFO's communication with the Uintah Basin children through an Ouija Board was an occurrence that he did not even know how to approach in a scientific medium.

Generated Images

Looking first to the physical appearance of the UFOs and their occupants can be enlightening. Much of the literature documents how UFOs initially "resolve" themselves from a dispersed mist into a sharply "focused" object. They then zip and zigzag about at phenomenal speeds, only to "dissolve," or disappear in a blink. As in the cases of the French Dr. "X" or Betty Luca, some UFOs are reported to transform their shape or size, or even merge with a second UFO as the witness looks on. The cry of "superior science" is drowned out by the roar of "projected image" when it comes to these kinds of displays. An image generated by a simple slide projector can travel quite quickly and erratically along a wall by the slight pivoting of the projector at its source. Can this rudimentary concept be applied to UFO sightings?

There are those who believe that UFOs may be nothing more than mere projections—laser or holographic. Although this theory is possible, and interesting, we have little evidence that anyone possesses the level of technology required to put on such a light show. However, the technology is not too far in advance of state-of-the-art projection capabilities, and the possibility should not be overlooked. The question then arises, Who would go to such extravagant, sophisticated, and expensive lengths to fool so many people? Only persons looking for power, as we discuss below, would conduct such a campaign. This would limit them to the political or religious realms.

Although this theory seems workable, it is not a practical one. The risk of being caught in the act of setting up the necessary equipment is too high for never having been discovered. This is especially true in light of the massive investigation that attends many UFO sightings. Besides these difficulties, this theory fails to account for victims' close encounters with, and examinations by "aliens," unless we include the use of drugs and hypnosis in the equation. Then, however, we have the radar and photographic images that have been produced by these phenomena to explain. UFOs seem to be solid objects—semisolid, at least.

Spiritual Projections

If not laser or holographic projections, then what kind? Does Satan have the ability to resolve a semisolid image before a human, complete with a messenger delivering a message? As so many witnesses (including prophets)[1] have testified, the response is a resounding "Yes." How does he do it? We can only guess, but we know that he can. Dr. Curt Wagner, a physicist whose doctoral degree was earned in the field of general relativity theory explains how he believes it is done.

> Drawing from what we know can happen in seances and poltergeist activity, it seems that these supernatural forces can manipulate matter and energy, extracting energy from the atmosphere, for example (which manifests as a local temperature change), to manipulate matter and produce an apparent violation of the second law [of thermodynamics], and I guess my feeling is that on a larger scale this is what a UFO could be. I'm not saying I know that it is, but only that it could be. It seems to me likely that UFOs are largescale violations of the second law in which energy is arranged to take on enough of a force field appearance so that it appears to look like matter, yet it's really just energy concentration—it's not really solid matter in the usual sense.[2]

Another researcher similarly concludes: "Demons, as fallen angels, apparently retain great powers, such as the manipulation and restructuring of matter, as well as the ability to influence or control human consciousness and experience through classic possession or by direct psychic implantation of a set of experiences."[3] The extraction of "energy from the atmosphere, for example (which manifests as a local temperature change)," refers to the classic "cold spot" that is experienced during negative spiritual manifestations.

---

[1] *See e.g., D & C* 128:20, 129:8.

[2] *SCP Journal,* August 1977, p. 20.

[3] *SCP Journal,* August 1977, p. 19.

As discussed below, UFO phenomena are often accompanied by such cold spots. Often, in fact, the larger the scene, the colder the temperature.

A New Age spokesperson and a prominent New Age writer, Brad Steiger frankly admits: "I have even come to suspect that, in some instances, what we have been terming 'spaceships' may actually be a form of higher intelligence rather than vehicles transporting occupants . . . . I feel, too, that these intelligences have the ability to influence the human mind telepathically in order to project what appear to be three dimensional images to the witnesses of UFO activity."[4] Steiger's suspicious observations appear to support our theory. He, however, does not assume that the spirits involved are Satanic. His explanation, although tentative, is more innocuous: "I cannot help questioning whether the Space brothers might not be angels, spirit guides, and other messengers hiding themselves in more contemporary, and thereby more acceptable, personae."[5]

Physical Spirits

The question has often been raised, is Satan capable of physically intruding on our world, manipulating objects with mass, and "touching" or otherwise physically affecting humans? Because I do not feel that an examination of the full range of Satanic "abilities" is necessary or proper in a work like this (or any work, possibly), I will forego such a discussion. However, a look at the very first miracle of the Restoration demonstrates that demonic spirits are indeed capable of affecting us physically.

Joseph Smith records that he had spoken often with Newell Knight about the Gospel and its restoration. Newell was very impressed, but was reluctant to pray. His reluctance turned to inability. He retired to the woods to attempt prayer, but was unable. Joseph chronicles:

> He began to feel uneasy and continued to feel worse both in mind and body until upon reaching his own house his appearance was such as to alarm his wife very much. He requested her to go and bring me to him. I went and found him suffering very much in his mind, and his body acted upon in a very strange manner. His visage and limbs distorted and twisted in every shape and appearance possible to imagine. And finally he was caught up off the floor of the apartment and tossed about most fearfully.
>
> His situation was soon made known to his neighbors and relatives and in a short time as many as eight or nine grown persons had got together to witness the scene.

4 Brad Steiger, *The Fellowship*, Ivy Books, p. 49.

5 *Revelation: The Divine Fire*, A Berkley Book, p. 148.

> After he had thus suffered for a time I succeeded in getting hold of him by the hand, when almost immediately he spoke to me and with great earnestness requested me to cast the devil out of him saying that he knew he was in him and that he also knew that I could cast him out. I replied, "If you know that I can it shall be done." And then almost unconsciously I rebuked the devil and commanded him in the name of Jesus Christ to depart from him. When immediately Newell spoke out and said he saw the devil leave him and vanish from his sight . . . . This scene was entirely changed for as soon as the devil departed from our friend his countenance became natural, his distortions of body ceased, and almost immediately the spirit of the Lord descended upon him and the visions of eternity were opened to his view. [*History of the Church* vol. 1, pp. 82-83]

Church history and those who have had the misfortune to experience demonic attacks bear witness to the fact that there exists a very real physicality to Satan's powers. This principle is borne out in latter-day revelation: "There is no such thing as immaterial matter. All spirit is matter, but it is more fine or pure, and can only be discerned by purer eyes; We cannot see it; but when our bodies are purified we shall see that it is all matter." (*D & C* 131:7-8) We often assume that Satan has little control over the elements because he is a spirit. However, this scripture, which we all well know, instructs that Satan is a physical being, or semiphysical at least.

We can only assume that Satanic powers are increasing as we approach the Second Coming of Christ. Although there are many ideas and teachings in the Church that attempt to delineate such powers, LDS testimonies clarify that few are immune from their effects—children under the age of eight years included. This must be kept in mind as we examine the "abduction" aspect of UFO encounters.

The UFO phenomenon parallels these Satanic attacks. Ed Walters's description of his first encounter in Gulf Breeze, Florida, is instructive.

> The blue beam had hit me like compression. It was pressing me firmly, just enough to stop me from moving.
> I screamed, with my mouth frozen half open, but the sound was hollow. Dead, like a vacuum. I couldn't even move my eyes or eyelids. I thought I was dying. I was trying to breathe, there was air, each breath shallow . . . .

Walters then described how he attempted to speak, but could merely make unintelligible sounds.

This scene is reminiscent of Joseph Smith's description of how he was attacked by Satanic forces just before receiving the visitation from the Father and the Son.

> I had scarcely done so, when immediately I was seized upon by some power which entirely overcame me, and had such an astonishing influence over me as to bind my tongue so that I could not speak. Thick darkness gathered around me, and it seemed to me for a time as if I were doomed to sudden destruction. [*Joseph Smith—History* 1:15]

Many others who have been similarly attacked relate the same feeling of being bound by an unseen force, body and tongue, accompanied by a feeling of imminent doom. These people report their experiences in the context of UFO encounters as well as spiritual encounters—the only difference is the presence or absence of a UFO or an "alien."

In addition to these strictly physical attacks, many victims (including Church members) complain of being attacked by spiritual beings (sometimes in a UFO context) while in a semiconscious, or semiphysical state. Although astral projection, and other forms of out-of-body experiences are part and parcel of forbidden occult practices, some Latter-day Saints have related to me how they preceive that they are attacked and wrestled away while in a state in which they are outside of their bodies—generally as they are waking from sleep. As related, this is a truly terrifying and exhausting experience. According to the Roper Organization poll we have elsewhere discussed, a full 18% of American adults report "waking up paralyzed. With a sense of a strange person or presence or something else in the room."

Solid Objects Without Mass

Other physical aspects of UFOs that alert us to their possible spiritual origin are manifested in the accounts included in Part II. For instance, Ed Walters described his first sighting as though the UFO had no physical effect on its environment. "It glided along without a whisper of sound. In all of the reports of these Gulf Breeze UFOs, the observers are unanimous that none of the UFOs made a sound. There was no hum, no wind, not a single disturbance to the air, trees, or houses as it passed over them." This description of the UFO having no effect on the wind or air is classic. UFOs shoot past observers at tens of thousands of miles per hour, and fail to create a wisp of wind or a sonic boom. Is this possible?—not for an object with mass—not in our space/time continuum. Others report walking on solid, metallic UFO floors, but being unable to make any sound of footsteps.

Synchronous Specters

The physical makeup of the "aliens," entities, or beings, is also of great interest from a Satanic-origin viewpoint. We have many testimonies, for instance, that the "small grey" variety often float along without touching the ground, or that they walk and otherwise move in unison. The floating is easily explained in terms of spiritual manifestations. The aspect of moving and walking in "lockstep" unison is somewhat more intriguing. If we were looking at the problem from an extraterrestrial visitor theory viewpoint, we would think that the small greys are in some kind of controlled telepathic communication. That is the initial appearance, anyway. However, why would spiritual beings walk and act in unison?

One aspect of demonic entities that comes to mind is that if a scene is being generated by just one of these beings, the movement portions of the manifestations may require more brainpower, or whatever the source of their manifestation abilities, than the being possesses. When Betty Luca was asked to observe a particular scene as an observer, the scene slowed to half speed, apparently due to the "double processing" of the images. Assuming that she was being directly "fed" the images she was experiencing under hypnosis, a subject discussed below, this could explain the phenomenon. As any cartoonist or computer animator can attest, the more movement that is generated in an image, the more work and power that is required. Although we are not on well-trodden ground when discussing these aspects of demonic abilities, we can safely assume that when presenting any manifestation, demonic forces are taxed in the process—the more glorious or complicated, the more taxing.

I Am Legion

Another characteristic of demonic entities that could explain the "unison" aspect of these apparitions is the "legion" principle. When Christ spoke to the spirit entity that had possessed a young man, asking the entity's name, the entity "answered, saying, My name is Legion: for we are many." (Mark 5:9) After receiving this information Christ listened as the spirits begged him not to send them out of the country: "And all the devils besought him, saying, Send us into the swine, that we may enter into them." (Mark 5:12) They entered into the *2,000* swine "and the herd ran violently down a steep place into the sea" and drowned. Reserving for a later discussion the overwhelming demonic desire to possess bodies, we well remember the many "alien" encounters in which multiple telepathic voices spoke in unison. For example, speaking of the "visitors'" attempts to control his will and behavior, Whitley Strieber recounts:

> I remembered the visitors' admonition about sweets and decided, experimentally, to toss away the [ice cream] cone. The moment I discarded it, three young voices shouted in unison, "He threw away ice cream for us!"
>
> This sounded totally real, but so close to my ear that it couldn't have been generated by somebody, say, hanging out of an apartment window or standing across the street. I had never heard disembodied voices before the visitor experience started.[6]

Strieber describes how these "disembodied voices" would occasionally speak to him, either within his head or just outside of his ear. He was quite disturbed that he may have developed a brain disease or schizophrenic condition, resulting in his many abduction and disembodied voices experiences, so he underwent thorough psychological and medical testing to determine if he had a diagnosable disorder. He did not.

Betty Andreasson Luca, as well as many others, similarly reported that many of her lifelong contacts with the beings included their speaking in a "chorus" of voices to her. It is important that these beings feigned divinity—speaking in terms of the Savior being "my Son."

> Betty defensively proclaimed her Christian faith . . . . "There is nothing that can make me fear. I have faith in Jesus Christ!"
>
> "We know, child, that you do. That is why you have been chosen. I am sending you back now. Fear not . . . . It is for your own fear that you draw to your body, that causes you to feel these things. I can release you. But you must release yourself of that fear *through my son.*"
>
> The words "through my son" suddenly became the catalyst for the most moving religious experience that I have ever witnessed. Betty's face literally shone with unrestrained joy as tears streamed down her beaming face.
>
> "Oh, praise God, praise God, praise God. (Crying) Thank you, Lord. (Crying, sobbing) I know, I know I am not worthy. Thank you for your son. (Uncontrollable sobbing) Thank you for your son."[7]

Ghostly Abilities

Another characteristic of the entities that indicates a spiritual origin is their practice of walking through walls and other solid objects. Their explanation that they are able to change their vibrational levels at will, and pass through solid objects in that state, is not convincing. Although this explanation sounds *possible,* it seems more of a smokescreen to mask a clearly spiritual manifestation or feat than an explanation of superior science or brainpower.

---

6 *Transformation*, p. 147.

7 Raymond Fowler, *The Andreasson Affair*, Bantam Books, New York (1980), p. 87.

Invasion Of The Body Snatchers

The "disembodied" characteristic to which we have referred in the prior two topics leads us squarely into a third indicator that these are demonic spiritual beings. *They have a need of bodies.* As is clearly manifest throughout the abduction and contactee literature, the procurement of bodies for their species is an overriding element in the motivation of these beings. Their stated reasons for requiring bodies vary with each contactee, but the theme is constant. There are three methods that they could employ to secure these bodies: genetic engineering; mechanical invention; and, corporeal possession.

Theory 1: Genetic Engineering

In the television movie *Intruders,* the "Laura Davis" character comments on the hybrid baby nursery aspect of Kathie Davis's experiences on the UFOs to the "Psychiatrist" character, and queries, "Why do you think they created them—to start a new world?" The Psychiatrist responds pensively, "Maybe—or to save an old one." Although this exchange is a dramatization produced to editorialize on the hybrid baby phenomenon, the question and answer are common in UFOlogy. Abductees report that they "perceive" the answer to be (1) to save the "genetically imperiled" alien race, (2) to save our own "soon to become extinct" race, or (3) to create a new hybrid race, possibly to inhabit a new world somewhere in space.

We have already discussed some of the problems associated with these responses. First, if an extraterrestrial human race, genetically compatible with our own (which we would assume to be the case), were to be having such difficulties with their genetic stock, why would they pursue the entire abduction scenario course, when their *claimed* superior capabilities enable them to engineer such stock or to at least steal the human samples unnoticed? The "aliens" have no intention of working unnoticed! They fly their craft through our dark night skies lit up like neon Christmas trees! They do everything they can to be detected, while pretending to work surreptitiously. They inadequately seal the abduction memory into the subconscious regions of their victims' minds knowing that it will be recalled in a dramatic investigation. I believe that the genetic experimentation spectacle is a sham.

Why Hybrids?

Nothing about the "hybrid baby" farce makes the least bit of sense. Why "hybrids" instead of "aliens" if they want to preserve their own species? If this were their true purpose they could use a small amount of human genetic coding for minor physical improvements. If their race is truly superior to ours, which claim they make frequently, why pollute their offspring with inferior genetics? Understanding that some will think these observations sophomoric, from a genetic engineering viewpoint anyway, I challenge those who accept this theory to explain the necessity of a 50/50 genetic hybrid, instead of a genetically reinforced alien result. It is a smokescreen.

Not To Preserve The Human Form

The second response, "to save our soon to become extinct human race," has no basis in truth. As discussed above, our Earth has a fixed seven thousand year period of temporal existence. Our race will be saved without the help of "aliens." There is little probability of imminent, worldwide destruction of the human race. Prophetically, that is just not how it is going to happen. Abductee after contactee report how they are filled with visions of the Earth's imminent destruction. Whitley Strieber speaks of his very vivid induced dream in which he saw a nuclear power plant blow up and the moon explode, causing great catastrophes on Earth.[8] As a result of his "catastrophe" visions (common in UFOlogy) implanted by the entities, Strieber has written best-selling books decrying the use of nuclear energy (a common crusade of contactees) and generally promoting the Earthspirit doctrines of the New Age.

All telestial/probationary planets have their times and bounds fixed, just like the Earth—this would include those of the "aliens." God, who controls the destiny of the Earth and each of its inhabitants, has already decreed the end from the beginning—what will be is written in granite. Perhaps some readers will say that this is either not necessarily true (even though the prophets have made it perfectly clear), or they may say that the "aliens" might not know this fact. Even allowing for the ignorance of the superior intellect, any claim to preserve the human race by collecting specimens before the holocaust is untrue—it is not "our race" that is being preserved in the UFO nursery—it is a purported hybrid race.

---

8 *Transformation*, pp. 58-59.

The third response, "to create a new hybrid race," likewise fails to pass scriptural muster. The question returns again and again, Why hybrids? If they want to save their own race, then do it—but 50/50 hybrids are not their own race. The same is true of saving our race. So why hybrids? Only one answer presents itself—to create a superior human race—certainly not to create an inferior alien race. For what purpose? To populate another planet? The gospel says "no." It is clear that God's offspring are assigned to specific planets and the human/Adamic family that populates each. Is it possible that we could get around such a principle, and retain our planetary/family identity, yet explore the universe in *Star Trek* fashion? Not if any interplanetary marriages produce offspring. Granted, this is a mere academic exercise, but we must face the fact that little possibility exists that extraterrestrial humans are mixing with our own race to populate another planet or save either of the donor races.

The Superhumans

What could be the benefit of creating a superior human race then—assuming that such is the case? I can think of two possible scenarios. The first hypothesis: the only hybrids, assuming that there are any, are those rendered from the altering of human bodies. We know that human devolution is a reality, and its source has often been connected with ungodly practices. (*Mormon Doctrine*, p. 616) These bodies are made available to unembodied demonic spirits, whose driving compulsion is to possess a body, no matter what its source. We have too little revealed on the matter to speculate further, but the subject has been debated for centuries by speculating theologians who have argued about the sin of copulating with demons:

> The devil does not have a body. Then how does he manage to have intercourse with men and women? How can women have children from such unions? Theologians answer that the devil borrowed [possessed] the corpse of a human being, either male or female, or else he forms with other materials a new body for this purpose . . . .
> The devil then is said to proceed in one of two ways. Either he first takes the form of a female succubus and then has intercourse with a man, or else the succubus induces lascivious dreams in a sleeping man and makes use of the resulting "pollution" to allow the devil to perform the second part of the operation.[9]

Many ancient theologians theorized that it is by this very process that Antichrist (or, the Man of Sin, if Antichrist will be a political entity rather

[9] *Dimensions*, p. 146.

than an individual man), must be born, which brings us to our second possible scenario for the creation, actual or pretended, of a superior human race.

The second hypothesis: The entire New Age movement is based on the belief that mankind is about to evolve into a new, improved, superior, enlightened race. The elite of the New Age are believed to be made up of "early evolving" ones of the coming superhumans. Their superhuman abilities—intellectual, spiritual, and physical—will enable them to take the reigns of government and religion, and save the world from the imminent catastrophes that threaten its certain destruction. They will be supported by the "space brothers" and "ascended masters" who are concerned for the welfare of our planet and its inhabitants. Anyone wishing to receive the benefits of their leadership must abandon their outdated, superstitious beliefs, and embrace the New Age. Antichrist will thus come to power with the aid of these men.

Lewis and Shreckhise, Fundamentalist Christian New Age watchdogs who adhere to this UFO/Satanic Conspiracy theory speculate:

> If our calculations are right there will be a massive open manifestation of alien presence and power on Earth. Something big is about to happen! Kings, prime ministers, and presidents will tremble before the "ascended masters." How could they refuse the help so generously offered when Earth is about to self-destruct? They will play right into the hands of Antichrist if they follow the aliens' suggestions. Some rulers may be executed by angry mobs for taking a stand against the "space brothers."
>
> An axis-shift and concurrent disasters are related to the "paradigm shift" that New Age devotees expect in the near future. This shift in humanity's worldview will be precipitated by massive demonic deception and even possession. [10]

The second reason for creating a seemingly superhuman race, then, is to convince humanity to follow the superhumans into whatever paths the superhumans may choose. Whether these superhumans are merely humans with Satanic powers, hybrid-appearing humans endowed with Satanic powers, hybrid-appearing demons, or human-appearing demons, the predicted result is the same. How likely is it that the superhuman race theory is true? In one of the four forms just enumerated, I believe that the scriptures support the probability of such a ruse—in at least partial implementation of Satan's latter-day, premillennial rise to world domination. The Man of Sin, the head of Antichrist will be such a man.

> [The man of sin] opposeth and exalteth himself above all that is called God, or that is worshipped; so that he as God sitteth in the temple of God, *shewing himself that he is God* . . . . Even him, whose coming is after the working of Satan with *all power and*

---

[10] *UFO: End-Time Delusion*, p. 160.

signs and lying wonders, And with all deceivableness of unrighteousness in them that perish; because they received not the love of the truth, that they might be saved. And for this cause *God shall send them strong delusion,* that they should believe a lie. [2 Thessalonians 2:3-11; emphasis supplied]

Satanic Science

Are aliens or demonic spirits carrying out genetic engineering experiments for any of the reasons discussed above? There exists a low likelihood that extraterrestrial humans are involved in such an activity for the reasons allegedly proffered by them. The question of Satanic involvement in such physical pursuits is intriguing, and opens the floodgates to many questions involving "Satanic Science." We, of course, do not know to what extent Satan may involve himself in human reproductive activities to promote his diabolic purposes in the Earth. Furthermore, we know even less about his ability to enter and possess such custom-engineered flesh.

One example that we have of spiritual intervention in human insemination is the conception of the Savior's body. When Mary was told by the angel Gabriel, "And, behold, thou shalt conceive in thy womb, and bring forth a son, and shalt call his name JESUS," she responded, "How shall this be, seeing I know not a man?" (Luke 1:31, 34) Gabriel then explained, "The Holy Ghost shall come upon thee, and the power of the Highest shall overshadow thee: therefore also that holy thing which shall be born of thee shall be called the Son of God." (Luke 1:35) This "explanation" has spawned a plethora of theories and debates concerning the nature and origin of Christ Himself.

Modern prophets have rejected all of the "Son of the Holy Ghost" theories and have assured us that Christ is the literal Son of the Father—a physical being. Yet Mary was a virgin. Nephi explains that Mary was "carried away in the Spirit" at the time she conceived. (1 Nephi 11:19) Modern prophets say, without elaboration, that she conceived just like any other woman conceives. How was it done? Is any confusion eliminated by all of these clarifications?

I believe that modern fertilization techniques enlighten us as to how it occurred. We are now capable of taking physical seed from a man and artificially implanting it in the ovum of a woman. I would not think that this would be too arduous a task for the Holy Ghost—to take a small seed from the physical, glorified body of Heavenly Father and place it in the ovum of a mortal woman. So doing, all of the known facts regarding the conception of Christ are undisturbed. Although this conclusion leaves room in the world for numerous virgin births, there is only one Only Begotten Son of the Father.

Having considered the uniqueness of the conception of the Savior, it is more than curious that much of the activity described on UFOs is centered in artificial insemination and the premature removal of hybrid fetuses from artificially inseminated human women. What drama is being played out here? A counterfeit of the virgin birth?—a probable claim that will be made by the superhumans, in all of their glorious modesty.

Theory 2: Mechanical Invention

As mentioned above, there exists a little-discussed subject that must be raised here in an effort to determine if the "aliens" are of a mechanical nature, or of some other "manipulation and restructuring of matter" as also mentioned above—is there such a thing as Satanic Science? As discussed, Heavenly Father metes out technology in His own time, for His own purposes. Does Satan do the same? Surely, any technology that has been had among any of the planets of God is known to Satan. He has this kind of knowledge, and uses it to his own advantage every time he sees an opportunity. For example, we have been specifically informed by latter-day prophets that communications technology has been revealed in these latter-days for the primary purpose of spreading the Gospel throughout the Earth. Yet, Satan has exploited these Godgiven gifts for his own evangelism. Possibly, Satan is aware of even greater technology than is had on any planet, he having filled the position of the Great Bearer of the Light before his rebellion and fall. Our technology is simple and crude. The microprocessor and wave technology are the only real advancement made in centuries. Before that, the printing press—not very impressive. Our question is then: Does Satan conduct technological enterprise and/or dispense technology to his human recruits for his own purposes?

Because we were unable to answer the question, Does God personally use technology?—we may be equally unable to answer whether Satan does, for similar reasons. However, we know that God dispenses it to man and we have no indication that Satan cannot. The only force that could prevent Satan's employment or dissemination of technology for his purposes is God's disallowance. Would God disallow it? We know that he puts many limitations on Satan to control the level of his attack on humanity. (*D & C* 121:4) We also know that in these latter-days God will allow Satan more power in the Earth. How much, we do not know.

Is Satan involved in creating robotic or materialistic bodies for him and his demons to possess and control? We know that Satan can enter and control the bodies of animals, and that he can influence objects with mass. Therefore, little reason exists to doubt his ability to control mechanical devices, including sophisticated robots, as though they were alive. In fact, some of our most eerie accounts of supernatural displays are centered in just such acts of animating objects.

Is this the answer then to UFOs or their occupants? Within this line of reasoning two possibilities exist. First, Satan creates physical crafts and bodies, then animates them through spiritual control, like possession. Second, Satan recruits humans to his cause, arming them with technology sufficient to build and pilot the craft, and to build and control the robots, if such are employed under this theory. This latter explanation could also account for the "remote timetraveler" who comes to this century on a Satanic mission if given the proper technology as we discussed above. This, however, is quite unlikely.

It is often reported that the small greys and other "aliens" are seen moving in a very mechanical, robotic fashion. This could also explain the phenomenon of why they are seen moving in unison, even when the movement of the second entity has no effect on the object being manipulated by the first. Whether these fabrications are mechanical (made by Satan or human recruits) or illusion, the operation and results are the same—they are centrally controlled. This would also explain why communication with the beings is telepathic—they do not have the power of human speech.

The fact that the smaller, gnomelike, or robotlike beings are often seen in the presence of, and are subservient to, human-looking beings supports these theories. Are the human-appearing entities behind the UFO phenomenon Satan's human recruits who are employed in his service? Are they demonic beings projecting an angelic or human appearance? Are they too robots—controlled spiritually or mechanically? We, of course, have no firm answers. But we know for sure that none of these "message bearing" beings is what it claims to be. They are all lying—a prime indicator that we are dealing with Satan.

Whitley Strieber had an experience that lends credibility to our discussion. After being embarrassed by the beings in a bizarre drama, he recounts:

> I was forced by my [ballooning paper gown] clothing to move like an arrogant prince—which made me feel even more like a toad. Carrying myself as best as I was able, I

left the room. We were going down the curving corridor again when one of the blue beings looked up at me with his wide face. I saw it clearly this time, and it was really startlingly horrible. Awful! The eyes glittered as if they were shiny black membranes, with something moving behind them that made lumps and pits as it seethed within the eyeball. He smiled, showing the tips of his grey, spongy-looking teeth. His companion pulled open one of the [many] drawers [that lined the corridors].

In that drawer were stacks of bodies like their own, all encased in what looked like cellophane. Their eyes were open, their mouths wide as if with surprise. I did not know what to make of it. The oddest thing was the way the drawer was opened with a prideful flourish. I was being shown something the two of them clearly thought was wonderful. [11]

An arsenal of readied bodies. Ready for what? For whatever it was that propelled the two gnomes that so proudly exhibited the contents of one of the many drawers. If these were manufactured bodies, Why these hideous little gnome appearing creatures instead of handsome humans or angelic beings? After all, if you are going to create your own tabernacle through some kind of technology or manipulation of matter, it is just as easy to generate a Lamborghini as a Pinto. I believe that the answer lies in the fact that this is a drama—a theatrical production—and the actors are costumed appropriately for their parts. It is apparent that these inanimate bodies were lifeless, just as those of the escorts had been prior to animation.

Similar Encounters Have Historical Precedents

In analyzing the beings and their behavior, some researchers have shown the parallels between human encounters with nonhuman beings throughout history, and these UFO encounters. Noted scientist and UFO researcher Jacques Vallee has produced a wealth of information concerning these parallels. Some of them are included in the previous chapter as paranormal parallels.

One such encounter is cited by both Whitley Strieber and Jacques Vallee, albeit for different reasons. The tale is well documented and relates how a young teenage boy disappeared for two years. One day his mother, who had grievously mourned his death, was shocked to see him at the door. Upon seeing him she was astonished that he had not aged at all during this period of traditionally accelerated maturation. Vallee cites the story because, as in many such cases, the boy insisted he had been away with the little people

---

[11] *Transformation*, p. 40; emphasis supplied.

for less than two full days. Strieber, however, found interesting the fact that the boy carried a bundle containing a white, seamless paper gown, exactly like the one given to Strieber in the above-quoted story, that the boy told his mother the little men had given him to wear while he was with them.

Following is a story quoted by a researcher cited by Vallee to further demonstrate the similarities between traditional encounters with the "Gentry" and modern UFO occupant encounters.

> The folk are the grandest I have ever seen. They are far superior to us and that is why they call themselves the Gentry. They are not a working-class, but a military-aristocratic class, tall and noble-appearing. They are a distinct race between our race and that of spirits, as they have told me. Their qualifications are tremendous: "We could cut off half the human race, but would not," they said, "for we are expecting salvation."
>
> They take young and intelligent people who are interesting. They take the whole body and soul, transmuting the body to a body like their own.
>
> I asked them once if they ever died and they said, no; "We are always kept young." Once they take you and you taste food of their palace you cannot come back. They never taste anything salt, but eat fresh meat and drink pure water. They marry and have children. And one of them could marry a good and pure mortal.
>
> They are able to appear in different forms. One once appeared to me and seemed only four feet high, and stoutly built. He said, "I am bigger than I appear to you now. We can make the old young, the big small, and the small big.[12]

To further illustrate the similarities Vallee says:

> The parallel between these modern claims and the medieval legends is closer than ever. The same theory was presented about intercourse with the elves. I have shown that fairy tales are full of stories about the stealing of human babies, changelings, and the abduction of both males and females for procreation with the Gentry. Even the scars sound familiar.[13]

The entities' assertion is quite interesting: "We could cut off half the human race, but would not, for we are expecting salvation." Again, the number two billion comes to mind. Interestingly, the Gentry describe themselves as "a distinct race between our race and that of spirits."

By this time it should come as no surprise that for centuries clergymen and town officials have documented the testimonies of thousands who have recounted tales of abduction, procreative experimentation, and other encounters with nonhuman beings, which closely resemble modern accounts of UFO close encounters. The top thinkers in UFO research, including Vallee, believe that the phenomena spring from a common source—whatever it is. Whitley Strieber writes in his forward to *Dimensions:*

---

12 *Dimensions*, p. 54.

13 *Ibid.*, at 267.

> [Vallee] reveals an appalling truth: the phenomenon has been with us throughout history, and never have we been able to deal sensibly with it. Whatever it is, it changes with our ability to perceive it. The fifteenth century saw the visitors as fairies. The tenth century saw them as sylphs. The Romans saw them as wood nymphs and sprites. And so it goes, back into time. [*Forward,* pp. vi-vii]

As we have seen, the procurement of bodies is an underlying compulsion of the UFO occupants. Are these genetic experimentations, hybrid children, and inventoried bodies all part of Satanic Science, providing what God has denied the angels that kept not their first estate—mortal tabernacles? Are Satanic forces, demonic or human, literally manufacturing physical bodies for demonic habitation and animation?—or, are these characteristics of the UFO phenomenon just more smoke and mirrors to create an illusion for their audience? Again, we cannot know the answers to these questions absent divine revelation. One thing we know for certain—from this time forward we cannot rely solely on our five physical senses to discern what we think we are seeing or hearing. More than ever it will be imperative that we have as our constant companion the Holy Ghost to bear witness of the truth or falsity of any manifestation or representation.

Theory 3: Corporeal Possession

Demonic infestation and possession of humans is well documented throughout the entire history of the Gospel. Again, this results from Satanic spirits' overwhelming drive to unite with the elements and "feel" the physical world—it is the only means by which the sensual lusts of depraved, unembodied beings can attain any degree of satisfaction. We see activity in this arena escalating as we approach the winding up scene. Spiritual merging with these entities is the affirmative pursuit of most Eastern and New Age religions and cults. Even unwilling, righteous people, including Church members, have become plagued by the infestation of such vile spirits. Does "demonic possession" play a role in the UFO phenomenon? To at least some degree, the response is a clear "yes."

New Age guru Ruth Montgomery explains that the Earth is being visited by foreign beings:

> To the limit of my understanding, it would seem that the Guides have identified three types of beings who have achieved sufficient advancement to enter our earth plane, and appear in solid form to us . . . .
>
> Apparently the highest achievers in this category are the avatars, who can come and go at will, and who, according to the Guides, are in touch with outerspace beings as

well as with humans on Planet Earth. The second type is the Walk-ins, who have always been Earthlings but are high-minded, advanced souls who return to adult bodies in order to accelerate the progress of their fellow-men. The third class is the extraterrestrials, who, still few, have allegedly found the means of penetrating the earth's atmosphere and occupying bodies of adult humans, for limited scientific experiments and observations of our planetary changes.[14]

Montgomery further clarifies on another occasion:

I asked about the different means used by space beings to enter our culture, and the Guides said that some are being born into human bodies for the first time, some have lived here upon occasion before, some are arriving as Walk-ins, and others are temporarily exchanging bodies with Earthlings "with or without permission."[15]

We must remember while reading these New Age writings that Ms. Montgomery is not apologizing or making excuses—corporeal possession is a common occurrence and completely accepted by New Agers as a natural means of spiritual communication and interaction. Channelers like Montgomery receive the above tidbits of information frequently from their "spirit guides," spiritual entities who profess to be advanced, enlightened beings, but who are indeed, the very same demonic spirits that serve Satan. (*Mormon Doctrine*, pp. 195-96, 759)

This self-admitted practice of entering the bodies of Earthlings "with or without permission," to carry out extraterrestrial activities is a strong indicator that corporeal possession is pursued at some level. And whether the assertion is true or not we at least know that the "extraterrestrial" contacts feeding us this information are demonic spirits.

New Age author Brad Steiger quotes the words of a channeled extraterrestrial who explains the process in more innocuous terms: "By mutual agreement between a planetary dweller and an inhabitant of our craft, the knowledge and the memory of one of us may be blended with the planetary inhabitant without the loss of the receiver's identity."[16] However, in assessing the communications and New Age gospel message being delivered by the UFO occupants Steiger is hesitant to accept the entities at full face value. "I had the uneasy feeling that the ecstatic flame may, in reality, have been kindled by multidimensional beings who have a kind of symbiotic relationship with man and who may exploit their 'prophets' for selfish, parasitical purposes."[17] I agree.

---

[14] *Strangers Among Us*, pp. 147-48.
[15] *Aliens Among Us*, p. 13.
[16] *Revelation*, p. 141.
[17] *Revelation*, p. 8.

Mystic Knowledge

The spiritual "knowledge" passed from the UFO entities to "planetary dwellers" bears a strong resemblance to the mystical knowledge with which Eastern initiates are endowed at the pinnacle of their spiritual quest. As discussed earlier, the transference of such spiritual knowledge is another counterfeit employed by Satan to mock the true principle of the ministering of the Holy Ghost. As we know, the Holy Ghost radiates His influence throughout the universe on an ongoing basis. However, on special occasions He personally merges with the spirit of a worthy person and shares eternal truth at a level that transcends any worldly communication. The recipient is endowed with spiritual truth that is unmistakable and undeniable.

"Memory implanting" is the means by which Satanic forces convince people that they have experienced past lives or other mystical phenomena. In stating their conclusion about the origin of UFOs and their deceptive purposes, Christian Fundamentalists Lewis and Shreckhise declare their belief that memory implanting is the same method used to convince percipients that they have seen UFOs and their occupants.

> The spirituality that the New Age/UFO religion offers is a false hope. It is based upon subjective human feelings and observations that are being manipulated by demonic forces. The psychic implantation of deceptive experiences is changing the way [abductees] perceive reality. What they experience is a real experience—deceptive and manipulative in character. It is not, however, an experience of reality. It is an illusion of reality used solely for the purpose of convincing people to turn away from the Creator.[18]

Although this conclusion is somewhat premature for the purposes of our discussion, it points out how the authors believe spiritual memory implants are being employed by Satan in the UFO phenomenon. Of course, even if we accept the fact that UFOs are a Satanically generated phenomenon, the psychic implant theory is not as amenable to photography and radar detection as are materialization and manifestation generation. Of course, the psychic implant is very amenable to the more peripheral aspects such as alien encounters and communications and the attendant visions of alien worlds or UFO interiors. I suspect that a mixture of techniques is employed to create a panorama of special effects in a UFO/abduction experience.

Whitley Strieber recounts how the aliens touched his head with a "wand," producing realistic, three-dimensional images that swirled about in his mind, reminiscent of the images of dogs and naked women that were thrust into

---

[18] *UFO: End-Time Delusion*, p. 235.

the mind of Ed Walters during an "attempted" abduction. The visitors would communicate with Strieber (and countless others) any time they wished. He periodically would hear voices speaking to him as if standing next to him or within his head that would give him information and instructions on what was going on around him. This all sounds very much like psychic implanting. Was Strieber "possessed"? He worried about this possibility, saying "I realized that they must have been aware of my attempts to walk in the woods. I felt more than watched; I felt entered and observed from within."[19] Did he feel menaced?

> Increasingly I felt as if I were entering a struggle that might be even more than life-or-death. It might be a struggle for my soul, my essence, or whatever part of me might have reference to the eternal.
> There are worse things than death, I suspected. And I was beginning to get the distinct impression one of them had taken an interest in me.
> So far the word *demon* had never been spoken among the scientists and doctors who were working with me. And why should it have been? We were beyond such things. We were a group of atheists and agnostics, far too sophisticated to be concerned with such archaic ideas of demons and angels.
> Alone at night I worried about the legendary cunning of demons.[20]

Strieber worried:

> I could not shake the idea of the soul predator. I took my midnight walks regularly now, and every time I reached the darkest part of the woods the thought would come whispering back.
> I had no evidence that it was true. I just couldn't rid myself of the notion that there was something predatory about the visitors. I had terrifying memories of them—memories of leering visitor faces, of long, four-fingered hands, of recoiling at their touch.
> Those moments remain as if sealed behind smokey glass. I couldn't tell where the memories came from. There were dozens, maybe hundreds of them. [*Ibid.*, p. 176]

It is interesting that Strieber reached a point in his hypnotic regression therapy at which he felt that he could no longer trust these memories whose origins he had come to doubt. He knew the memories were of external origin, but doubted their veracity—as if they were a "mask" of something else that had actually occurred.

Strieber had the clear impression that the "visitors" as he called them, were evil—unnatural.

> In the wee hours of the night I abruptly woke up. There was somebody quite close to the bed, but the room seemed so unnaturally dark that I couldn't see much at all. I caught a glimpse of someone crouching just behind my bedside table. I could see by the huge, dark eyes who it was.

---

19 *Transformation*, p. 136.

20 *Transformation*, pp. 44-45.

I felt an absolutely indescribable sense of menace. It was hell on earth to be there, and yet I couldn't move, couldn't cry out, couldn't get away. I lay as still as death, suffering inner agonies. Whatever was there seemed so monstrously ugly, so filthy and dark and sinister, of course they were demons. They had to be. And they were here and I couldn't get away. I couldn't save my poor family.

I still remember that thing crouching there, so terribly ugly, its arms and legs like the limbs of a great insect, its eyes glaring at me.

And there was also the love. I felt mothered. Caressed. Then the terrible insect rose up beside the bed like some huge, predatory spider. The eyes glittered as it tilted its head from side to side.

Every muscle in my body was stiff to the point of breaking. I ached. My stomach felt as if it had been stuffed with molten lead. I could hardly breathe.

The next thing I knew, something had been laid against my forehead. I felt it there, a light electric pressure vibrating softly between my eyes.

Instantly I seemed to be transported to another place, a stone floor with a low stone table in the middle of it. The table was a bit more than waist high and on it there was a set of iron shackles. A man was led down some steps and attached to these shackles. He was right in front of my face, not two feet from me, looking directly at me with eyes so sad that I almost couldn't bear it. [*Ibid.*, pp. 181-82]

Whose Will?

At that point the holographic (or otherwise projected) man was tortured for Whitley's lack of obedience to the commands and requirements of the visitors. When returned to his bed, Strieber was also forced to listen to his son's screams downstairs as punishment for his disobedience.

These forms of psychological abuse to supplant the will of the victim for their own will is reminiscent of Satan's plan to direct the affairs of the Earth through coercion. This, of course, is in direct opposition to the Lord's Plan of Salvation, through which man chooses good or evil of his own free will. Remember Betty Luca's report that the beings were perplexed and obstructed by man's free will. It seems to be a constant theme that runs through the UFO phenomenon.

Strieber describes being raped by an "alluring, yet despicable-looking" alien or hybrid female. Horrified, he screamed out, "You have no right to do this to me. I am a human being!" The female sternly replied, "We do have a right!" This single, affirmative claim of the visitors has perplexed researchers. It would be one thing to conduct experimentations on lower lifeforms with neutral moral intentions, much as we do with our own medical research or migration/habitat tracking. It is another thing altogether, however, to positively assert that one has an affirmative *right* over another creature.

This would imply "ownership," which is an aspect of the visitor experience heretofore undiscussed.

One night, Strieber felt that the aliens were returning for him. He tried to resist, but he finally lost his strength and became resigned to his fate.

> There was no question of my doing anything about the fact that I knew the visitors were here. It was all I could do to climb the stairs to the bedroom . . . . I felt an absolutely indescribable sense of menace. It was hell on Earth to be there, and yet I could still not move, couldn't cry out, couldn't get away. I lay as still as death, suffering inner agonies . . . . I thought I was going to suffocate. My throat was closed, my eyes swimming with tears. The sense of being infested was powerful and awful . . . ."[21]

As we read through Whitley Strieber's accounts of his encounters with the visitors, we wonder if he hasn't possibly employed his proven ability to research and write on unusual subjects. After all, he earned more money for *Communion* than most of us earn in a lifetime. Strieber concludes *Transformation* with his testimony:

> Of course, one could take the comfortable road and say that I am lying, that the descriptions in my book are hyperbole or hallucination. But they are not. I am telling the truth of what happened to me, and the implications are there for anyone to see. Not only are we not alone, we have a life in another form—and it is on that level of reality that the visitors are primarily present.
>
> I call them visitors, but now I am beginning to think that is a misnomer. I have had the impression that they think of themselves as family, and perhaps that is exactly what they are. [*Ibid.*, p. 201]

Dozens of people have added their testimonies to support Strieber's story— they claim that they too saw many strange events at Strieber's remote cabin. An officer with the publisher of *Communion* relates that he was essentially accosted by two hybrids in obvious disguises at a bookstore as he was passing by the new *Communion* display. The book had just been put out, and had not been available to the public—no one even knew that the famed fiction writer had produced a nonfiction exposé of the visitors. The two characters, having no apparent way of knowing that this fellow passing through the store was with the publisher, flipped through the pages in just seconds repeating "that's not how it was, that's not how it happened at all." In the Whitley Strieber case, the theatrics of the entities knows no bounds. Why should the visitors go to these lengths to support Strieber's incredible story? Because they want us to believe every incredible word.

Strieber's comment, "I have had the impression that they think of themselves as family," is noteworthy. These bizarre beings who communicate through theater and abuse their victims with the most vile forms of psychology have

---

21 Whitley Strieber, *Transformation*, pp. 189-92.

a purpose behind their eccentricity—could it be that they still think of themselves as our brothers and sisters? Are they truly still expecting salvation?

Many Indicators Of Corporeal Possession

There exist many indications that demonic spirits are involved in spiritually contacting humans with UFO messages. The case of Marion Keech, discussed in Part II, is instructive. Dr. Vallee quotes her as she explains her initial contact with the entities: "I had the feeling that somebody was trying to get my attention. Without knowing why, I picked up a pencil and a pad that were lying on the table near my bed. My hand began to write in another handwriting."

Vallee narrates:

> Through the messages she got, this woman was gradually introduced into something she regarded as the realms of the life beyond, until one day she received a message of comfort from an "Elder Brother" as described in Leon Festinger's book *When Prophecy Fails,* "I am always with you. The cares of the day cannot touch you. We will teach them that seek and are ready to follow in the light. I will take care of the details. Trust in us. Be patient and learn, for we are there preparing the work for you as a connoiter. That is an earthly liaison duty before I come. That will be soon."
>
> . . .
>
> Mrs. Keech came to think of this as genuine channeling with higher entities and began telling people that amazing new knowledge was coming through. Soon a small sect formed in the midwestern city where she lived.

Some truly anomalous phenomena were experienced by members of Keech's group. When, in the end, the prophesied cataclysms failed to occur, the testimonies of many of the faithful were actually reinforced, while others left in disillusionment.[22]

Automatic writing, like that experienced by Mrs. Keech, has been common in trance channeling and alien contacting. Again, its source is demonic—the foreign spirit controls the body of the writer and the writer produces formerly unknown works in an unfamiliar hand. A female college professor has produced an entire "Bible" of sorts through this type of interplanetary communication.

When analyzing the "message" given to Betty Luca for later delivery to the world, it is important to first consider the method of its delivery—first to Betty, then to the world. As discussed previously, except for a couple of

---

[22] *Dimensions,* p. 242.

brief anomalous experiences, Betty, like most abductees, had no conscious memory of her abductions. It was only as she underwent regressive hypnosis that she was able to "recall" her experiences. Raymond Fowler emphasizes Betty's exceptional ability to summon her lost memories under hypnosis:

> Under hypnosis, Betty not only recounts but *relives* her UFO encounters. She does this in intricate detail—with corresponding emotion, trauma, and body movements. She is able to provide detailed drawings that tally exactly with her verbal testimony. Weeks, months, and even years later she is able to relive selected segments of her experience upon demand by a hypnotist.[23]

Not too surprisingly, many of the abductees who have undergone similar experiences and investigations have such detailed recall to the point of "reliving" the experiences, including Kathy Davis and Bob Luca. Budd Hopkins claims that physical manifestations such as hypothermia (abductees often complain of being in very cold environments) return as the abductee relives the experience under hypnosis. He always has warmed blankets on hand during such hypnotic sessions. One might easily dismiss these occurrences as mere psychosomatic manifestations of a perceived experience, but the phenomenon appears to go beyond that, as related by the following:

> The aliens placed Betty on a soft, rubbery, cushion-like mat on the floor of a section of the craft that was roofed by a large transparent dome. A mouthpiece was installed that kept her tongue held down. When describing it to us under hypnosis, she actually talked as if something were holding her tongue down. Betty began sinking into the rotating circular mat as the craft accelerated upward. Incredible as it may seem, her body actually sunk into the hypnotist's chair! The psychosomatic effects on Betty's face and voice were fantastic to behold. All present were amazed to actually see the effect of the g-forces on her face. The skin got very tight around her face and her mouth was pulled way back. She experienced difficulty talking.[24]

These manifestations of physical forces on the body of Betty Luca and others during hypnosis give me great pause. No answer exists in modern science to explain Betty's sinking deeper into the hypnotist's chair as she experienced a mere "recall" of rapid upward acceleration. This is clearly not within the realm of psychosomatic reaction. Some outside force had to be present to compress Betty's body into the cushion of the chair. The researchers present assumed that there exists a latent effect originating with the experience, which remanifests itself as the abductee relives the experience under hypnosis—an effect completely unknown to us. This does not seem like a workable solution to me.

---

23 *The Watchers*, p. 353.
24 *The Watchers*, p. 10.

There is every indication that demonic forces are at work on Betty during her hypnosis. Is this why she, like others, becomes very cold at times during hypnosis—is this a "cold spot" manifestation? Is this why no memory exists prior to the hypnotic session—because the memory is directly "downloaded" to her during the session? We know that it is often during these hypnotic trances that people with no prior recollection of abnormal memories are suddenly deluged with vivid, panoramic recollections of past lives. These, we know to be Satanically induced. Others are known to levitate during hypnotic trance. These paranormal experiences are common occurrences in both UFO encounters and the occult.

Or, does hypnosis merely unlock or reinitiate an already experienced demonic encounter? Some victims, Whitley Strieber for instance, feel that the encounter really occurred remotely, and it was masked or altered in the subconscious. That is why, they believe, some people who have anomalous, vague memories of animals (generally large-eyed animals like deer or owls), are recalling a masked memory instead of the actual visitor encounter. Deeper than this, some believe that the entity encounter recovered memory is only a mask for a more profound experience—one that the entities really do not want the victim to remember.

Hypnosis—A Spiritual Revolving Door?

The entire process of hypnotic retrieval of suppressed memories is suspect from a spiritual viewpoint. The Church's stand on hypnosis is fairly conservative. In *Mormon Doctrine,* under the heading of "Hypnotism," Elder McConkie quotes President Francis M. Lyman of the Council of the Twelve as writing,

> From what I understand and have seen, I should advise you not to practice hypnotism. For my own part I could never consent to being hypnotized or allowing one of my children to be. The free agency that the Lord has given us is the choicest gift we have. As soon, however, as we permit another mind to control us, as that mind controls its own body and functions, we have completely surrendered our free agency to another; and so long as we are in the hypnotic spell—and that is as long as the hypnotist desires us to be—we give no consent in any sense whatever to anything we do. The hypnotist might influence us to do good things, but we could receive no benefit from that, even if we remembered it after coming out of the spell, for it was not done voluntarily. The hypnotist might also influence us to do absurd and even shocking, wicked things, for his will compels us.[25]

---

[25] *Era,* vol. 6, p. 420.

Although this "lounge show" viewpoint of hypnosis may seem surprisingly antiquated to most who have more than a passing acquaintance with modern psychology and the use of regressive hypnosis to ascertain the origin of unknown trauma, there is a fundamental purpose behind the belief. It is, although not well articulated in Church literature, that the hypnotic process lowers barriers that normally protect our bodies from negative spiritual intrusions. This belief is not unique to the LDS Church, and is, in fact, the accepted belief of most "Christian" churches. Does this indicate that under no circumstances should anyone undergo any form of hypnosis? Elder McConkie continues:

> Reputable doctors sometimes use hypnotherapy, a limited form of hypnotism, in connection with the practice of their profession. Their sole apparent purpose is to relieve pain and aid patients in perfecting their physical well-being. It is claimed that there are many people who have been benefitted materially by this practice and that the ills normally attending hypnotic practices have not resulted. This medical practice of hypnotism obviously does not carry the same opprobrium that attaches to hypnotism in general.

It is unclear to me if this modification to President Lyman's counsel sheds any new light, but we are apparently given to understand that certain limited forms of hypnosis, performed therapeutically by medical professionals, that do not produce certain unnamed harmful effects, are condoned. Personally, I would not undergo hypnosis out of the presence of a discerning Priesthood holder.

Spiritual Psychology

The "Men In Black" phenomenon, referred to above, is that in which men in "official" looking apparel show up at the home or other location of a witness or abductee, demanding any and all evidence of a close encounter. They often threaten the witness if he or she ever divulges the details of the close encounter. These experiences are usually alternated with "official" looking helicopters that buzz the location of the witness. It is reported by witnesses that these MIBs are often somewhat alien looking (in the eyes), and that the helicopters have sometimes transformed themselves from disks or spheres, and back again.

Noting that the techniques of the MIBs are closely akin to spiritual brainwashing methods used by cults and Satanic groups to negatively enforce their will and control over initiates, Brad Steiger suggests that the "Brothers of the Shadow, like the MIB, are known for threatening students of the occult whenever they get too close to lifting the Veil of Isis [reaching the spiritual pinnacle]." As Madame Blavatsky says when referring to the Brothers of the Shadow, they are "the leading stars" on the great spiritual stage of "materialization."[26] The key words here are "stage" and "materialization." What Madame Blavatsky is conveying is that the occult is very "manifestation" oriented—Satan provides the curious with many signs and wonders to prove his powers. When the curious become practitioners of the occult arts, it is they who provide the uninitiated with signs and wonders. This is the great proselyting effort of Satan's kingdom. Levitating, flying, astral projection, corporeal transformation, and other manifestations of magical power are the bait. Once baited, proselytes are controlled through psychological manipulation, such as that described by Steiger.

Negative psychological "warfare" has long been a control device of the occult, inhumane POW captors, and others with evil, dominating tendencies. As pointed out by Lewis and Shreckhise, the "aliens" appear to be playing "Good Cop/Bad Cop." Any television police drama watcher knows that this is a scenario wherein one police officer will act as the "heavy," projecting a threatening image to the targeted person. The second officer will then make an appearance, offering sympathy and hope—befriending the target— convincing the target that he is the target's friend and advocate. Manufacturing "bad" spirits or aliens drives the terrified victim into the open arms of the "good" spirits or aliens, accepting their message as beneficent, no matter how much pain is caused thereby or how at odds it may be with revealed truth. Remember that visiting spirit entities, as well as "aliens," come in the good and bad varieties by their own accounts. We know that the spirit entities are all of the same origin (Satanic), and I believe that most of the "aliens" spring from the very same source.

Lewis and Shreckhise further observe that the threat of superhuman retribution for pursuing the "forbidden fruit" of secret knowledge has always been too tempting for man to withstand. The threats whet the appetite, and the victim is drawn more deeply into his captor's sphere of influence.

Speaking of one woman victimized by Men In Black, Steiger notes, "At times she seemed almost to be possessed."[27] Lewis and Shreckhise speculate: "This is the purpose of MIB: to bring a person into subjection and control.

---

[26] Brad Steiger, *Alien Meetings*, Ace Books, p. 114, quoting *New Atlantean Journal*, March 1975.

[27] *Alien Meetings*, p. 117.

By using the initial hallucinatory experience of UFO contact and subsequently the MIB threat, the contactee is subjected to a mindcontrol, brainwashing technique designed to break down his will and resistance to eventual possession."[28]

The Control System

Jacques Vallee has researched and reasoned, pondering the extraterrestrial behavior and message. He has articulated a "control" theory of his own.

> I propose there is a spiritual control system for human consciousness and that paranormal phenomena like UFOs are one of its manifestations. I cannot tell whether this control is natural and spontaneous; whether it is explainable in terms of genetics, of social psychology, or of ordinary phenomena—or if it is artificial in nature, under the power of some superhuman will. It may be entirely determined by laws that we have not yet discovered.
>
> I am led to this idea by the fact that, in every instance of UFO phenomenon I have been able to study in depth, I have found as many rational elements as absurd ones, as many that I could call friendly as I could call hostile. This is what tells me that we are working on the wrong level. And so are all of the believers, and this definitely includes the skeptics, because they believe that they can explain the facts as strongly as the most enthusiastic convert to Ms. Dixon's vision of Jupiterians![29]

Vallee explains how the system works through a deceptive reinforcement schedule:

> If the phenomenon is forcing us through a learning curve, then it has no choice but to mislead us. When Skinner designs a machine that feeds a rat only when the right lever is depressed, this is extremely misleading for the rat. But if the rat doesn't depress the right lever, he becomes extremely hungry. Man is hungry for knowledge and power, and if there is an intelligence behind the UFOs it must have taken this fact into account. We also tend to forget that we have no choice either: we *must* eventually study UFOs, and that study, unavoidably, will in turn contribute to the reinforcement itself.[30]

Vallee suggests that it is possible to convince a major sector of our population to believe in the existence of superior extraterrestrial beings "by exposing them to a few carefully engineered scenes the details of which are adapted to the culture and symbols of a particular time and place." He then explains *why* he believes the UFO phenomenon/control system has been engineered.

> Could the meetings with UFO entities be designed to control our beliefs? Consider their changing character. In the United States, they appear as science fiction monsters. In South America they are sanguinary and quick to get into a fight. In France, they

---

28 *UFO: End-Time Delusion*, pp. 137-38.

29 *Dimensions*, p. 272.

30 *Ibid.*, p. 275.

behave like rational, Cartesian, peace-loving tourists. The Irish Gentry, if we believe its spokesman, was an aristocratic race organized somewhat like a religious-military order. The airship pilots were strongly individualistic characters with all the features of the American farmer.

. . . .

What is the variable being controlled in this control system? Thermostats control temperature; gyroscopes control the direction in which a rocket flies. What could a paranormal phenomenon control? *I suggest that it is human belief that is being controlled and conditioned.*[31]

I agree with Vallee's conclusion—the UFO phenomenon is "presented" to us in a manner designed to elicit human response sufficient to manipulate human beliefs. He hesitates in his many books to forthrightly identify the source of the presentation—in his opinion anyway. It is significant that Jacques Vallee is a top computer scientist, specializing in the analysis and processing of scientific research data. In fact, it was while creating systems for observatories that he became interested in UFO research—as he saw UFO tracking tapes destroyed as a matter of policy. After many years of inquiry, what does Vallee conclude about the origin of the UFO phenomenon? In an interview given to the *SCP Journal,* Vallee revealed the following: "We believe that the thousands of cases of transformation represent one aspect of the ultimate purpose of UFOs. They are part of a plan to deliberately move significant portions of an entire culture, or world, into acceptance or involvement in the occult, and a collective alteration in world view. This is preparatory for and necessary to the events surrounding the rise of the Antichrist." It is no wonder that Vallee hesitates to share his ultimate conclusions in his books.[32]

Does Vallee believe that UFO occupants are demonic? In explaining why the phenomenon operates as it does, he relates that some witnesses assume that they are. He says, "In fact, some witnesses have though that they had seen demons because the creature had the unpredictability and the mischievousness associated with popular conceptions of the devil." Vallee further explains why he believes that "UFO" and "alien" encounters are so bizarre, illogical, and internally inconsistent:

If you wanted to bypass the intelligentsia and the Church, remain undetectable to the military system, leave undisturbed the political and administrative levels of a society, and at the same time implant deep within that society far-reaching doubts concerning

---

[31] *Ibid.*, p. 276.

[32] August 1977, p. 23.

its basic philosophical tenets, this is exactly how you would have to act. At the same time, of course, such a process would have to provide its own explanation to make ultimate detection impossible. In other words, it would have to project an image just beyond the belief structure of the target society. It would have to disturb and reassure at the same time, exploiting both the gullibility of the zealots and the narrow-mindedness of the debunkers. This is exactly what the UFO phenomenon does.[33]

New Ideas

In describing various psychological techniques employed to open human minds to heretofore-unacceptable precepts, Vallee notes further similarities between occult methods and those of UFO messengers:

> Is this confusion technique deliberately used to effect change on a major scale? Answering such questions could also help us to understand the strong resemblance that anyone who has examined the beliefs of esoteric groups could not fail to note between certain UFO encounters and the initiation rituals of secret societies. This "opening of the mind" to a new set of symbols that is reported by many witnesses is precisely what the various occult traditions also try to achieve.[34]

Is this "opening of the mind" of a major portion of the population actually occurring? Yes! With the cooperation of the popular media the "extraterrestrial savior" dream has been fostered and championed. All of our ills—pollution, energy, war, property, hunger, poverty, and social injustice—will soon be cured; just as soon as we establish permanent ties with these superior lifeforms. With the promotion of these intergalactic messiahs by the New Age movement, occult spiritualism is now centered in the cosmos—*extraterrestrials are God.*

In summing up the UFO message Raymond Fowler concludes that the significance of their message is revolutionary. He says, "It is now time to review *what* the aliens told Betty about their *identity* and *operations.* They were brief and to the point but what they revealed will revolutionize every aspect of our lives—science, religion, philosophy, sociology—nothing will be spared." Most observers, no matter what their background or which ax they choose to grind, agree on this one point—that if nothing else, the UFO phenomenon is changing world (at least Western) beliefs in God.

Lewis and Shreckhise [Christian Fundamentalists]:

> The menace is that they lure people into an alternative philosophy and world-view that stands in direct contradiction to the Christian faith as found in the Bible.[35]

---

33 *Dimensions,* p. 178.

34 *Ibid.,* p. 188.

35 *UFO: End-Time Delusion,* p. 20.

Whitley Strieber:

The only thing now needed to make the UFO myth a new religion of remarkable scope and force is a single undeniable sighting. Such a sighting need last only a few minutes—just long enough to be thoroughly documented. It will at once invest the extraterrestrials channels, the "space brothers" believers, and the UFO cultists with the appearance of revealed truth.[36]

I cannot forget my memory of the visitors' claim, "We recycle souls." It had also been said to other participants. I thought of Jo Sharp's experience, of the whole tone of what was happening to me. It was becoming clear to me that the visitors were concerned with the life of the soul as well as the body.[37]

Jacques Vallee:

The experience of a close encounter with a UFO is a shattering physical and mental ordeal. The trauma has effects that go far beyond what the witnesses recall consciously. New types of behavior are conditioned, and new types of beliefs are promoted. Aside from any scientific consideration, the social, political, and religious consequences of the experience are enormous if they are considered over a timespan of a generation.

Faced with the new wave of experiences of UFO contact that are described in books like *Communion* and *Intruders* and in movies like *Close Encounters of the Third Kind,* our religions seem obsolete. Our idea of the church as a social entity working within rational structures is obviously challenged by the claim of a direct communication in modern times with visible beings who seem endowed with supernatural powers.[38]

Randall Baer [former New Age Guru]:

UFO sightings and contacts have made deep inroads into the everyday fabric of much of the New Age. More than seventy-five percent of New Agers firmly believe in the existence of hosts of alien beings within and around planet Earth to help in the birthing of the New Age. It is noteworthy to point out that the strong upsurge in this trend also parallels the crystal craze and the huge increases in channeling activities in the mid-to-late 80s.[39]

Kenneth Grant [Occult Leader]:

Some believe that the UFO phenomena are part of the "miracle," a mounting mass of evidence seems to indicate that mysterious entities have been located within the Earth's ambience for countless centuries and that more and more people are being born with innate ability to see, or in some way sense their presence.

Prayer for deific intervention in ancient times has now become a *cri de coeur* to extraterrestrial or interdimensional entities, according to whether the manifestations are viewed as occurring within man's consciousness, or outside himself in apparently objective but often invisible entities. New Isis Lodge has in its possession the sigils of some of these entities. The sigils come from a *grimoire* of unknown origin which forms part of the dark quabalahs of Besqul, located by magicians in the Tunnel of Qulielfi.

---

[36] *Dimensions, Forward,* p. v-vii.

[37] *Transformation,* p. 198.

[38] *Dimensions, Introduction,* p. xiii.

[39] Randall N. Baer, *Inside the New Age Nightmare,* Huntington House, pp. 145-46.

The *grimoire* describes Four Gates of extraterrestrial entry into, and emergence from, the known Universe.[40]

Brad Steiger [New Age writer]:

Again the "angels" i.e. the space intelligences, are speaking to the prophets, the UFO contactees, in order that we might be guided through the difficult period of transition as a new world rises from the ashes of the old.[41] [Remember the Phoenix theme?]

[T]hese UFO prophets have not only brought God physically to this planet, but they have created a blend of science and religion that offers a theology more applicable to modern mankind.[42]

The UFO contactees may be evolving prototypes of a future evangelism. They may be heralds of a New Age religion, a blending of technology and traditional religious concepts.[43]

The Cosmic Gospel

Brad Steiger enumerates the salient points of what he terms the Outer Space Apocrypha, a distillation of the "Cosmic Gospel" being preached by contactees and channelers alike:

- Man is not alone in the solar system. He has "Space Brothers" and they have come to Earth to reach him and teach him.
- The Space Brothers have advanced information that they wish to impart to their weaker brethren. The Space Brothers want man to join an intergalactic spiritual federation.
- The Space Brothers are here to teach, to help awaken man's spirit, to help man rise to higher levels of vibration so that he may be ready to enter new dimensions . . .
- Man stands now in the transitional period before the dawn of a New Age. With peace, love, understanding, and brotherhood on man's part, he will see a great new era begin to dawn.
- If man should not raise his vibratory rate within a set period of time, severe Earth changes and major cataclysms will take place. Such disasters will not end the world, but shall serve as cataclysmic crucibles to burn off the dross of unreceptive humanity. Those who die in such dreadful purgings will be allowed to reincarnate on higher levels of development so that their salvation will be more readily accomplished.[44]

---

[40] Kenneth Grant, *Outside the Circles of Time,* London, Frederick Muller (1980), p. 1. Grant shares hair-raising accounts of confrontations between leaders of his group and some of these spirit beings or entities.

[41] Brad Steiger, *The Fellowship: Spiritural Contact Between Humans and Outer Space Beings,* New York, Dolphin/Doubleday (1988), p. 194.

[42] *The Fellowship,* p. 1.

[43] Brad Steiger, *The Fellowship: Spiritual Contact Between Humans and Outer Space Beings,* New York, Dolphin/Doubleday (1988), p. 4.

[44] *Revelation,* pp. 157-58.

Steiger says that there "is an enormous amount of New Age revelatory material that has been given to the UFO contactees" and that the "Space beings seem very concerned with the spread of what has come to be known as New Age concepts . . . ."[45] He was told by an alien that he channeled, Ox-Ho:

> People of Earth, you are becoming fourth dimensional whether you are ready or not. Leave the old to those who cling to the old. Don't let the New Age leave you behind . . . . Earth must be cleansed. There can be no transition into a new dimension without this cleansing.
>
> The world right now is feeling the effect of the Karmic pattern of the Atlantean culture . . . .[46]

Vallee discusses the "new" religious and other belief systems being adopted (and promoted in some cases) by contactees and many who read about their encounters, and offers his analysis of the results of the "control system" being imposed on us. He observes that in the same manner that science has gradually undermined faith in religion, now, faith in science is deteriorating with the advent of the New Age "science-spiritualism" being heralded by the UFO occupants.[47] This new belief system disregards the revealed truth of religion and the discovered truth of scientific experimentation and observation, leaving believers with the mysticism of the East and the dogma of the Dark Ages—centered in telepathic alien humanoids who claim to be the Father of Christ.

Are people with strong Christian backgrounds easily duped into accepting this new religion? I have received telephone calls from longtime Church members who have learned that I have conducted in-depth research into the UFO phenomenon from the LDS viewpoint—assuming that I, like they, have come to accept the message of our Gospel brethren hailing from other worlds created by God. They find that the UFO message is "compatible" with the Restored Gospel. They believe that the extraterrestrials are part of Heavenly Father's plan to usher in the Millennium. The UFOs are the signs and wonders in the heavens foretold by the prophets they say. The extraterrestrials will direct the latter-day events from their spacecraft. They might even be the angels who will sound the trumps according to some LDS "believers." When I propose that although there may be genuine extraterrestrial encounters, possibly like that of Udo Wartena, the vast majority of UFO encounters appear to be spiritually generated counterfeits, they recoil as though I had lost the faith. Yes, this new compatible alternate to the Restored Gospel is catching on—in Zion, and around the world.

---

45 *The Fellowship*, p. 39-40.

46 *Revelation*, p. 204.

47 Jacques Vallee, *Messengers of Deception*, pp. 221-23.

Latter-day Heralds

Here, we should discuss what has become a popular theory among UFO intellectuals—those who accept that the UFO phenomenon, extraterrestrial or otherwise, is actually a continuing dialogue with interdimensional beings—for our purposes, demonic spirits. Researchers such as Jacques Vallee, who have studied the great Madonna encounters of history, shamanistic apparitions, occult contacts with disembodied spirits including extraterrestrials, and similar phenomena, in the context of how they parallel UFO encounters, have lumped Joseph Smith in with other contactees. However, they have the insight to discuss him as the ultimate contactee. If ever there were a "beam down" scenario, the following constitute textbook cases. Although we looked at these scriptures above in a different context, they are worth reproducing here.

> I saw a pillar of light exactly over my head, above the brightness of the sun, which descended gradually until it fell upon me. It no sooner appeared than I found myself delivered from the enemy which held me bound. When the light rested upon me I saw two Personages, whose brightness and glory defy all description, standing above me in the air. [*Joseph Smith—History* 1:16-17]
>
> While I was thus in the act of calling upon God, I discovered a light appearing in my room, which continued to increase until the room was lighter than at noonday, when immediately a personage appeared at my bedside, standing in the air, for his feet did not touch the floor . . . . Not only was his robe exceedingly white, but his whole person was glorious beyond description, and his countenance truly like lightning. The room was exceedingly light, but not so very bright as immediately around his person . . . . After this communication, I saw the light in the room begin to gather immediately around the person of him who had been speaking to me, and it continued to do so until the room was again left dark, except just around him; when, instantly I saw, as it were, a conduit open right up into heaven, and he ascended till he entirely disappeared, and the room was left as it had been before this heavenly light had made its appearance. [*Joseph Smith—History* 1:30-43]

In addition to angelic appearances in beams of light, researchers point to the following as parallels between Joseph Smith's experiences and those of UFO contactees: the delivery of semireligious messages (classically bizarre); instructions to organize a cult; the binding of the tongue and paralysis of the body during a visitation (good angels vs. bad angels); the delivery of a secret book with hieroglyphs; the use of crystals (Urim and Thummim and the Seer Stone); telepathic communications including 3-D pictures; unwakable roommates during bedroom visitations; healing or comforting by the laying on of hands; speaking in unknown tongues; paranormal activities; and, social isolation of the contactee and his followers.[48] These UFOlogists

---

[48] *Dimensions*, pp. 210-218.

believe these various Restoration events and occurrences to be classic indicators of UFO/entity encounters. In a sophisticated book dedicated to debunking every sort of supernatural event ever reported, *The Paranormal Borderlands of Science,* an article chronicling the experiences of Betty Andreasson Luca, "Betty Through the Looking Glass," similarly observes:

> The same lack of inquiry [e.g., sexual imagery and birth trauma] arises in other areas as well. Consider theology. We have seen that religion was an important part of Betty's life. Three aspects of her narrative are of particular interest from a theological point of view: (1) During her trip she was from time to time comforted by the laying on of an alien hand. (2) In the later sessions she began to speak in an unintelligible tongue. (3) She received, from an entity she at first thought might be an angel, a book containing important messages for man but written in unintelligible symbols. Here are three striking parallels with the Mormon religion: The founding of that church was based upon the alleged finding, by Joseph Smith, of the "Golden Bible," a book of metallic plates, given by an angel; the plates were covered with incomprehensible writing that Joseph "translated" by means we needn't go into here. And the concepts of speaking in tongues and the laying on of hands have been important parts of Mormon doctrine from that church's beginning. Was Betty familiar with this history? We need to know the answer to this and other questions, but no information is provided.

I assume that you have retained your testimony in the face of these observations. The researchers are placed in a bind that they conveniently fail to address. Although it is true that the events of the Restoration parallel many UFO contacts, they simultaneously parallel the experiences of most of the major prophets throughout recorded history. Although the von Danikens will quickly claim that this "proves" that historical religious contacts have been nothing more than ongoing UFO contacts, the intelligent researchers know better. Therefore, they remain silent—writhing inwardly.

The answer is, as we have discussed at length above, that we must use the experiences of the prophets, including Joseph Smith, as a standard against which we measure the veracity of any alleged contact with Divinity—Satan will make every attempt to cloak his delivery of false messages in the garb and guise of angelic visitations. By this late hour, he has managed to furnish his deceptive encounters with promises of false messiahs—coming soon to save the world from its human infestation. Most UFO encounters, like Blessed Virgin Mary encounters, are nothing more than theater—played out on the premillennial stage of Satanic deception. These are counterfeits, like Perry Mason's hired actresses, employed to confuse those who know the truth.

The Priesthood—Our Only Defense

Let us again consider the prophetic words of Joseph Smith, warning us of the cunning of the evil one: "for as no man knows the things of God, but by the Spirit of God, so no man knows the spirit of the devil, and his *power and intelligence, which is more than human,* and having unfolded through the medium of the Priesthood the mysterious operations of his devices . . . ." (*Teachings of the Prophet Joseph Smith,* pp. 204-05; emphasis mine) This warning counsel appears very appropriate in light of what we have discovered about the UFO phenomenon.

Whitley Strieber, who like many others (including Church members) has been plagued by the visitors or entities throughout his life, adds his testimony: "Never, in those bleak April days, could I have imagined the subtlety of the plan that they were carrying out. Nor could I have seen the magnificent brilliance of the mind behind it."[49] Yes, Strieber, who considers himself to be of high intellectual stock, is overwhelmed by the "power and intelligence" of the visitors—he too believes it to be "more than human." Strieber worries:

> If I had been having these encounters throughout my life, then what had I become? Why were my visitors so secretive, hiding themselves behind my consciousness? I could only conclude that they were using me and did not want me to know why.
>
> Frankly, I found this idea deeply disturbing. What were the visitors' motives? *Communion* had become a number-one bestseller. What if they were dangerous? Then I was terribly dangerous because I was playing a role in acclimatizing people to them. And if they were benevolent? Then the agonizingly difficult task of bearing witness to their reality would turn out to be worthwhile.
>
> My desperation increased as I searched across the years of my past, seeking answers.[50]

Rather than twist helplessly at the end of Satan's rope, never knowing what is true and how to act as lamented by Whitley Strieber, we have the path marked clearly before us by the prophets of God—only the power of the Priesthood can discern and control Satan's latter-day deceptive devices. I believe that Joseph's counsel is worth repeating one last time:

> Or who can drag into daylight and develop the hidden mysteries of the false spirits that so frequently are made manifest among the Latter-day Saints? We answer that no man can do this without the Priesthood, and having a knowledge of the laws by which spirits are governed; . . . A man must have the discerning of spirits before he can drag into daylight this hellish influence and unfold it unto the world in all its soul-destroying, diabolical, and horrid colors . . . . [*Teachings of the Prophet Joseph Smith,* pp. 204-05]

---

49 *Transformation,* p. 55.

50 *Transformation,* p. 96.

16
Conclusion

There is no question that extraterrestrial human life exists. It is found in exponential quantities, strewn throughout the universe. Our own Heavenly Father creates worlds without number through His Only Begotten Son—probationary globes like our Earth—and populates them with His children, who like us are progressing through their second estate. Each of these orbs passes through creation, the terrestrial garden, the fall to a broken telestial desert, and baptism by water and fire, eventually being raised to a terrestrial paradise for a millennial reign of its sovereign, the universal Savior. Then, when the allotted probationary period is spent, each planet is celestialized in the fire of the great refiner, becoming a crystallized globe, a Urim and Thummim to its eternal inhabitants.

These trillions upon trillions of children of the second estate are humans, created in the image of Heavenly Father. With some variation they look like us. They are tempted by denizens of demonic spirits who kept not their first estate, and who seek to frustrate the Plan of Salvation and Exaltation—possibly to gain a second chance for their own salvation. The inhabitants of these far-away planets live through cycles of good and evil, famine and plenty, and wisdom and foolishness. They have prophets, whom they accept at times and reject at others. When they learn of the Savior, they look to the heavens and contemplate the beastly world that could have crucified the Son of God. They live their lives, one day or a thousand years, it does not matter, because they die and move into the spiritual plane that coexists with their own world. They are resurrected and judged according to their faith and works while in the flesh. Those who have kept their covenants inherit their celestialized planet. Those who have fallen short of that glory inherit a planet prepared for them, terrestrial or telestial. And those who have rejected pure light, once having discerned by its radiant glory, go to that place where there is no light and no glory—with Satan, who deceived them by his cunning craft.

Within these parameters all of life's questions are answered—universally. Herein we can discover the origin of UFOs and their occupants. Any communication that fails to fit within this Gospel paradigm is false. Any assertion that is contrary hereto is from the Father of Lies. With this understanding, we posses a standard by which we can measure the UFO phenomenon.

Many investigators and writers are philosophizing about the origin and nature of UFOs and their occupants. More and more we read that there is something "evil" about them—something "inhuman." This is the apparent, even obvious conclusion being reached by researchers. But many abductees, of all people, are telling us that even though they were violated by the entities, they feel that no malice is intended, that the beings are benevolent. They tell us that the UFO occupants are just so advanced that they have difficulty communicating effectively with us at our level—much as a zoologist inadvertently offends a chimpanzee when attempting to communicate or teach a lesson. Extraterrestrial proponents would have us believe that the entities "act out" their message and fill our minds with mythical symbolism in an effort to convey their higher message in a universal language. Is this really what the "aliens" are up to? I do not think so.

Our first consideration is the multiplicity of alien types. We have presented to us a scenario in which there appear to be good aliens and bad aliens. Even the aliens make this assertion—however, it appears to be the bad aliens that make it. First, the gnomes, or small greys. They profess love at times, but demonstrate unpredictability and rage at others. They lie, kidnap, blaspheme, mislead, inflict pain and suffering, exploit, torment, invade, steal, control, mutilate, impregnate, take babies, frighten children, teach reincarnation, and possibly kill. However, they do warn us about the dangers of nuclear energy. Reflect now on their counterparts, the human-appearing aliens. They seem benevolent, caring, and superior in every way. Yet, they appear to be associated with the gnomes and indulge in, and even direct, the activities of the small greys just enumerated above. Some do, anyway.

Jesus taught us that we would "know them by their fruits." (Matthew 7:16) He explained, "Even so every good tree bringeth forth good fruit; but a corrupt tree bringeth forth evil fruit." (Matthew 7:17) By analogy, the fruit of many of these "aliens" is corrupt and evil. The cries of those who say that we need to give the misunderstood aliens a chance are the dysfunctional chants of enabling victims. Those who claim that the "aliens" are establishing a symbiotic relationship with our race ignore the unmistakable indicators that they are, in fact, imposing a parasitic enslavement on us. This is the appearance of their design, anyway. If we were to put our very best brains to the task of procuring the voluntary enslavement of the world's population, the elements present in the UFO phenomenon would be essential. Appearing as superior visitors from afar, bearing higher technology, has always been a workable rouse. The only thing these brains would lack to fulfill their design is the technology. Whoever the "aliens" are, they have the technology—real or perceived. Either way, it is sufficient to entrap a world hungry for an easier, *Star Trek* lifestyle.

If the gnomes and angelic humans are evil, then what about the humans—those who act like courteous, noninterfering explorers? These are the type encountered by Udo Wartena. These profess to be extraterrestrial, yet act very much like well-mannered, educated humans. They explain their purposes and their methods. They obey law and ethics. They speak with their mouths and shake with their hands. They have no message, but would happily speak of the Gospel, the Savior, and the Priesthood if they were permitted. Are these any different, any more feasible or trustworthy than the humans that accompany the gnomes? We cannot know for sure, but their fruits appear good—so far, at least.

Perhaps there are good aliens and bad aliens, then. Or perhaps there are only human extraterrestrials who, like us, have their good and their bad citizens—but their bad citizens are not allowed to travel to underprotected outposts, like Earth. If the extraterrestrials of Udo Wartena are good, then what of the abducting gnomes? Are they physical extraterrestrial beings with superior technology, who are delivering a message to mankind, true or untrue? This is possible. Are they demonic spirits masquerading as beneficent New Age messiahs?

After wading through the literature describing UFO encounters; interviewing abductees and investigators; and poring over the details of abductions, the messages, and the paranormal and metaphysical phenomena associated with UFOs, I have my own conclusion. My conclusion, however, is only that—conclusory—based on my personal analysis of the available data. The conclusion is volatile, and is not based on special enlightenment or personal revelation. The Lord so far has specifically withheld express instruction on these matters, from the body of the Church, anyway. Does this indicate that they are not important? No, there are many important things on which He has remained silent—many of them dealing directly with latter-day events preceding the Second Coming.

I first believe that there is every indication that Earth *can* be visited by extraterrestrial human explorers. Furthermore, there is strong evidence that some limited, discrete visitation is conducted by these persons. I also believe that the Earth is visited often by angels and translated beings, although these fail to account for the UFO phenomenon. I believe that the abducting "aliens" are untruthful and imperialistic. I further believe that they are purposefully deceiving and controlling our world population by selectively planting psychological devices in handpicked persons and selected media. I also believe that these manipulative "aliens" are not physical extraterrestrials as they present themselves to be. Because they act exactly like Satan acts, there is every reason to believe that they act for him, or in concert with him.

This theory is supported by the fact that the small grey gnomes and their asserted activities and messages fail to fit within the Gospel paradigm—especially within the positive "last days" parameters. However, they fit quite neatly into the elements and events that will lead to the rise and world dominion of Antichrist and the Man of Sin, whose master is Satan.

Whatever its source, it is obvious the extraterrestrial presence *will* continue to escalate. Whether the "aliens" are demonic or not, demonic hordes *will* utilize the concept, in part at least, to help establish Satan's premillennial kingdom. This we know from the many "alien" contacts already present in the New Age movement. Will there be a large-scale invasion by bad aliens, or a war between good and bad aliens locked in battle over our planet? Will there be emissaries from afar, or supermen from our ranks, enlightened by the intergalactic mind? What drama awaits us in the final scene? However the drama unfolds, it is only that—theater.

It matters little *how* Satan deceives the nations—we know he will. Beware of the Prince of the power of the air and of false messiahs and false christs, coming in power and glory and invoking the holy names of God. Beware of false prophets and superhumans who work miracles in our sight and console us with dispensations of forgiveness and extensions of time. These will come, speaking in dignified tones and reasoning with superior intellects. They will offer hope and answers to a world poised on the precipice of certain destruction. They, and they alone will present workable solutions to seemingly insurmountable problems. Their price? It will be much higher than that required by the Savior who says, "Take my yoke upon you, and learn of me; for I am meek and lowly in heart: and ye shall find rest unto your souls. For my yoke is easy, and my burden is light." (Matthew 11:29-30)

The Prophet Joseph Smith saw our days and the events of which we speak, in full panoramic vision. The subtle cunning of Satan cannot be overstated. He is the Great Deceiver. Again, Joseph's counsel to us is essential if we are to find our way through Satan's grand illusion, and his guidance warrants reiteration:

> Or who can drag into daylight and develop the hidden mysteries of the false spirits that so frequently are made manifest among the Latter-day Saints? *We answer* that *no man can do this without the Priesthood, and having a knowledge of the laws by which spirits are governed;* for as no man knows the things of God, but by the Spirit of God, so no man knows the spirit of the devil, and his power and intelligence, which is more than human, and having unfolded through the medium of the Priesthood the mysterious operations of his devices . . . . *A man must have the discerning of spirits before he can drag into daylight this hellish influence and unfold it unto the world* in all its soul-destroying, diabolical, and horrid colors . . . . [*Teachings of the Prophet Joseph Smith,* pp. 204-05; emphasis supplied]

As the events of the winding up scene begin to beseige us, the Lord has given us a type of what we must do. As Israel was required to look up to Moses and his serpented staff for temporal deliverance, in similitude of the requirement to look to the uplifted Savior for spiritual deliverance, so must we look to the Prophet of God for deliverance as darkness and confusion gather in around us. As it was difficult for ancient Israel to lift their eyes from the immediate danger of the poisonous serpents, so shall it be difficult to see through the life-threatening complexities of the world as Antichrist rises to world reign.

The "mist of darkness" witnessed by the Prophet Lehi, which prevented many from clinging to the iron rod leading to eternal life, is the confusion created by Satan to distract us and divert us from the path that leads to salvation and exaltation. Those mists of darkness that are even now drifting toward us are made up of the most sophisticated deceit and lies that this planet has ever known. Only by looking to the living oracle of God and following the established Priesthood order can we escape the snares that are so carefully being laid for us. Only by employing the powers of discernment that accompany the righteous exercise of the Priesthood can we hope to keep ourselves unspotted from the sins of the world and the blood of this generation. Whether aliens, superhumans, or deceiving spirits, Satan's servants will come working miracles and ensnaring the world. One of the greatest blessings of membership in the Kingdom of God is knowing what to watch for and how to discern between good and evil as promised by the Apostle Paul. Although Satan will have power to enslave the world through his deceit, those who possess the gift of the Holy Ghost, the children of light, need not be deceived if they will exercise their God-given gifts and reject the great latter-day lie.

But of the times and the seasons, brethren, ye have no need that I write unto you. For yourselves know perfectly that the day of the Lord so cometh as a thief in the night. For when they shall say, Peace and safety; then sudden destruction cometh upon them, as travail upon a woman with child; and they shall not escape. But ye, brethren, are not in darkness, that that day should overtake you as a thief. Ye are the children of light, and the children of the day: we are not of the night, nor of darkness. Therefore let us not sleep, as do others; but let us watch and be sober. [1 Thessalonians 5:16]

Afterward

There may be readers who have either experienced "alien" encounters or who have loved ones that have. The information provided in this book is calculated to familiarize the reader with the UFO phenomenon and to offer an analysis of the possible origins of, and purposes behind the phenomenon. Although I have attempted to supply the reader with a thoughtful analysis, there is no guaranty that I am correct in my conclusions. Therefore, anyone who has experienced a close encounter, and has any residual effects from that experience is well advised to seek out whatever counseling that he or she deems appropriate. I believe that many of these difficulties may be spiritually centered, and therefore, advise that spiritual counseling be sought. Psychological counseling could also be an effective tool in combatting any latent effects of these encounters—I ardently suggest a counselor with a strong knowledge and testimony of the Gospel and significant spiritual insight.

Having concluded that many UFO sightings and alien encounters have negative spiritual origins, I must emphasize that a percipient is *not* a participant. A victim of spiritual "attack" is only that—a victim. To be targeted for an apparition of any kind is no sin or disgrace. Therefore, let no one believe that witnesses of paranormal activity have necessarily invited Satanic ventures into their lives. However, we have discovered a correlation between UFO-related phenomena and occult activity in certain geographical areas. For example, there was a great deal of occult practice in the Snowflake, Arizona, region at the time of Travis Walton's abduction. This correlative principle appears to hold true in many locations thus far. How can we protect ourselves? As I have made clear in the main text, the power of the Priesthood is the best defense against demonic influences.

Because this research is ongoing, I would appreciate hearing from LDS Church members who have experienced close encounters with "aliens." I am especially interested in the spiritual aspects of such encounters—how you "felt" during the experience, or did you perceive anything spiritually. Information regarding spiritual confrontations would be most welcome. You decide what is important about your encounter—I will be happy to research your report.

Anyone wishing to submit a report of an experience is assured complete discretion and confidentiality. Send your materials to me, James Thompson, c/o this publisher.

Appendix A

Extraterrestrial Life Survey

1. Do you believe that any form of life exists on planets other than Earth?
   Yes _____ No _____ No opinion _____

2. Do you believe that human-like life ("aliens") exists on planets other than Earth? Yes _____ No _____ No opinion _____

3. Do you believe that aliens travel in space ships to planets other than their own?
   Yes _____ No _____ No opinion _____

4. Do you believe that aliens have indirectly contacted humans (e.g., electronic signals, telepathy)? Yes _____ No _____ No opinion _____

5. Do You believe that aliens have travelled into Earth's atmosphere?
   Yes _____ No _____ No opinion _____

6. Do you believe that aliens have landed on Earth?
   Yes _____ No _____ No opinion _____

7. Do you believe that aliens have landed on Earth and contacted humans directly?
   Yes _____ No _____ No opinion _____

8. Do you believe that humans have gone onto alien space ships?
   Yes _____ No _____ No opinion _____

9. Do you believe that angels use space vehicles to travel to Earth?
   Yes _____ No _____ No opinion _____

10. Do you believe that God uses space vehicles to travel to Earth?
    Yes _____ No _____ No opinion _____

11. Have you ever seen an alien space craft or UFO? Yes _____ No _____

12. Do you know anyone that claims to have seen an alien space craft or UFO?
    Yes _____ No _____

    ABOUT YOU— (please circle) Sex: M F   Age: 20-30, 30-40, 40+
    Educational Level: High School, College, Masters, Doctorate

If you have had any experiences with aliens or UFO's, or know of any LDS people that have had a UFO experience, please give a brief description on the back, with your identity if you wish, or contact:

> James or Lynne
> (801) 298-4672
> P.O. Box 53
> Bountiful, UT 84011

Please feel free to expand or explain any answers on the back.

269

Selected Bibliography

LDS Bibliography

Brough, R. Clayton, *They Who Tarry,* Horizon Publishers, Bountiful, Utah. 1976.

Crowther, Duane S., *Prophecy, Key to the Future,* Bookcraft, Salt Lake City, Utah. 1962.

Crowther, Duane S., *Prophetic Warnings to Modern America,* Horizon Publishers, Bountiful, Utah. 1977.

Doctrine and Covenants, The. A Scripture of The Church of Jesus Christ of Latter-day Saints, Salt Lake City, Utah. 1968.

Holy Bible, The. Old and New Testaments—King James Edition. Missionary copy bound for The Church of Jesus Christ of Latter-day Saints, Salt Lake City, Utah. 1969 edition.

McConkie, Bruce R., *Doctrines of Salvation: Sermons and Writings of Joseph Fielding Smith,* Bookcraft, Inc., Salt Lake City, Utah. 1954. Vols. 1-3.

McConkie, Bruce R., *Mormon Doctrine,* Bookcraft Inc., Salt Lake City, Utah. 1966.

Nibley, Hugh, *The Message of the Joseph Smith Papri: An Egyptian Endowment,* Deseret Book, Salt Lake City, Utah. 1975.

Pearl of Great Price, The. A Scripture of The Church of Jesus Christ of Latter-day Saints, Salt Lake City, Utah. 1968 edition.

Richards, LeGrand, *A Marvelous Work and A Wonder,* Deseret Book Compnay, Salt Lake City, Utah. 1969 edition.

Roberts, Brigham H., *A Comprehensive History of the Church,* Brigham Young University Press, Provo, Utah. 1956. Vols. 1-6.

Roberts, Brigham H., *Defense of the Faith and the Saints,* Deseret News, Salt Lake City, Utah. 1912. Vols. 1 & 2.

Smith, Hyrum M. & Janne M. Sjodahl, *Doctrine & Covenants Commentary,* Deseret Book Company, Salt Lake City, Utah. 1974.

Smith, Jospeh, *(The Documentary) History of the Church,* Deseret Book Company, Salt Lake City, Utah. 1946-1951. Vols. 1-7.

_____. *Teachings of the Prophet Joseph Smith,* Deseret Book, 1954.

Smith, Joseph F., *Gospel Doctrine,* Deseret Book Company, Salt Lake City, Utah. 1919.

Smith, Joseph Fielding, *Answers to Gospel Questions,* Deseret Book Company, Salt Lake City, Utah. 1957.

Smith, Joseph Fielding, *Doctrines of Salvation; Sermons and Writings of Joseph Fielding Smith* (compiled by Bruce R. McConkie), Bookcraft Inc., Salt Lake City, Utah. Edition: 1973. Vols. 1-3.

Smith, Joseph Fielding, *Essentials in Church History,* Deseret Book Company, Salt Lake City, Utah. 1969.

Talmage, James E., *Jesus The Christ,* Deseret Book Company, Salt Lake City, Utah. 1961 edition.

Talmage, James E., *The Articles of Faith,* Deseret Book Company, Salt Lake City, Utah. 1961 edition.

Whipple, Walt, *A Discussion of the Many Theories Concerning the Whereabouts of the Lost Ten Tribes.* A research paper prepared at Brigham Young University, Provo, Utah, 1958-1959.

Widtsoe, John A., *Discourses of Brigham Young,* Deseret Book Company, Salt Lake City, Utah. 1954.

UFO/Occult/Fairy Bibliography

Berlitz, Charles, and William L. Moore. *The Rosewell Incident.* New York: Berkley Books, 1980.

Bloecher, Ted, with Aphrodite Clamar, Budd Hopkins, and Elizabeth Slater. *Final Report on the Psychological Testing of UFO "Abductees."* Mt. Rainier, MD.: The Fund for UFO Research, 1987.

Briggs, Katherine. *Encyclopedia of Fairies,* New York: Pantheon/Random House, 1976.

Bullard, Thomas E., Ph.D. *On Stolen Time: A Summary of the Comparative Study of the UFO Abduction Mystery.* Mt. Rainier, Md.: The fund for UFO Research, 1987.

Conroy, Ed, *Report on Communion*. New York: William Morrow & Company, 1989.

Davis, Lorraine, "A Comparison of UFO and Near Death Experiences," *Journal of Near Death Studies,* Vol. 6, No. 4 (1988).

Evans, Hilary. *Gods, Spirits, Cosmic Guardians: Encounters with Non-Human Beings.* Wellingborough, England: Aquarian Press, 1987.

_____. *Visions, Apparitions, Alien Visitors: A Comparative Study of the Entity Enigma.* Wellingborough, England: Aquarian Press, 1984.

Evans-Wentz, W. Y. *The Fairy Faith in Celtic Countries,* New York: University Press, 1966.

Fawcett, Lawrence, and Barry J. Greenwood, *Clear Intent: The Government Cover-Up of the UFO Experience.* Englewood Cliffs, N.J.: Prentice-Hall, 1984.

Festinger, Leon, with Henry W. Riecken and Stanley Schachter. *When Prophecy Fails: A Social and Psychological Study of a Modern Group That Predicted the Destruction of the World.* New York: Harper and Row, 1956.

Fowler, Raymond E. *The Andreasson Affair.* Englewood Cliffs, N.J.: Prentice-Hall, 1980.

_____. *The Andreasson Affair, Phase Two.* Englewood Cliffs, N.J.: Prentice-Hall, 1982.

_____. *The Watchers: The Secret Design Behind UFO Abductions,* New York: Bantam Book, 1990.

Frazier, Kendrick, ed., *Paranormal Borderlands of Science.* Buffalo: Prometheus Books, 1981.

Fry, Daniel W. *The White Sands Incident.* Louisville, Ky.: Best Book Company, 1966.

Fuller, John G. *Aliens in the Skies: The New UFO Battle of the Scientists.* New York: G. P. Putnam's Sons, 1969.

_____. *Incident at Exeter: Unidentified Flying Objects Over America Now.* New York: G. P. Putnam's Sons, 1966.

_____. *The Interrupted Journey; Two Lost Hours Aboard a Flying Saucer.* New York: Dial Press, 1966.

Gardner, Martin. *The New Age: Notes of a Fringe—Watcher.* Buffalo: Prometheus Books, 1988.

Good, Timothy, *Above Top Secret: The Worldwide UFO Cover-UP.* New York: William Morrow and Company, 1988.

Grant, Kenneth, *Outside the Circles of Time.* London: Frederick Muller Ltd., 1980.

Hartland, E. S. *English Fairy and Folk Tales,* London: Walter Scott, 1893.

_____. *The Science of Fairy Tales: An Inquiry into Fairy Mythology.* Walter Scott, London, 1891.

Hassan, Steven. *Combatting Cult Mind Control.* Rochester, Vt.: Park Street Press, 1988.

Hasted, John. *The Metal Benders.* Routledge & Kegan Paul, 1981.

Hopkins, Budd, "The Extraterrestrial—Paraphysical Controversy." MUFON UFO *Journal,* no. 153, 1980. 3-5.

_____. *Intruders: The Incredible Visitations at Copley Woods.* New York: Random House, 1987.

_____. *Missing Time: A Documented Study of UFO Abductions.* New York: Richard Marek Publishers, 1981.

Hynek, J. Allen, and Jacques Vallee, *The Edge of Reality: A Progress Report on Unidentified Flying Objects.* Chicago: Henry Regnery Company, 1975.

Jacobs, Joseph. *Celtic Folk and Fairy Tales.* New York: G. P. Putnam's Sons, 1968.

Keel, John A. *Why UFOs?: Operation Trojan Horse.* New York: Manor Books, 1981.

Kinder, Gary. *Light Years: An Investigation into the Extraterrestrial Experiences of Eduard Meier.* New York: Atlantic Monthly Press, 1987.

Kirk, Robert, *The Secret Commonwealth of Elves, Fauns and Fairies.* Stirling, England: Mackay, 1933.

Larson, Robert, *Straight Answers on the New Age,* Tennessee: Nelson Publishers, 1989.

Lewis, David Allen and Shreckhise, Robert, *UFO: End-Time Delusion,* Arkansas: New Leaf Press, 1992.

Loosely, William Rober, with David Langford, ed. *An Account of a Meeting with Denizens of Another World 1871.* New York: St. Martin's Press, 1980.

Lorenzen, Coral, and Jim Lorenzen. *Abducted: Confrontations with Beings for Outer Space.* New York: Berkley Publishing Corporation, 1977.

Maccabee, Bruce, Ph.D. *Documents and Supporting Information Relating to Crashed Flying Saucers and Operaton Majestic Twelve.* Mt. Rainier, Md.: The Fund for UFO Research, 1987.

Monroe, Robert A., *Journeys Out of the Body.* New York: Anchor Press/ Doubleday, 1973.

Montgomery, Ruth. *Aliens Among Us.* New York: Fawcett Crest, 1985.

Neal, Richard, M.D., "Generations of Abductions—A Medical Casebook," and "The Alien Agenda," *UFO Magazines,* vol. 3, no. 2, 1988. 22, 25.

Nyman, Joseph, "The Latent Encounter Experience—A Composite Model," *MUFON UFO JOURNAL,* no. 242, 1988. 10-12.

Ring, Kenneth, *Heading Towards Omega: In Search of the Meaning of the Near-Death Experience.* New York: William Morrow and Company, 1984, 1985.

Rojcewicz, Peter M., "Men in Black' Experiences: Analogues of the Traditional Devil Encounter," *Fortean Times,* issue no. 50, London, 1986.

Salisbury, Frank B., *The Utah UFO Display: A Bioligists Report.* Connecticut: Devin-Adair, 1974.

Spencer, John, and Hilary Evans, *Phenomenon: Forty Years of Flying Saucers.* New York: Avon Books, 1988.

Steiger, Brad, *The Fellowship: Spiritual Contact Between Humans and Outer Space Beings.* New York: Dolphin/Doubleday, 1988.

_____. *Mysteries of Time and Space.* New York: Confucian Press, 1973.

_____. *The UFO Abductors.* New York: Berkley Publishing Corporation, 1988.

Story, Ronald D., *The Encyclopedia of UFOs.* Garden City, N.Y.: Dolphin Books/Doubleday and Company, 1980.

Strieber, Whitley. *Communion: A True Story.* New York: Morrow/Beech Tree Books, 1987.

_____. *Tranformation: The Breakthrough*. New York: Morrow/Beech Tree Books, 1988.

Vallee, Jacques. *Dimensions: A Casebook of Alien Contact*. Chicago: Contemporary Books, 1988.

_____. *The Invisible College: What a Group of Scientists Has Discovered About UFO Influences of the Human Race*. New York: E. P. Dutton and Company, 1975.

_____. *Messengers of Deception: UFO Contacts and Cults*. Berkely, California: And/Or Press, 1979.

_____. *Passport to Magonia: From Folklore to Flying Saucers*. Chicago: Henry Regnery Company, 1969.

_____. *UFOs in Space: Anatomy of a Phenomenon*. Henry Regnery Company, 1965.

von Daniken, Erich. *Chariots of the Gods?* New York: G. P. Putnam's Sons, 1970.

Walters, Ed, *The Gulf Breeze Sightings,* New York: William Morrow and Company, 1974.

Walton, Travis, *The Walton Experience*. New York: Berkley Publishing Corporation, 1978.

Yeats, W. B. *Irish Fairy and Folk Tales*. New York: Dorset Press, 1986.

Zaleski, Carol. *Otherworld Journeys: Accounts of Near-Death Experience in Medieval and Modern Times*. New York: Oxford University Press, 1987.

Index

Hypnosis, 81, 88, 97, 105-107, 109, 110, 111-113, 114, 123, 125, 126, 130, 227, 231, 245, 249-251.

I

Implant, 113-114, 122, 127, 224, 226, 227, 244, 254.
Impregnate, pregnant, 48-49, 106-107, 132, 210, 237-238, 241, 263.
Invisible, 92-93, 188, 190, 194, 196, 197, 206, 207, 226, 256.
Italy, 97, 156.

J

John (beloved Apostle), 39, 43, 220.

K

Kelley, Kentucky, 100-101.
Kimball, Spencer W., 25-26, 36, 41-42.
King, George, 120.
Kolob, 28-34, 134.

L

Lameck, 26, 48, 49.
Landing site, 82-83, 93, 94, 103-104, 142-143, 153, 161, 210.
Larson, Robert, 171-172.
Latter-day Saint, LDS Church, 3, 4, 16, 18-20, 24, 44, 49-51, 59, 63, 96, 100, 102, 115, 121, 136, 137, 138-166, 168, 173, 176, 184, 204, 209, 212, 219, 222, 225, 229, 230, 242, 251, 258, 260, 261, 264, 266.
Lazar, Robert, 86-88, 91.
Lehi, 4, 266.
Lewis, David, and Shrekhise, Robert, 173, 205, 236, 244, 252, 255.
Light (and balls, beams), 14, 46, 47, 53-60, 64, 65, 66, 68, 73-74, 75-76, 80-81, 92, 98-99, 100, 103, 105, 108, 113, 116, 117, 123, 125, 126, 127, 128, 131, 137, 138, 139, 140, 141, 143, 144-145, 149, 151, 154-155, 156, 157-158, 159, 160, 180, 189-191, 194, 197, 198, 201, 202-204, 205, 207, 213, 214, 224, 229, 259, 262, 267.
Lost Ten Tribes of Israel, 25, 217-221.
Love, 109-110, 111, 120, 121, 128, 129, 130, 133, 143, 168, 201, 212, 214, 237, 246, 257, 263.
Luca, Betty (Andeasson), 79, 81, 96, 106, 122-137, 150, 162, 191, 198, 207, 214, 226, 232, 246, 248-249, 255, 260.

M

Mack, John E., M.D., 13.

Madonna (Virgin Mary), 66, 80, 202-204, 224, 259, 260.

Master, the One, 119, 120, 123-127, 129, 171, 172, 173, 175, 177, 179, 181, 183, 236.

Media, 3, 63, 65, 67, 69, 72, 73, 81, 82, 84-86, 94, 104, 142, 147, 162, 169, 174, 176, 177, 208, 210-211, 252, 255, 265.

Memory, 97, 102-104, 106, 107, 109, 111-113, 114-116, 122-123, 127, 128, 145-146, 149, 150, 152, 154-156, 161, 163, 164, 166, 191, 193, 203, 224, 233, 243, 244, 245, 249-250, 256.

Menger, Howard, 120, 121.

Men in Black (MIB), 79, 155, 207, 251-253.

Message, 4, 20, 21, 42, 47, 67, 118, 119, 121, 122-123, 127, 128, 129, 130, 131, 133, 136, 137, 166, 167, 168, 172, 173, 176, 180, 186, 202-204, 205, 207, 208, 213, 217, 220-222, 223-261, 263, 264.

Miracle, 53, 54, 66, 181, 182, 184, 191, 196, 201, 202-204, 207, 228, 232, 256, 259-260, 265, 266.

Monster, 67, 95, 176, 253.

Montgomery, Ruth, 172, 206, 242.

Moon, 32, 34, 67, 92, 119, 124, 158, 162-163, 234.

Moroni, 37, 60.

Moses, 22, 24, 26, 27-28, 39, 41, 43, 49, 53, 181, 184, 266.

Mutual UFO Network (MUFON), 73, 147-148.

Moudy, Judi, 102-104.

N

Nevada (Area 51, S4), 86-88.

New Age, 3, 4, 51, 89, 92, 120, 121, 123, 124, 125-126, 128, 130, 135, 168-186, 187, 206, 208, 228, 234, 236, 242-243, 244, 255, 256, 257-258, 264, 265.

Newhouse, Delbert, 71.

Nibley, Hugh, 33, 54, 59, 126, 198.

Noah, 26, 48-49, 60.

Noise, silence, 56, 58, 65, 75, 76, 78, 85, 88, 100, 101, 103, 128, 138, 139, 141, 142-143, 151-152, 156, 157, 159, 160-161, 163, 190-191, 195, 196, 203, 207, 214, 230.

O

Occult, 3, 4, 51, 113, 120, 125, 126, 135, 148, 168-177, 180, 193, 230, 242, 251-252, 254, 255, 259.

Ouija board, 174, 203-204, 226.

Old age, longevity, 96, 110, 132, 142, 214.

Out-of-body experience (OBE), 14, 19, 125-126, 136, 165, 191-193, 230.

P

Paranormal, supernatural, 19, 21, 63, 65, 66, 74, 79, 80, 87, 90, 92-93, 100, 103, 110, 113, 115, 116, 131, 135, 148, 149, 156, 165, 174, 175, 180, 181, 182, 184, 187-207, 218, 220, 226, 227, 230, 232, 240, 241, 249-251, 254, 256, 259, 260, 264.

Phelps, William W., 37.

Photograph, 70-71, 72-79, 82, 83, 85, 88, 90, 98, 99, 101, 113, 140, 147, 148, 205-206, 210, 226-227, 244.

Plan, The, 172, 173-174, 175, 184.

Planet, 3, 19-20, 22-23, 25, 27-39, 41-47, 52, 58, 72, 87, 95, 96, 118, 119, 120, 129, 133, 143, 152, 167, 174, 183, 207, 208, 209, 213, 215, 216-217, 219, 221, 234, 238, 257, 262, 265, 266.

Polygraph, 72, 145, 146.

Possession, spiritual, 75-79, 81, 88, 115, 122, 123, 125, 130, 132-133, 170, 171, 174, 179-180, 184, 185, 224, 226, 227, 230, 231, 233, 235, 236, 237, 239, 242-245, 247-252, 258.

Portals, portholes, windows, 73, 87, 103, 105, 139, 145, 147, 149, 151, 157, 160, 187, 189, 194.

Pratt, Orson, 40, 45, 46-47.

Priesthood, 42, 59, 60, 139, 143, 166, 184, 198, 213, 214, 221, 225, 251, 261, 264, 266.

Projection, 226-228, 230, 231, 246, 255.

Prophet, prophecy, 20, 32, 35-39, 41, 42, 47, 49, 50, 120, 134, 178, 182, 203, 207, 218, 227, 234, 238, 257, 260, 261, 262, 265, 266.

R

Reincarnation, 120, 169, 170, 171, 173, 178-180, 244, 250, 256, 257, 263.

Religion, 3, 20, 47, 49, 57, 59-60, 65, 66, 90, 123, 126, 128, 129, 167, 168-177, 182, 186, 193, 196, 198, 200, 201, 202-204, 214, 224, 226, 232, 236, 242, 254, 255, 256, 257-258, 260.

V

Vallee, Jacques, 65, 156, 187, 195, 197-198, 199-200, 203, 204, 240-241, 248, 253-255, 256, 258, 259.

Venus, Venusians, 3, 67, 119, 120.

Vibrations, 122, 130, 135, 171, 172, 173, 177, 232, 257.

Victim, 6, 20, 60, 246.

Video, 72, 74, 90.

Villas-Boas, Antonio, 107-108.

Visitation, 6, 20, 42, 58, 59-60, 81, 82, 88, 95, 96, 101, 116, 128, 131, 164-166, 172, 180, 193, 206, 216, 219, 220, 259, 264.

Voice, 56, 58, 75, 77-79, 112, 115-116, 120, 123, 124, 129.

von Daniken, Erich, 48, 49, 51, 109, 260.

W

Walters, Ed and Frances, 72-78, 92-93, 96, 97, 98, 112-117, 135, 137, 140, 198, 207, 229, 230, 245.

Walton, Travis, 109, 144-146.

Wand, hand-held device, 38, 54, 57, 98, 99, 116, 127, 156, 195, 198, 244.

Wartena, Udo, 59, 121, 135, 138, 142-143, 213-214, 258, 264.

Water, 56-57, 58, 59, 76, 96, 113, 115-117, 124, 141, 142, 214, 231, 262.

Whitmer, David, 54.

Whitney, Orson F., 44.

Y

Year 2,000, 172.

Young, Brigham, 38, 39-40, 184, 225.

Z

Zeta Reticuli, 88.

Zion, 24-29, 31, 43, 45-46, 182, 184, 217, 219, 220, 258.